THE GREAT BOOKS:

A CHRISTIAN APPRAISAL

VOLUME IV

Identical with this volume:

THE GREAT BOOKS, VOL. I ($2.75)

THE GREAT BOOKS, VOL. II ($2.75)

THE GREAT BOOKS, VOL. III ($2.75)

(Four volumes $10.00)

Published by The Devin-Adair Company

THE
GREAT BOOKS

A CHRISTIAN APPRAISAL

A Symposium on the Fourth Year's Program
of the Great Books Foundation

Edited by
Harold C. Gardiner, S.J.
Literary Editor of "America"

❀ IV ❀

THE DEVIN-ADAIR COMPANY

NEW YORK

Printed in the United States of America

Foreword

THIS IS Volume IV of the four-volume series *The Great Books: A Christian Appraisal.* It follows the scheme and the purpose of the first three volumes, namely, to evaluate by the standards of Christian thinking the books which are selected for study by the Great Books Foundation. As the first three volumes considered the books of the first three years in the Foundation's four-year course, so Volume IV takes in order those used in the fourth year. The substantial success of the first three volumes, and the large measure of appreciation which has been accorded them have made it eminently worth while to complete the series.

From time to time the Great Books Foundation has elected to "change books." Subsequent printings of these volumes will follow such changes when possible.

Introduction

IN OFFERING this fourth and final volume of Christian interpretations of the Great Books, I must beg the reader's indulgence, as I have done in the three preceding volumes, to call attention to the fact that three authors treated in this volume are listed in the *Index Librorum Prohibitorum*. They are Descartes, Hume and Voltaire. This, of course, is of particular interest only to Catholics who may be following the Great Books discussion, and prudence demands that I make this statement so that those who wish to discuss the three authors realize that they ought to obtain the necessary permissions so to do—and particularly if they feel impelled from this acquaintanceship with the authors to go on to read other works from their pens. Non-Catholics, of course, may find themselves understandably irked by this practical direction. I have only to beg the patience they have obviously extended in the preceding three volumes.

HAROLD C. GARDINER

Contents

THE GREAT BOOKS:

A CHRISTIAN APPRAISAL

VOLUME IV

Hippocrates: Selections

"WHY IS IT that doctors, although they admire Hippocrates, do not read his writings, or if by chance they do, do not understand them, or if they have the good fortune to understand them, do not put their principles into practice and develop the habit of their use?" It was six centuries after Hippocrates that the great Galen asked this of his contemporaries in an address entitled "That the Good Physician Is a Philosopher."

The timelessness of Galen's observation is in part communicated by his reference to a perennial sports event: "The fate reserved for the majority of athletes who, while aspiring to win victory in the Olympic games, do nothing in order to attain it, applies equally well to the majority of doctors. These last, indeed, praise Hippocrates, regarding him as first in the art of healing, yet they do everything except what should be done to resemble him."

The timelessness is better substantiated by the high role Hippocrates has played through the ages. It is of note that when William Harvey, M.D., fellow student of Galileo, was graduated from the University of Padua in 1602, he was responsible in his final examination for an hour's discourse on any one of the aphorisms of Hippocrates.

Today many diverse tributes are to be found which are not simply historical in interest, but contemporary, as if Hippocrates held the answers to some of our urgent problems. A distinguished medical scientist and educator, A. C. Ivy, has this to say:

Though I had been in medicine for thirty years, I realized for the first time at the Nürnberg trials the full meaning of the contributions of Hippocrates and his school to medicine and human welfare. Hippocrates contributed the scientific philosophy of medicine as we know it today. . . . He contributed a technical philosophy when he taught that diligence, accuracy, thoroughness in

1

observation and skill were essential for success in the practice of medicine. He apparently realized that a scientific and technical philosophy of medicine could not survive through the ages unless it was associated with a sound moral philosophy. One cannot conceive of a sound society with medicine that does not have a sound moral philosophy.

Again, an astute observer and practitioner of medicine, Bernard Aschner, has written, "Today Hippocratism is still the worshiped ideal of educated physicians. But during the last 100 years it has remained more or less lip-service." An actively practicing physician, he indicts modern medicine in these terms:

Through the whole history of medicine there runs, like a bright thread, a more or less permanent struggle between two principal tendencies—empiricism and rationalism. The former, or empirical trend, lays its emphasis on helping and the cure of the sick. The latter, or rationalistic trend, lays its main emphasis on "scientific" explanations for the causes of disease and the methods of treatment.

He continues:

Today we are living once more in such an era of extreme intolerant rationalism. We can see the displacement of simple, valuable— nay, fundamental and indispensable—traditional methods of healing in favor of a more sophisticated, theorizing, experimental and technical trend, guided by an exaggerated application of such auxiliary sciences as physics, chemistry and physiology. This trend has even gone so far that established clinical experience has been replaced by the [neorationalism] of natural science.

He further observes:

Nor is this state of affairs a mere academic proposition, since it influences decisively the fate of the sick. . . . Moreover, our up-to-date medicine is wavering between the therapeutic nihilism of internal medicine and a too-far-reaching operative radicalism in the surgical branches.

He asks for a return to Hippocratic principles.

A third tribute indicating an additional dimension of Hippocrates' message for us was expressed by the present writer at a recent convocation for medical students and faculty members:

Hippocrates, the Father of Medicine, knew thoroughly that humanistic studies and piety in a physician were not a substitute for technical knowledge. But as a leading educator, he also knew, as few do today, that the intimate and complex relationship between one human being, the physician, and another human being, his sick charge, necessitated something above and beyond, something more inclusive and comprehensive than the pinning on of disease labels, and the execution of their attached medical and surgical recipes. This comprehension is manifest throughout his works in his persistent concern for what pertains to the whole of the patient. He would have been aghast at the notion that the newest of our specialties is psychosomatic medicine, that the patient ever could have been thought of as anything other than a person, an inseparable unit of *psyche* and *soma!* He would have held with St. Thomas (against the Cartesian duality that pervades contemporary thought) that "since the soul is united to the body as its form, it must necessarily be in the whole body, and in each part thereof."

As we have seen, there is professional witness to Hippocrates' capacity for making contributions of perennial value. We also have another type of witness—perhaps a more provocative type. This is the witness of a public as it reflects and cogitates on its collective experience. The testimony is negative; it arises from a sense of disharmony or disruption, an awareness of a deficiency or hidden hunger that permeates our seemingly robust present-day medicine. To bring these thoughts into sharper focus, to evoke any latent discontent with contemporary medicine should prove valuable in a true appreciation of Hippocrates, especially when one reads the works of the father of medicine. All readers of Hippocrates are patients, potential or actual. They should be concerned with medical tradition, for they are the ultimate gainers or losers.

Furthermore, the more vivid the critical insights that arise from one's reflections, the better the background for a reading of Hippocrates. And vividness, like a cure, often can be best achieved by highlighting the defects rather than the assets in the backdrop of our living experiences. Everyone applauds the rescue of men and women from premature death and the sharp reduction in mortality rates which modern medicine has achieved. But even these accomplishments make more manifest the anxieties and morbidities of the living. Let us view, then, the panorama of modern medical practice and sharpen our vision by characterizing—or caricaturing, as the case may be—the dissatisfactions we feel.

We see patients' stomachs turned into apothecaries' crucibles, and the patients perversely enjoying it; the substitution of varishaped and varicolored pills for knife-and-fork nutriments—the tasteless for the tasteful; the push-button electric shock-therapy approach to the psychiatric manifestations of our age; neurosurgeons competitively solving personality difficulties by whittling away irreplaceable brain tissues. We see surgeons displaying their skills in removing so-called nonvital organs, and an increase of medical literature on iatrogenic illnesses.

We witness the growth of highly technical assembly-line medical centers; the disappearance of the humanly sensitive person—the family physician—and his replacement by the automaton concentrating on the mechanically sensitive X ray, electrocardiography and laboratory procedures; complexities of treatment substituting for simplicities, for no other reason than that they are complex and duly impress physicians and patients alike; overspecialization and the consequent decline of the general practitioner; the false separation of the patient's ailment from the ecological environment of home, work and human association.

Finally, we see the veterinarian approach replacing the anthropomorphic approach, with growing confusion as to man's dignity and destiny; the perverse transmuting of normalities into abnormalities, as in obstetrics and pediatrics, and, in general, the over-all substitution of scientism for nature's norms and goals.

Confronted with such a picture, we suspect, to borrow a phrase from T. S. Eliot, that today we have answers for everything but exact ideas about nothing.

Our insensitivity to tradition and its wisdom is not without effect. It gives us modern man, who goes through life with fear of death; who, fearing death, expends his health in hypochondriacal distress; who becomes a vitamin-taking, antacid-consuming, barbiturate-sedated, aspirin-alleviated, weed-habituated, alcohol-inebriated, benzedrine-stimulated, psychosomatically diseased, surgically despoiled animal. Nature's highest product becomes a fatigued, peptic-ulcerated, depressed, sleepless, headachy, nicotinized, overstimulated, neurotic, tonsilless creature.

The reader can judge best to what extent such a characterization is a caricature. In any case, it should heighten our sensibility and increase our docility to Galen's warning that, though we praise Hippocrates, we do not read him or do not understand him or do not put his principles into practice. Reading Hippocrates may reward us with unexpected and needed insights.

In an age when patients markedly dictate the forms of medical practice, there is a certain appropriateness in the fact that Galen was speaking to laymen as well as physicians. The Hippocratic physician recognized the need for the layman to be educated. And, as Jaeger has shown, Hippocratic thought on this matter played a major if not a decisive role in establishing as a basis for the cultural pattern of Greek life the notion of the liberally educated person. His concept of man as being free when he is liberated by the "library" of the liberal arts received its fullest expression in later Greek thought. Aristotle definitively voices it in the opening paragraph of his biological work *Parts of Animals,* where he states that "every inquiry . . . the humblest and the noblest alike, seems to admit of two distinct kinds of proficiency; one of which may properly be called scientific knowledge of the subject, while the other is a kind of educational acquaintance with it. For an educated man should be able to form a fair off-hand judgment as to the goodness or badness of the method used by a professor in his exposition." That this is to include medicine is corroborated by his reference in the *Politics* to the three kinds of "physician": " . . . the ordinary physician, the physician of the higher class [the medical scientist], and thirdly, the intelligent man who has studied the art, to whom we attribute the power of judging quite as much as to the professors of the art."

This cultural pattern, so profoundly crystallized by the Hippocratic school, arose not from a preoccupation with disease but from a concern for optimum health. In their hands, medicine was freed from the domination of the demonstrative sciences, such as mathematics and natural science, and was the first discipline of a practical nature to become precisely formulated as such. As a consequence, medicine became the exemplar for other practical sciences, such as ethics and politics. Much of our insight into the Greek concept of medicine comes indirectly from the analogies that were drawn to it, especially by Plato and Aristotle, to clarify less familiar notions in other fields.

Thus, in the *Politics,* Aristotle, when classifying the medically educated layman with the practicing physician and the medical scientist, is trying to show the relationship of the electorate to the statesman and the political scientist. He concludes that the electorate, like the medically educated layman, the "user," so to speak, may "turn out to be a better judge" than the others.

We have from the Hippocratic school varied works, prepared for public discussion, on the nature of disease (e.g., "On The Nature of Man," "The Sacred Disease") and, at a more practical level, on things similar to present-day texts in personal hygiene (e.g., "Regimen in Health").

It would be sheer naïveté to think that these and other Hippocratic works spell out complete answers for us. They are not a true-or-false compendium in the modern manner. They suffer the handicaps of having to be translated from a terse and ancient language. They will be in part obscure, with an aphoristic obscurity not unlike that of metaphysical poetry. They will communicate through the flux of a past age much that is strange and foreign to us who are enmeshed in our contingencies. Finally, Hippocrates will come to us in a corpus diversified in time and authorship, with some parts duplicated, some parts missing, and some parts contradicting one another but achieving a wholeness through a living catechetical and functioning tradition. Thus, we should not expect an expository work form-fitted to a Great Books audience of the latter half of the twentieth century.

On the other hand, we do start with a common bond: the reality of man and nature and deity, and the eternal problems of a rational, social, divinely inspired animal, with his love of life and his capacity for health, with his subjection to disease, disorder and even irrationality, who is also unfortunately a money-paying animal. Our effort must be to take from the father of medicine (who like all fathers has the perspective that comes from looking both backward and forward) that wisdom which is common to all ages.

Unfortunately, the wisdom that can be found in Hippocrates is not foolproof. After we have recovered from the initial surprise of discovering that the first essay of the father of medicine is entitled *Ancient Medicine,* we must not make the mistake of thinking that our function as a reader is simply and smugly to look backward at former errors as if they were buried once and for all. On the contrary, we must look forward with him. For, no matter how well they are embalmed, the errors of physicians, unlike their patients, will be resurrected frequently—by later physicians. Actually we will discover in this essay and in other writings of his school that medicine which was ancient to Hippocrates possessed truths that medicine contemporary to him had lost because of the scientism of the day. If we are astute we will pluck the parallel that Hippocratic medicine, ancient to us, possesses truths that medicine, contemporary to us, has lost through a similar scientism.

What wisdom did the father of medicine possess that we, perhaps, lack? In the most general terms we may state that the Hippocratic physician would have had the opportunity of acquiring an active *philosophy* of medicine. This philosophy would give him an understanding of the ends of medicine, of the nature of medicine, of the nature of health and disease, of the nature of the medical act. Furthermore, it would give him a comprehension of the nature of the man who possesses health and disease and the realization that health is not man's ultimate end.

Again, he would be habituated in the attributes necessary to the physician as the maker of health. First, he would be clear in his obligations as a human being living in society. This would demand a liberal education. He would have to know metaphysics and theology in the manner of an educated man, because man has being and a divine goal. He would have to know natural science, because human beings are interconnected with all nature. He would have to be a moralist, possessing a practical knowledge of ethics and knowing how virtue operates among men. He would have to be educated in politics to know his functions and obligations in a society.

Second, he would be habituated in the attributes that belong to him as a physician working for the common good through a particular profession. He would have to be the kind of natural scientist who knows his science as serving an artistic end; he must know nature not simply for the sake of possessing truths about her but to the end of ordering those truths to the restoration and maintenance of optimum health. He would be a medical artist, for he must have the habit of right reason in respect to making health in cooperation with nature, the exemplar of medical artists. He would have medical experience so that he could recognize that to which he is to apply right reason. He would have prudence or practical wisdom so that he might have right reason in respect to the fitness of his medical acts, which are also human acts.

Finally, he would be able to communicate, for he is not a veterinarian dealing with dumb animals; he must possess his art in an intelligible and communicable way and thus be a rhetorician.

The Hippocratic Oath conveys and epitomizes some of the more general relationships and reveals a series of obligations: to the deities, to the teacher, to the Art (to cure, to conform to its ends, to harm not), to the patient as patient, to the patient as human being, and finally to the physician himself.

In more specific terms, there are endless facets to be explored and understood, especially as they illuminate the shadows of medical education and practice. That these facets seem inexhaustible testifies to the greatness of these works of the Hippocratic school. The reader will have the opportunity to discover some of them for himself. In passing, perhaps a few should be emphasized and commented upon briefly.

Here, then, are some propositions and prescriptions the writer finds in the Hippocratic school of medicine:

The practice of medicine can never be a science: medicine is an art, having a good to achieve, not a truth to possess. The final goal is the cure, not the diagnosis. Better a cured patient with no diagnosis than an autopsied patient with an exact diagnosis. There may be much intellectual confusion associated with the surgical or medical act; an exciting research experiment for the physician may be an experience of suffering for the patient; and the beautiful pathology found in a patient is hardly such to the person. The physician clearly must separate his scientific instincts from his artistic obligations. Perhaps this would be accelerated if he had to pay rather than render a fee when he sacrificed artistic obligations to satisfy scientific instincts.

The art of medicine cooperates with and imitates nature. It does for nature what nature would do for itself if it could. Hippocrates observes, "though physicians take many things in hand, many diseases are also overcome for them spontaneously. . . . The gods are the real physicians, though people do not think so." (*Decorum* 6.) Thus, it may be better to do nothing —which requires more thinking but creates less of an impression—than to do something—which frequently requires less thinking but creates a greater impression. There would be agreement with Benjamin Franklin's observation that there is a great deal of difference between a good physician and a bad physician, but very little difference between a good physician and no physician at all. There would also be agreement with Oliver Wendell Holmes's observation that a pair of substantial mammary glands are more advantageous than the two hemispheres of the most learned professor's brain in the art of compounding a nutritive fluid for infants.

A patient cannot be known adequately apart from his environment. The modern hospital-centered training of a physician can well be contrasted with the wider approach exemplified in part in the opening section of *Airs, Waters, Places.*

The positive production of optimum health, not the cultivation of the hypochondriacal state, is the ultimate goal in medicine. To borrow from the Greeks, the problem is not to educate diseases but to graduate them into health; not to nurse the real or imaginary diseases along (as in the abuse of bed rest) and encourage their presence as if every person should be a patient till he dies, struggling to old age through the modern extension of the ancient "invention of a lingering death." Hippocrates would have been puzzled at the amounts of patent and prescribed medicine consumed by the public today. He would be amused to observe that self-medication seems to increase in proportion to newspaper, periodical and radio concentration on bodily ills, as in the United States, and that prescribed medicine disproportionately increases with economic accessibility of physicians and druggists, as witnessed in England in recent years.

Health education is ordered toward health and not toward morbid preoccupation with disease. One out of five dies of cancer, we hear. Lesser health organizations find that one out of ten dies of lesser diseases. The fact is that one out of one dies of something. And so we worry about what we do not have, while we do nothing about what we do have; whereas, if we did something about what we do have, we might not develop what we don't have. This is the state of affairs, for instance, in obesity, which is our most prevalent abnormality and which predisposes to all chronic diseases and cancer.

The proper order of treatment is, first, regimen, then medication and lastly, surgery. Regimen for Hippocrates took in the entire dimension of one's habits of life: eating, working, resting, exercising, massaging, sleeping. On the whole, it called for active cooperation in the cure on the part of the patient and not simply for passive participation or resignation. One may contrast the current tendency to the reverse order of treatment, which is epitomized by the fact of a disproportionately high fee paid the surgeon. It is not unrelated to the worship of the hand-minded, the somatic and the material in modern society. Regimen was also ordered to what today is most neglected, positive health. The purpose of regimen here was twofold: a perfective part which attempted to promote optimum health in the present, which was interrelated with a preventive part to protect against disease in the future.

We treat an individual, not a universal. Our diagnostic and prognostic considerations should be based on individuating characteristics which will lead to an individuated therapeusis, not to a routine procedure nor one in which the patient is used as a target for the physician's armamentarium.

Clinical observations should be exact and not colored by our preconceptions; conclusions should record mistakes. Since we learn from mistakes, we should not overemphasize successes, which are frequently short-range and apparent. ". . . those things also give good instruction which after trial show themselves failures and show why they failed." (*On Joints*, 47.) *Epidemics*, which introduced the concept of an accurate case history and recorded more deaths than cures, should therefore remain a model for us.

The true physician will suffer from the ignorance and stylish therapies of others. "For they praise what seems outlandish before they know whether it is good, rather than the customary which they already know to be good; the bizarre rather than the obvious." (*On Wounds of the Head*, 1.)

Medicine is a profession; as such it becomes the measure of the physician's work and fee. A basic understanding of a professional fee (hardly touched upon in the modern medical school) needs "our consideration as it contributes somewhat to the whole." The following two passages from Hippocrates speak for themselves:

So one must not be anxious about fixing a fee. For I consider such a worry to be harmful to a troubled patient, particularly if the disease be acute. For the quickness of the disease, offering no opportunity for turning back, spurs on the good physician not to seek his profit but rather to lay hold on reputation. Therefore it is better to reproach a patient you have saved than to extort money from those who are at death's door. (*Precepts,* 4.)

And if there is an opportunity of serving one who is a stranger in financial straits, give full assistance to all such. For where there is love of man, there is also love of art. For some patients, though conscious that their condition is perilous, recover their health simply through their contentment with the goodness of the physician. (*Precepts,* 6.)

But Hippocrates was a pagan and we may examine, in conclusion, the loss to a physician that results from the absence of the Judeo-Christian tradition. Certainly Hippocrates could have no fundamental awareness of our intrinsic disharmony or of the cause and cure of the underlying spiritual disorder. Though "where there is love of man, there is also love of the art," the man we love may easily turn out to be ourselves. Love of ourselves, against which the pagan had incomplete immunity, has a diabolical way of interfering with love of man and thus with love of the art. In redirecting love to its highest object, St. Luke, the Patron of Physicians, elevates medicine and so completes and perfects Hippocrates in the manner of grace perfecting nature. St. Luke signifies much for the physician striving for cure (which in its derivation means "care"), and through the physician much for the patient hungering for a care proportionate to his human worth and destiny.

We must remember, however, that grace acts only through nature. Grace does not replace nor dispense with nature. Grace subsists in and elevates nature. Hippocrates did a profound job of reading the Book of Nature, that book which, St. Thomas says, "God, like a good teacher, has taken care to compose [for us—along with the Book of Holy Scriptures] . . . that we may

be instructed in all perfection." Thus St. Thomas, who declares
that in this Book of Nature there are "many excellent writings
which deliver the truth without falsehood. Wherefore Aristotle,
when asked whence it was that he had his admirable learning,
replied: 'From things, which do not know how to lie.'"
(*Sermo V in Dom. 2 de Adventu.*) Hippocrates could have answered similarly.

We can best appreciate the worth of Hippocrates by considering modern medical schools in this connection. They purport to give their students an integrated medical education,
but fail to achieve this comprehensive grasp of nature and fail
to realize its prior and basic necessity. The fact is, they are
essentially technical schools rather than professional schools.
This makes it difficult for them to deal with nature adequately. As a result, the catalytic forces of the Judeo-Christian
tradition have little to catalyze. What little they do in this
direction is more anatomic than physiologic and more divisive
than reparative. Furthermore, they add the tradition of St.
Luke to medicine as though they were transplanting a baptized appendix to an unbaptized body. They hardly know that,
in many instances, their body is not living but dead. Therefore,
in a choice between the pagan medicine of Hippocrates and
contemporary medicine—and we may remember here that the
natural law is implanted in the hearts of all men—there is reason
to believe that Hippocrates comes closer to God in his vision
of medicine that do those myopic ones who miss nature or
muddle the application of a God-given tradition.

Medical educators with an insensitivity to the Hippocratic
tradition and an insensitivity to the Judeo-Christian tradition
miss truth, therefore, in a twofold way. They fail to ascend *to*
the wholeness which comes from a comprehensive understanding of the patient, the physician, and the Art, through their
respective natures; and they fail to descend *with* the wholeness
of God's teaching into nature and the concrete world. They
narrow the teachings of nature and they narrow the teachings
of God. As a result, in these modern times we are becoming
more and more of a paying animal and less and less of a
praying animal, as if health were a commodity that could be
bought rather than a state which should be sought, not alone
through the ministerial functions of the physician but through

a wise accommodation of one's nature to nature, and a loving subjection of one's being to God.

Hippocrates is a major step on the road back to a fully integrated and properly humanized medicine and is a prime example of one type of contribution of the Great Books to modern culture and society.

HERBERT A. RATNER

SELECTED BIBLIOGRAPHY

The Hippocratic Collection, translated by W. H. S. Jones. Loeb Classical Library.
The Genuine Works of Hippocrates, translated by Francis Adams. Williams & Wilkins.
The Medical Works of Hippocrates, translated by John Chadwick and W. N. Mann. Charles C. Thomas.
CELSUS, *On Medicine,* Vol. 1, *Prooemium,* translated by W. G. Spencer. Loeb Classical Library.
REIDEL, William Arthur, *Hippocratic Medicine.* Columbia University Press.
PETERSON, William F., *Hippocratic Wisdom.* Charles C. Thomas.
HIPPOCRATES, *Selections.* Regnery.

Plato: Republic, *Books VI and VII*

IN THE FIFTH BOOK of the *Republic*, Plato has argued that
only the union of political power and philosophical wisdom
can secure to the citizens and the City "a possibility of life,
light, and happiness." This follows logically from his understanding of *real* justice as distinguished from specious justice,
of the intelligibility of real justice, and of its relevance to an
enduring, just social order. The Ideal State must contain a
permanent embodiment of its constitutive principles of objective justice through the infallible knowledge and agency of
the philosopher-king.

This repeated insistence of Plato is consequent to his radical
distinction between empirical and ideal truth. What experience gives us is, at best, a right opinion about things; it is not
scientific, that is, infallible, knowledge of reality. But sound
political philosophy is essentially a true metaphysics, the unfailing knowledge of "causes," "forms" and "first principles"
about the order among men as comprised within the all-com-
prehensive order of the universal cosmos. Empirical prescriptions and practical exigencies are too variant and unreal to be
the determinant norms of a just social order.

If, then, there could be found a man who could transfer the
perfect law, of which he has scientific knowledge, into the
character and institutions of men, he could help realize *in*
men as well as *among* men the fulfillment of the objective
demands of their natures. For Plato felt that the Socratic demand for self-knowledge and self-realization could not be fulfilled without a real insight into the character and scope of
political life. The soul of the individual is characteristically of
a social nature; we cannot separate one from the other. Private
and public life are so interdependent that if the latter is unjust
and corrupt the former cannot develop and reach its end.

Actually, the Greek *polis* was, like the Roman *res publica,* "the common thing," *to koinon.* It was "common" because it embraced universally or entirely the private and public life of its citizens, and no distinction between society and the State was conceivable for the Greek. It was the "thing" because it was the most tangible reality in their daily experiences. The citizen was related to the State as a part to the whole, and he was in duty bound to conform his behavior with patterns prescribed by the State, not because the State spoke with the absolute imperative of supernal authority but because it was the supreme embodiment of right reason among men. Plato's *politeia,* far from ignoring the historical nature of the Greek State, insisted that eternal principles must underlie its laws and institutions in order that *true* justice may exist in the City and its citizens. Plato's rejection of all empirical schemes of social engineering or statecraft as precarious contrivances is made on the metaphysical basis that they are ultimately unreal, unrelated to the objective order of lasting reality.

It is most imperative, therefore, to ascertain the course of study and way of life by which men, selected for their greater philosophic insight, can be trained to possess knowledge adequate for the governance of society. Philosophy, the knowledge of reality, *of that which is as it should be,* will thrive in society if society survives through philosophy.

Since the object and objective of speculative thought is to issue in practical reason for the conduct of human affairs, Plato is led to the study of the various sorts of intellection and of their corresponding import.

When Plato says of something that it truly *is,* or exists, he always means that its nature is both necessary and intelligible. Material and sensible things cannot truly be said to be, for the simple reason that, ceaselessly changing as they are, knowledge of them either completely loses its object or no longer answers to its object. The relativity of sense and sense perception, however, does not lead Plato to a universal relativism but only to the conclusion that sense perception on the part of both subject and object is too elusive to provide the objects of scientific knowledge. The object of absolute and infallible knowledge must be capable of being grasped in clear and scientific definition, which is of the universal.

Truly *to be* means to be immaterial, immutable, necessary and intelligible. That is precisely what Plato calls "Idea" or "Form." The eternal and intelligible Ideas are reality itself. The only thing that truly *is*, or exists, in a given individual, for example, is not that accidental combination of characters which constitutes him as distinct from every other individual within the same species; it is rather his own sharing in the eternal essence of this species. It is this participation of man in the eternal Idea or Form of human nature that constitutes his reality and intelligibility.

The import of this doctrine of Ideas for politics is clear. If the functions of political governance are the noblest and of greatest significance for all, then the philosopher-king, unmoved and uninfluenced by the things of change and opinion, will contemplate these eternal Ideas. His practical judgment being thus regulated by the unfailing vision of the eternal exemplar of justice, he can communicate a pattern of *right* order as the guiding inner principle for the just and orderly integration of political society. Now, among the Ideas there is one which dominates all the others, because they all share in its intelligibility. It is the Idea of the Good, the supreme and adequate object of the philosopher's study.

The doctrine of the Idea or Form of the Good is the central metaphysical doctrine of the Republic and it is indeed remarkable, as Jowett has observed, that although Plato speaks of it as the first principle of Truth and Being, it is nowhere mentioned in his writings except in the *locus classicus* of the *Republic*. Just as the sun, according to Plato's theory of light and sight, is the source of vision in the eye and of visibility in its object, so too the Good is the source of intelligence in the mind and of intelligibility in the object. Secondly, as the sun is the source not only of sight and visibility but also of generation, nourishment and growth of the organic world, so the Good is the author not only of truth and knowledge but also of the being of the world. The world is intelligible and the soul truly cognoscent in proportion as the Good is reflected and discerned. The Idea of the Good dominates the intelligible world because all that *is*, in so far as it is, is good.

Through this imagery of the sun, Plato teaches that the Idea of the Good is the source of being, intelligibility and intelligence. It is not, however, an object among objects, as the sun is. It is above being because existence, in the sense in which we experience it ourselves and which we assert of the objects we see, is mutable and defective. There we have the essence of Platonism, the belief in the reality and more than reality of the "ideals," as his Ideas may properly be called. That which is as it ought to be, transcends in dignity and power that which simply is. Since it is assumed in the *Republic* that scientific knowledge is knowledge of Forms, the objects which are thus said to derive their being from the Good must clearly mean the whole body of Forms. Consequently, the philosopher's knowledge must have its culmination in the actual apprehension of this transcendental Good as clue to the whole teleological scheme of existence.

Plato then proceeds by the use of another simile, that of the Line, to illustrate the process of mental development by which the Idea of the Good becomes known to the few men endowed with a greater philosophic capacity than the generality of men have. Draw a vertical straight line crossed into two main sections, each subdivided into two more. The upper level, *episteme,* is properly the domain of infallible knowledge, since it possesses the absolute certainty of understanding (*dianoia*) and reason (*nous*) of the intelligible world, and it contrasts sharply with the essentially lesser assurance of opinion (*doxa*) comprehending sensate perception (*pistis*) and the lowest species of cognition, that of shadows, reflections, images, and second-hand imitations (*eikasia*). While the two main divisions apparently suggest an antithesis of the sensible and the intellectual, an opposition of the permanent and the transient, of the universal and the particular, there is no break between the visible and the suprasensible world, since the former by reason of any meaning inherent in it must conduce to the world of Ideas.

Further, the simile of the Line aptly stresses the continuity of the progression from defective and imperfect cognizance of any sort to the knowledge which is perfect, knowledge of first principles, according to the correlative consideration of the character of the object of mental apprehension and the corresponding state of mind. The successive aspects that the world presents to the mind of man as it advances to a greater

power of discernment, do not connote four different classes
of real objects but rather four different views of the same objects.

Among the chief evils which vitiated the political life of the
Greek *polis* were the distorted views of justice circulated
among the populace by the sophistical persuasion of the rhetoricians. What the people were led to consider justice, was, in
Plato's linear scale of intellection, but a caricature of the empirical justice of the Athenian Constitution, which itself, according
to Plato's theory of Ideas, is at most only an image of the universal Idea of Justice. This acceptance of second-hand imitations as final is the most superficial kind and lowest level of
cognizance, which Plato aptly designates *eikasia*.

When man recognizes it for what it is—and this he does in
referring the distorted representation to the justice embodied
in a particular Constitution (or in a particular man)—he is no
longer in a mental condition of *eikasia*, but of *pistis*, the opin-
ionate state of mind whose ultimate objects of cognition are
the empirical data of the external world and of our experience.
When we discern that sensible objects are, in turn, but imperfect embodiments in the particular of the universal Idea or
Form, then we ascend beyond the region of opinion to the
superior mental level of scientific knowledge. The uncertain-
ties and conjectures of the domain of opinion are harmful and
must be dispelled only in so far as one believes the objects of
sense perception to be ultimate truth. Statesmen and rulers
would indeed be blind leaders of the blind if they mistook for
Absolute Justice the shadow world of *eikasia* and the variables
of *pistis*.

When the particular objects of sense perception are recognized for what they are, shifting and changing impressions of
sense or of subjective opinion, they compel the mind of man to
seek by the instrumentality of these very sense phenomena the
"Forms" or "principles" underlying this changing and elusive world. Particular constitutions change in time and vary
from city to city, but the essence of justice remains fixed, and it
is in reference to this objective immaterial reality that we ap-
praise the justice of particular Constitutions. The dissatisfaction that comes with the admission that the sense objects of
doxa are unreliable media of truth arises from the fact, which

Plato never questions nor demonstrates but simply assumes, that the mind of man can attain infallible knowledge of the *real*.

The mental process by which we attain to the unchanging reality, Plato calls *dianoia*. The objects of *dianoia* are the "Ideas," "Forms," "absolute essences" which the mind of man strives to ascertain by the use of the sensible observables of the lower level of *doxa*, and, starting from commonly accepted hypotheses, the mind proceeds not to a first principle but to a conclusion. The geometrician, for example, assumes that every number is either odd or even, or that there are just three kinds of angles. He employs figures and diagrams as sources of suggestion and illustration, but in his reasonings and demonstrations the "eye of his mind" is fixed upon the ideal and perfect objects of thought, the universal, and not upon the empirical circles or lines nor even upon the sensible particulars of geometrical diagrams. The validity of his theorems depends on the logical consistency with which they follow from the unquestioned hypotheses.

The sense world, however, is not wholly an illusion. The sensible particular, too, is real only in so far as it is subsumed under one of the Ideas as a class instance. In other words, not merely are our subjective universal concepts abstract forms devoid of objective content, but also to each true universal concept there corresponds an objective reality, and the corresponding reality is of a higher order than sense perception as such.

We can appreciate, therefore, Plato's preoccupation with science as the road to the vision of the Good. The sciences are great educational instruments to facilitate both in methodology and in content the transition (or "conversion") of the soul from the materiates of the phenomenal world to the higher and true multiplicity of the immaterial unitary realities of the exemplary Ideas. The sciences deal with specific forms of reality; each form is related to other forms by reason of its derivation from the Absolute Good, the ultimate principle of Unity, and, as thus constituted, provides a part of the hierarchic noetic structure by which the mind ascends to the Good.

However, to attain to this perfect intelligence, the mind must rise to the higher and more rigorous science of *dialectic*. The mathematical objects of *dianoia*, because they do not mount up above their hypothetical premises, constitute a class of "intermediaries" of intelligible particulars above the sensible particulars but below the true universals. The highest level of intellection is *noesis*, wherein the mind employs the initial hypotheses of the sciences solely as points of departure for the discovery of the first principles and, having done so, deduces the consequences which follow.

In this process, dialectic differs from the other sciences both in function and in methodology. The scientists, in their search for some one principle to unify a body of phenomena, proceed logically from hypotheses to conclusions, with the accessory assistance of sensible imagery. The dialectician, on the contrary, advances to the first principles from and through the hypotheses, independently, however, of any imperfect sensate aids. The dialectician will not, like the geometer, rest with the Idea of triangle, but will ascend to the first principle from which all geometrical sciences flow, to that which gives them their being and truth. In every instance his quest for knowledge will lead him to the first principle of that branch of knowledge.

But the dialectician proceeds still higher. Just as the lesser sciences strive to achieve a harmonious synthesis of all reality under the dominance of the Idea which they study as their proper object, so dialectics rises from the multiplicity of exemplary Ideas to the source of all being and intelligibility, the Idea of the Good, which, in its function of absolute unity, is the synthesizing reality of the transcendental sphere and the ultimate Exemplar. As a consequence of the difference in these two processes, the dialectician can give an exact account of his science, whereas the mathematician cannot. The latter assumes as a working hypothesis the being and truth of the absolutes of his science, of the absolute angle, for instance, but has not thereby attained to the causes of the intelligibility of that absolute. He assumes the validity of the major concept so as to have a guiding norm when descending through the various species of mathematical reality contained under it; and he seeks to draw conclusions, using the various species of mathematical reality as his basis. The objects of geometry are intelligible when considered in reference to the Idea under which they are contained, but the validity of geometry as a science has not thereby been established.

This, dialectics achieves. Once it attains to the ultimate of all being and truth, it descends by strictly abstract reasoning, in and by the Ideas themselves, to "destroy" the hypotheses and reveal them as truths now ascertained by reference to first principles and not as actually false, as they may well have turned out to be. In this epistemological ascent and descent, the dialectician discovers the place of each intelligible object in the hierarchy of reality, and thereby ascertains the validity of each science. The objects corresponding to *noesis* are forms and first principles, spiritual realities, free from matter, immutable, perfect, intelligible. They are epistemological and ontological truths; immanent in the things which embody and reflect them, indefinitely imitable and participable in sensible reality and transcendental realities beyond the subjective existence of our abstract concepts.

The discouraging difficulties of this Platonistic ascension of the soul from the darkness of sense to the light and truth of all being (*ex umbris et imaginibus ad veritatem*), Plato illustrates by the allegory of the Cave in which he develops conjointly the doctrines underlying two previous similes of the Sun and of the Line. The majority of the people are represented as spending their lives in a state of *eikasia*, entranced in a make-believe world of puppet-show realities and, like children, imprisoned in their own fancies. Should a person escape to the entry of the Cave, he must habituate himself to the glare of the light and strive perseveringly through the four successive cognitive stages, whereby the world becomes more intelligible and the mind more intelligent, until he beholds the sun itself, figure of the Idea of the Good, "universal cause of all things right and beautiful—the source of truth and reason." Then must the philosopher, from a compelling sense of public duty, constrain himself to descend to the cavernous darkness and, like Socrates, risk even his life at the hands of those he would release from the bondage of falsehood and misconceptions and lead to eternal and absolute truths and values.

The primacy of the spiritual in Plato and its moral and esthetic connotations should not mislead to a religious interpretation of the Platonic ascesis to the Supreme Good. His ascent is not "mystic" (like that of St. John of the Cross) nor "ecstatic"; it is dialectical, and the vision of the Good is by "pure intelligence." Further, the Good, though undefinable in its ontological nature, is surely not a person but an Idea; nor is it ever for Plato the object of adoration and supplication. Indeed, the Platonic gods are inferior to the Ideas. On the other hand, it is beyond doubt that the Neo-Platonists and the Christian philosophers, such as Plotinus and Pseudo-Dionysius, were interpolating the Platonic ascesis when they evolved a religious *via negativa* as a legitimate approach to the Absolute One, the Good. The figure of the sun to symbolize the source of intelligence and being in the suprasensible world persisted in Neo-Platonic literature, and finds essentially superior expressions in the Judeo-Christian revelation—*Dominus illuminatio mea et salus mea, lux mundi,* and the Pauline *per Ipsum, cum Ipso, et in Ipso.* In Dante's *Divine Comedy,* Beatrice, Divine Wisdom, is compared to "Light intervening between Truth and Intellect"—*che lume fia tra il vero e l'intelletto.*

An adequate critique of the metaphysics of the sixth and seventh books of the *Republic* is not the scope of this study, and so we may be content to select some profitable considerations underlying the doctrine of the Good as Plato refers it to the good of individuals and of society.

Plato gave full philosophical value to the Socratic principle that the universal and supreme cause in everything that exists is the intelligible Good. The fully real is the fully intelligible and the fully good, and it is not only the proper object of speculative thought but equally the true normative objective of all human endeavor. The first inference to be drawn about Plato's dialectic is that the mind of man is itself subject to orderly method. He guards it against anarchic expressions without at the same time destroying the mind's function of reaching beyond set bounds. This is not a prudential postulate for the possibility of knowledge and science; rather, Plato's hierarchic noetic structure is the supreme dictate of an objective world of reality. The mind of man does not fabricate the objects of its knowledge nor contrive arbitrarily the manner of intellectual discovery.

The significance of this conception lies in Plato's answer to the Socratic demand for self-knowledge and self-realization. In our experience we find an intellectual appetition effecting a final causation toward ideal ends which lie outside the mere physical tendency. The reason is that the soul has an innate affinity with the eternal Forms, else Plato would ask how it could yearn after them and guess about their nature. On account of that affinity it can strive to transform itself to the likeness of the Ideal through a dialectical purification from sensate experiences of the body and grow more and more conformable to the intelligible Ideas. Even artificial natures such as society and the arts can justify the meaning of their existence only as the counterpart of their exemplary archetypes. The conduct of human affairs is dominated by the recognition of philosophic insight into an all-pervading purpose *sub specie aeternitatis* that must issue into an objectively just social order.

The second profitable observation is that all valid knowledge mounts to the Good, and education for all, according to their innate capacity, must be of that knowledge which gradually leads to it. Plato's love of truth was not simply for its own sake but rested on his conviction that it was the ultimate condition of all values, moral, esthetic and intellectual, and that it is the objective pattern and motivation for the realization of justice in the individual soul and the achievement of a just social order among men.

Plato's interest in the epistemological ascension is therefore by no means a purely academic one: the argument of the *Republic* is the search after justice, and without knowledge of it the individual will not realize his own true good nor will the statesman be the salvation of his people. True, for want of an adequate metaphysics and sound theology, Plato did not provide the metaphysical basis for morality, God, the eternal and natural law, or for a human individuality that transcends the omnicompetence of the Greek *polis,* nor did he discern that the good of man is the good citizen *and more,* and that society and the state are distinct. But it is his everlasting glory that he struck at the roots of that individualism that is so anarchic in the expression of truth and values and is so divisive of social harmony.

Politics is but a part of the total reality, within which it must ever remain for the validity of its claims. We must wait till modern times to hear the word "politics" pronounced as an unsavory expletive. Lastly, Christian charity welcomes the import of the Platonic obligation whereby the truly competent, learned and wise should devote themselves to the good of society. Any separation of the intellectual life from its requisite context in human affairs is doubly disastrous. For it abandons practices and decisions to unregulated impulse or, at best, to temporizing and expedient endeavors. As for itself, such sterile intellectualism will lose magnanimity of soul for want of that charity which the contemplation of Divine Truth ever enkindles. To those who study him diligently, Plato may be, as he has been to many since the early Christian centuries, a guide to the vision of the Eternal Good, the God of revelation and of philosophy, lovable and adorable, that Divine Light wherein alone we see and ever shall see light. *Dominus Deus omnium scientiarum, Dominus illuminatio mea.*

JOSEPH F. COSTANZO

SELECTED BIBLIOGRAPHY

TAYLOR, A. E., *Plato, the Man and His Work.* Methuen.
STEWART, J. A., *Plato's Doctrine of Ideas.* Oxford.
BARKER, Ernest, *Greek Political Theory, Plato and His Predecessors.* Methuen.
NETTLESHIP, R. L., *Lectures on the Republic of Plato.* Macmillan.
HARDIE, W. F. R., *Study in Plato.* Oxford.
JOWETT, B., *The Dialogues of Plato, Vol. II, The Republic.* Scribners.
PLATO, *Republic,* Books VI-VII. Regnery.

Aristotle: Metaphysics, *Selections*

IF IMPACT upon the intellectual development of the West be the thing that gives a work a place on the list of the Great Books, a plausible case could be made out for putting the *Metaphysics* of Aristotle at the head of the list. For this work is the supreme achievement of the mind whose influence upon the evolution of Western thought has probably been deeper, more far-reaching and more enduring than any other. It makes no difference how you look at Aristotle; you can agree with Dante that he is "the master of those who know" and hold with Schelling that "no one will create anything enduring who has not come to terms with Aristotle," or you can prefer to think that his influence, on the whole, has been unfortunate, and to say with Bertrand Russell that "since the beginning of the seventeenth century almost every serious intellectual advance has had to begin with an attack on some Aristotelian doctrine." The fact remains that, either for good or ill, his ideas have been the strongest moving forces in the shaping of Western thought. And all his ideas have their roots in his *Metaphysics*.

The term "metaphysics" means literally "after physics" or "beyond physics"; most historians agree that it was first coined by Andronicus of Rhodes as a label for those lectures of Aristotle which were placed after the lectures on physics in his collected treatises. Originally signifying nothing more than a sequence of lectures, it was later taken to mean the very nature and substance of these lectures, which are precisely an inquiry into reality beyond the physical and sensible order. In any case, the title was never used by the author of the *Metaphysics* himself. He had three other names for it: sometimes *Wisdom*, again *First Philosophy*, still again *Theology*. And it is only by entering into the meaning of these three titles that some insight into the nature, scope and significance of this great work can be gained.

It is as *Wisdom* that Aristotle first presents his *Metaphysics* to the reader. In the two opening chapters of Book One (which are among the selected passages on the Great Books program) he analyzes the nature of wisdom and shows why the science he is undertaking to discuss eminently deserves this title. And he does so in typical Aristotelian fashion—not by laying down preconceived and ready-made notions, but through a dialectical procedure which seeks to disengage the characteristics commonly attributed to wisdom and to show how they are found in the subject under inquiry. Starting with the premise—long since become aphoristic—that all men naturally desire to know, and comparing the various ways in which men satisfy this desire, he discovers that knowledge is generally considered to have something of the nature of wisdom about it to the extent in which it gets at the causes of things. Already the reader is prepared for the constant preoccupation with the problem of causes which runs throughout the *Metaphysics*.

But knowledge of causes in general, though sufficient for science, is not sufficient for wisdom. The wise man must reach the highest and most universal principles of all reality. This, Aristotle shows by examining the characteristics commonly attributed to the wise man and pointing out how they are found only in one who has attained to the ultimate and most universal reasons for things. And nothing could better serve to bring out the true nature of the *Metaphysics* and its peculiar relevance for the times in which we live than a consideration of some of these characteristics.

The first quality people look for in the wise man, Aristotle suggests, is wholeness and fullness and breadth of view. The wise man is not a specialist, not a departmentalist. Still, he is not an encyclopedist either; he does not attempt the impossible task of getting to know all reality in its unlimited diversity. Rather he knows all things by rising above their multiplicity to their basic unities and ultimately to the most basic unity of all in which they find their summation and intelligibility and order. This means that he is concerned not so much with this or that particular type of reality or with this or that aspect of it,

but with the very inner core of reality or being itself. He wants
to know what it means to *be* and what are the primary attributes and principles of being in so far as it is being. And this, as
Aristotle never stops repeating throughout the *Metaphysics,* is
the proper object of all the interests of the metaphysician.

You cannot let go of these things, you cannot turn aside from
the first principles of all reality and lose your grasp upon the
basic unities in things without leaving human knowledge and
therefore human life fragmentized and departmentalized and
dispersed. The intellectual confusion resulting from the anti-
metaphysical bias of the modern mind has made this as plain
as anything could be. And against the background of this chaos
of an age of science without wisdom, the reading of Aristotle's
Metaphysics has taken on a significance it has never had before
in its history.

But no one should attempt to read it expecting to find it easy
going. Even if the whole intellectual climate in which we live
had not effectively conditioned the mind against reading of
this sort, the fact that metaphysics is wisdom would still make
it an extremely difficult experience. The great Arab philosopher Avicenna claimed that he had read the *Metaphysics* forty
times without being able to understand it fully; and Aristotle
himself seems to have been acutely conscious of the difficulty of
the inquiry he was undertaking, as the constant repetition of
the phrase "the science we are seeking," even in the latter books
of the treatise, might suggest. In any case, the second characteristic of the wise man is acquaintance not only with things easily
known but with difficult things as well.

It is impossible to get at the first principles and most universal causes of all reality except by transcending the realm of
the purely sensible and physical, and this is never easy for man
to do. Indeed, there will always be a kind of conflict between
man as man and man as metaphysician. For the more congenial
study of the human intellect is the physical and sensible world,
whereas the most proper study of the metaphysician transcends this world. Man is more naturally a physicist than a metaphysician, more naturally a scientist than a wise man. So true
is this that Aristotle, in the opening passages of the *Metaphysics,* warns the reader that the study he is undertaking is really

more divine than human: " . . . the possession of it might be justly regarded as beyond human power; . . . such a science either God alone can have, or God above all others."

This will help us to understand presently why Aristotle called his *Metaphysics* by the name of *Theology;* meanwhile it gives us reason to suspect that the fact that our culture since the Renaissance has been at the same time humanistic and anti-metaphysical is something more than a mere coincidence. But in this, as in everything else, man's life is ruled by that strange paradox from which there seems to be no escape: only by striving for things that transcend him, things that are proper to God, can man make his life truly human. The inhumanity of a culture of science without wisdom leaves no doubt about it: the knowledge that is most difficult for man is the knowledge that is most important for him.

The difficulty of the study of metaphysics is connected with another characteristic of wisdom noted by Aristotle. The wise man, he says, is one who is given not to the life of action and production but to the life of contemplation and speculation. And in the natural order there is no higher object of contemplation than the inner core of reality and the ultimate source from which all things flow. Metaphysics is therefore the most speculative of all the natural disciplines. And this means, says Aristotle, that it is also the most liberal. For practical knowledge is like a servant or slave: its whole function is to serve some purpose beyond itself; speculative knowledge is like a freeman: it exists in its own right and is its own end. For Aristotle, liberal education does not mean merely an acquaintance with a wide variety of subjects; it means essentially an education in speculative knowledge, and primarily in metaphysics, the most liberal discipline of all. And he does not hesitate to admit that precisely because it is the most liberal it is the most useless of all knowledge. But he adds: it is also the most valuable. "All the sciences, indeed, are more necessary than this, but none is better."

Unfortunately, it is difficult for man to appreciate this distinction between usefulness and value, difficult for him to rise to the highest level of speculation. For he is more a *homo faber* than a *homo sapiens,* more at his ease in the practical order than in the speculative. Or, as Aristotle puts it, "human nature is in many ways in bondage." Yet, if he rejects this knowledge, there will be nothing in the natural order to save him from his bondage. Once the most liberal of all disciplines is gone, true liberal education is doomed. The liberal character of the other speculative disciplines, all of which are completely orientated toward metaphysics, will gradually disappear. Education will be taken over by technology; and, in general, the practical will assume primacy over the speculative. And in a culture in which this has happened, it is inevitable that man's life should be ruled by ideologies; for an ideology is a rationalization of the appetites and consequently a subjection of the speculative to the practical. This we have seen in our own antimetaphysical age.

The implications of it all become clearer when viewed in relation to another quality of wisdom which Aristotle attributes to metaphysics. "The wise man," he says, "must not be ordered but must order." Metaphysics is the only natural discipline which attains to the first causes of things; it alone can grasp the ultimate final cause, the ultimate purpose of things. And that is why it alone can order all things to their proper ends. Remove this ordering principle, and everything in the speculative order is thrown into confusion.

As is well known, Robert Hutchins in his *Higher Learning in America* has made capital of this point in explaining the chaos in the modern American university. For the first time in history, he points out, higher learning has been without the ordering principle of wisdom: the Greeks had their metaphysics and the medievalists their theology; but the moderns are without any wisdom to give order to their learning. And since it is too much to expect our secular universities to make sacred theology architectonic, only a revival of metaphysics can bring order out of chaos.

The fact that metaphysics is the basic principle of order for all learning, and that it alone penetrates to the first causes of all reality, explains why Aristotle often calls it *First Philosophy*. By this he means that it is first in the order of dignity, in the sense that it studies the highest objects the human mind can get to know, and first in the logical order, in the sense that all the other branches of knowledge derive their fundamental principles from it. He does not mean that it is first in the pedagogical order, whatever those may think who, followers of Aristotle in name but of Christian Wolff in fact, insist on putting it at the beginning of the college or university curriculum. For Aristotle, metaphysics belongs at the very end of the process of learning, since it is the most difficult kind of knowledge and since the human mind can get at first causes only through a previous knowledge of secondary causes. This explains why readings from the *Metaphysics* are reserved for the fourth year of the Great Books program. But to make clear what is implied in this title of *First Philosophy* and how it is related to the title of *Wisdom,* some clarifications are necessary.

It is customary to contrast wisdom with science. The contrast goes back to Aristotle himself and is important for an understanding of the nature of metaphysics. But the modern reader of the *Metaphysics* will miss completely what Aristotle means by the distinction if he understands the terms involved in the sense in which they are now generally understood. He will find Aristotle contrasting metaphysics with mathematics and physics, and once again he will be misled if he takes the term "physics" in its modern meaning. Moreover, he will probably be confused when he finds Aristotle sometimes calling metaphysics science and sometimes distinguishing it from science. Even the term "philosophy" will be misleading, and he will not grasp the full import of the title *First Philosophy* if he takes it in its modern meaning.

To dissipate all these ambiguities, one has to understand first of all that the term "science" has a double meaning in Aristotle: a generic meaning which includes all certain knowledge through causes and which applies therefore to metaphysics, and a specific meaning which is limited to knowledge through secondary causes and which is therefore distinguished from metaphysics. For Aristotle, the term "philosophy" includes all the branches of science in the generic sense, even such disciplines as mathematics, chemistry and biology. The term "physics" includes not only physics in the modern sense but the whole study of nature: cosmology, psychology, biology, chemistry, and their multiple offshoots and hybrids. In modern times, however, the mathematical sciences and the more concrete branches of natural science and moral science have shed the name "philosophy" and have arrogated to themselves the name "science," which they once shared with the whole of philosophy. Thus has arisen the distinction between philosophy and science. The terms which for Aristotle were coterminous have now become antithetical.

One of the unfortunate consequences of this development is that since the days of Wolff this new distinction between philosophy and science has been identified with the old distinction between wisdom and science, and all the branches of philosophy are now considered to be a study of ultimate causes. This situation is completely alien to the thought of Aristotle; and to read the *Metaphysics* with this view in mind is to miss the central point of what he is trying to say about metaphysical knowledge and wisdom. Moreover, it is only when one remembers the scope which the term "philosophy" had for Aristotle that it becomes possible to see that the title *First Philosophy* means that metaphysics is the first of all the disciplines which fall under the generic notion of science, and that the "second philosophies" include all the sciences in the modern sense as well as the disciplines still called philosophy.

Since the student of "first philosophy" must come to grips with the first sources of all knowledge and reality, one of his tasks is to examine critically the basic notions involved in the study of being. The terms employed in this study are necessarily analogical, and if their various meanings are not carefully discriminated no end of confusion will result. This task Aristotle performs in Book V, which is the second selection in the Great Books readings. At first glance this lexicon seems to be a rather haphazard collection of terms without any particular design or continuity. But St. Thomas, in his *Commentary on the Metaphysics,* shows that Aristotle is following a very definite order. For every science deals with three things: a subject, its causes, and it properties. In this lexicon Aristotle examines first the terms which relate to causes, such as "principle," "cause" and "element"; secondly the terms which pertain to the subject of metaphysics, considering on the one hand those relating directly to the subject, such as "one," "being" and "substance," and on the other those relating to its divisions into actuality and potentiality, and into the categories of quantity, quality, etc.; and thirdly the terms which pertain to the properties of being, such as "whole" and "limit."

A careful and critical reading of this lexicon has more than scientific and academic significance. For the notions and distinctions it contains have become deeply imbedded in the whole cultural heritage of the West; they have shaped and determined our very habits of thought. Even the thinkers who have attacked them most vigorously have had their thinking processes deeply influenced by them. This was true of Descartes, who wrote of Aristotle: "Those who have not followed him have yet been imbued with his teaching in their youth"; it was true of Hobbes and of all the others. The yeast of Aristotelian notions is working everywhere in Western thought, and no one can consider himself truly educated unless he has acquired some kind of reflective and critical acquaintance with them.

Of all the thirty notions in this lexicon, none receives closer attention throughout the *Metaphysics* than that of substance. This explains why the final Great Books selections are passages dealing with substance and substantial change. The reason Aristotle gives so much attention to substance is that he is inquiring into the nature of being, and substance alone is being in the full sense of the word. And because it is impossible to understand substantial being without analyzing substantial "coming-to-be," the metaphysician must explore the problem of change.

It would be a serious mistake to find only museum interest in Aristotle's solution of this problem in terms of matter, form and privation. What he says about the necessity of explaining change in terms of contraries is just as alive today in the Marxian Dialectics of Nature as it was in the teachings of Heraclitus and of all the other Greek thinkers who preceded Aristotle. The Marxists have resurrected Heraclitus, as they willingly admit; and that is a sufficient reason, if not the only one, for revivifying the only adequate solution ever given for Heraclitus' problem of change.

But though the metaphysician must be concerned with all substances, there are some substances which are his primary object of inquiry—those immaterial beings which, because free of all matter, are above the problem of change. Though neither disregarding nor disdaining the material world as the metaphysics of Plato did, the metaphysics of Aristotle is completely orientated toward the immaterial world, where being is found in its fullness. So true is this that if there were no purely immaterial world there would be no metaphysics, and some other science would be "first philosophy" and wisdom. On several occasions he tells us that this would be the science of nature; elsewhere, as though suspecting that with the disappearance of metaphysics the practical would take precedence over the speculative, he suggests that it might be political science. Perhaps his thought could be paraphrased in this way: when the mind becomes materialistic, metaphysics will disappear and man will endeavor to make himself wise through the physical and social sciences. Is not this an accurate description of our decadent culture?

It is because the *Metaphysics* is centered in the immaterial world that it can be called *Theology*. For if it has a special interest in all immaterial substances, it is primarily concerned with that immaterial Being who alone is being in the fullest and most absolute sense, and who is the first cause and ultimate end of all reality. For Aristotle, the whole of metaphysics culminates in the study of God, as he suggests in the opening pages: "This science alone must be in two ways most divine. For the science which it would be most meet for God to have is a divine science, and so is any science that deals with divine objects; and this science alone has both these qualities; for God is thought to be among the causes of all things and to be a first principle, and such a science either God alone can have, or God above all others."

Reading what Aristotle has to say about God is bound to be a paradoxical experience for the Christian. He will be equally amazed by Aristotle's achievements and by his failures. On the one hand he will find the most refined and exalted ideas ever conceived by a pagan mind, such as the notion of God as pure intelligence and pure actuality; on the other there will be the obscure and inept handling of notions, like that of creation, which to the Christian mind seem elementary. The fact of the matter is that Aristotle's natural theology points to supernatural theology in a paradoxical way: its achievements provide the most perfect natural instruments for the exploration of the riches of faith; its failures show the weakness of even the best pagan mind in dealing with divine things, and thus call for a higher theology. Luther's statement that "the whole of Aristotle is to theology as darkness is to light" is not unequivocally true.

It is the title of *Theology* that gives this book its most valid claim to greatness. The *Metaphysics* is, in a sense, the supreme achievement of the Greek world, for in it the pagan mind reached its most penetrating and accurate knowledge of God and succeeded for the first time in making this knowledge into a strict and formal science. At the same time it is the chief link between the Greek and medieval worlds, for it was in the *Metaphysics* of Aristotle that the medievals found the best and richest natural resources for the erection of their vast theological structures. The most eminent theologians have never agreed with Luther's claim that "only without Aristotle can we become theologians." And from this point of view, a Christian appraisal of Aristotle's *Metaphysics* is unnecessary: it has already been appraised by the best Christian minds and found to be the greatest contribution of pagan intelligence to the Word.

BERNARD I. MULLAHY

SELECTED BIBLIOGRAPHY

ST. THOMAS AQUINAS, *Commentarium in Metaphysicam Aristotelis*. Cathala ed., Marietti.
GOMPERZ, Theodor, *Greek Thinkers*, Vol. IV. London, J. Murray.
JAEGER, Werner, *Aristotle: Fundamentals of the History of His Development*. Oxford.
ROSS, W. D., *Aristotle's Metaphysics*. Oxford.
ZELLER, E., *Aristotle and the Earlier Peripatetics*, Vol. I. Longmans, Green.
ARISTOTLE, *Metaphysics*, Selections. Regnery.

Sextus Empiricus: Outlines of Pyrrhonism, *Book I*

IT IS DUE only to an accident of history that Book I of the *Outlines* of Sextus Empiricus can lay any claim to be numbered among the Great Books. Of itself, the principal merit of Sextus —his exceptional competence as an industrious and clear-sighted compiler of the ideas of more ingenious minds than his own (to which he frequently acknowledges his indebtedness)—would not warrant the inclusion of any of his writings in an anthology of great thinkers. His contribution to the history of ancient philosophy is important not because of any philosophical or literary originality of his own, but solely due to the peculiar historical circumstance that, while the actual teaching of his masters, notably Pyrrho, Aenesidemus and Agrippa, has been lost, he has preserved for us in his writings a lucid and systematic presentation of the skeptical tradition, one of the most significant trends in Greek thinking.

Book I of the *Outlines of Pyrrhonism* is the earliest and the best of the writings of Sextus Empiricus. It purports to be a clear statement and defense of the skeptical position and, as far as possible, it adequately fulfills that purpose. What literary brilliance it lacks in discharging this function—in comparison, for instance, with the dialog *Hermotimus* of Lucian of Samosata—it amply compensates for by the mass of information which it imparts, by the clarity and precision of its exposition and by the good sense of the author. The general attitude, arguments and objectives of the later full-fledged Greek skeptics are precisely defined and are propounded with an exactness that descends to the minutest dialectical differences of meaning and to the finest nuances of terminology.

This concern with being comprehensive and precise neces-

sarily detracts from the literary excellence of the work, as it
generally does in any first-rate handbook, but the passion for
completeness and accuracy is pushed to such extremes in the
Outlines that it results in the exposition often becoming dis-
ordered and lacking in internal coherence and, at times, ends
in little more than the sheerest logomachy and sophistical hair-
splitting.

The other two books of the *Outlines* are simply applications
to various dogmatic theses of the general refutation contained
in Book I. Hence they are more polemical than expository, directly attacking all previous systematic philosophers on every
front, listing their counterarguments and turning these against
their proponents, principally by attributing to them the standard fallacies of ignorance of the issue, begging the question,
vicious circle, infinite regress, and so on. The one word
"against," which is featured in the titles of all of Sextus' other
works, signalizes the negative and polemical character of his
thinking and, at the same time, summarizes his whole philosophical—or, to be more precise, his antiphilosophical—position. In his *Against the Professors of All Arts and Sciences
(Contra Mathematicos)* five books are *Against the Dogmatists*
(logicians, physicists and ethicians) and six are directed against
grammarians, rhetoricians, geometers, arithmeticians, astrolo-
gers and musicians.

In short, Sextus is opposed, or at least pretends to be opposed, to any positive affirmation whatsoever, to anything that
smacks of theory or even of conjectural speculation. A thoroughgoing skeptic, he has little or nothing to offer that is positive or
constructive. This negative and disputatious attitude, however,
has been the occasion of much of the incidental renown that
has been attached to his writings. Since he felt it incumbent
upon himself to expound the doctrines which he proposed to
refute, his writings in general, and notably the present work,
rank with those of Diogenes Laertius as one of the chief sources
for our knowledge of ancient Greek philosophy.

Caution and discrimination, however, must be exercised in
using either of these sources. As a biographer Diogenes betrays
a penchant for the legendary; and Sextus, while professing and
apparently striving to be objective as a doxographer, seems
unwittingly to represent the opinions of his predecessors in

such a way as to make them less immune to the criticism of the skeptics than they deserve. Furthermore, with the outstanding exception of the Stoics, his acquaintance with the principal Greek philosophers, such as Plato, Aristotle and Epicurus, appears on the whole to have been superficial and, at times, even gives the impression of having been got at second hand.

If one were to trace the origins and antecedents of Greek skepticism, none of the classical schools of Greek philosophy would be found to be altogether without its share of blame in furthering the degeneration of the indigenous Greek love of wisdom (*philosophia*) into a skeptical negation of itself. There were Greek philosophers who, prior to Pyrrho, were skeptical in principle, but none of them was intellectually ruthless enough to carry out his skeptical premises to their logical conclusion. As Sextus frequently points out, even the skepticism of Sophists, such as Protagoras or Gorgias, and of members of the New Academy, such as Arcesilaus or Carneades, was half-hearted and tainted with a latent dogmatism. Even their positive assertions—that reality is contradictory or that nothing can be known with certitude *about external reality*—are theoretical pronouncements, hence foreign to the true skeptical attitude of complete intellectual neutrality. These philosophers were just as agnostic as the skeptics, but they differed from the latter in making too positive a protestation of their agnosticism and proclaiming it a dogma.

We stress the words "about external reality" advisedly. For the Greek skeptic did not attempt the physically impossible feat of questioning his own immediate experience, the evidence of his direct consciousness. In short, he did not doubt phenomena themselves, that is, his sense impressions and the feelings that necessarily result from them (*Outlines*, I, section 13); he simply declined to view them as apprehensions or to make any judgments about their objective validity (sections 19, 20, 198, 200). It would be anachronistic, however, to assume that he was an idealist. Though he suspended his judgment about the nature of the reality that lay beyond sensible appearances, he never raised the question of the existence of an external material world. As naïvely realistic as all the other Greek philosophers, he took this existence for granted.

Nor, again, was he a relativist in the proper meaning of that term. For the relativist is after his own fashion as dogmatic as any, whether he contends with Heraclitus that being itself is essentially "becoming," or with Protagoras concludes from this thesis that man is the measure of all things. Aenesidemus used to claim that the skeptical contention that the same reality *appears* to possess opposite qualities led to the Heraclitean conclusion that reality was actually constituted by contradictory attributes (sections 210-212). With this, Sextus disagrees. For, he argues, "the view about the same thing having opposite appearances is not a dogma of the skeptics but a fact which is experienced not by the skeptics alone but also by the rest of philosophers and by all mankind."

The skeptic, however, refuses to draw any inferences from these *apparently* contradictory attributes or to dogmatize about the nature of objective reality, as do the Heracliteans. Hence, "the skeptic way, so far from being an aid to the knowledge of the Heraclitean philosophy, is actually an obstacle thereto, seeing that the skeptic decries all the dogmatic statements of Heraclitus as rash utterances." Though the subjectivism implied in Protagoras' famous formula that man is the measure of all things seems at first glance identical with the phenomenalism of the skeptic, it is too dogmatic to suit Sextus. What does the formula mean? (Needless to say, it should not be wrenched from its historical context and interpreted in the idealistic sense of Berkeley's equally famous dictum that the *percipi* of things constitutes their only *esse*.)

According to Sextus (sections 216-219), Protagoras held that matter, though in a constant flux, contains within itself the underlying reasons (*logoi*) of its diverse and contradictory appearances to men; hence it is "in itself capable of being all those things which happen to all." But what appears will depend on the differences in the disposition of the percipient subject, whose matter is also in a constant flux. Sextus concludes: "We see, then, that he dogmatizes about the fluidity of matter and also about the subsistence therein of the 'reasons' of all appearances, these being nonevident matters about which we suspend judgment."

The skeptic's necessary acceptance of the *fact* of phenomenal experience is no reason to categorize him as an empiricist or sensist. Indeed, his reason for rejecting the pretensions of the empiricist would be that very positivism which some assume to be the distinguishing feature of Greek skepticism. For the empiricist distinguishes between the intellectual and the sensible only to reduce the former to the latter, assuming quite arbitrarily, according to the principles of skepticism, that in view of the origin of all knowledge in sensible experience, metempirical knowledge is invalid.

The skeptic, on the contrary, refuses to admit any source of knowledge to be valid or to pass judgment on the objectivity of his ideas. In short, he is the most thoroughgoing of agnostics, a confirmed intellectual nihilist. He will make no positive affirmation, not even the agnostic thesis that nothing is knowable or certain (sections 13-15; 196-201). For even the thesis of positive agnosticism is "included in the things to which doubt applies, just as aperient drugs do not merely eliminate the humors from the body but also expel themselves along with the humors." However seemingly categorical may be the formulas used by the skeptic, such as "I suspend judgment," "I determine nothing," "I apprehend not," "To every argument an equal argument is opposed," he does not intend these to be understood in any absolute sense or as connoting any theory about objective reality; rather, they are used "without precision and, if you like, loosely" (sections 206-207).

Hence, the state of mind of the Greek skeptic differs from that of pure nescience only by his acceptance of the factual or immediately experiential. For that reason Sextus protests against the view that skepticism constitutes a school of thought or follows any "doctrinal rule" (section 16). For this would imply some kind of positive affirmation. Skepticism, he claims, is nothing but a way of thought (agōgē) or method of inquiry. Etymologically, "method" in Greek simply designates a pursuit, specifically a pursuit of knowledge, just as "to be a skeptic" signifies to be a seeker or searcher of truth (section 7). It is the contention of the skeptic that in the course of his search he has found that the original object of his pursuit is unattainable, though he will not venture to affirm or deny that truth of its nature is such.

Disillusioned in the object of his quest, the skeptic seeks contentment in the pursuit itself and has no other aim than to continue in his state of inquiry or doubt (sections 3-4). The practical aim of his skepticism is not knowledge nor certainty. In this respect it is radically different from that of the so-called universal methodic doubt of Descartes, who in the third part of his *Discourse on Method* tells us that he has no intention to "imitate the skeptics who doubt only that they may doubt and seek nothing beyond uncertainty itself." Skepticism, as Sextus himself defines it (section 8), is rather "an ability, or mental attitude, which opposes appearances to judgments in any way whatsoever, with the result that, owing to the equipollence of the objects and reasons thus opposed, we are brought first to a state of mental suspense and next to a state of 'unperturb-edness' (*ataraxia*) or quietude." "Equipollence" (*isosthenia*), he explains (sections 10; 202-205), is synonymous with equal probability.

The aim of the Greek skeptic, therefore, is purely practical. He is a seeker after truth who, despairing of any theoretical certitude because of what he considers to be the equipollence of the rash dogmatic claims of the conflicting philosophical sects, is only too willing to sacrifice knowledge or theoretical certitude if, by suspending his assent (section 196), he can attain the practical end of all knowledge, which is temporal felicity. The ultimate happiness possible to man he envisages as "quietude in respect of matters of opinion and moderate feeling in respect of things unavoidable" (section 25), and this he believes to be possible only through systematic doubt. "For the man who opines that anything is by nature good or bad is forever being disquieted" (section 27).

He realizes, however, that thought is essentially ordered to action and that happiness can be acquired only through activity. Yet he is aware that not sheer activity of itself, such as the in-discriminate indulgence of his feelings or passions, will guaran-tee his happiness, but only that activity which, as befits a human being, is in some way guided by reason. He is conscious, there-fore, of the need of a moderation or "metriopathy" (section 25) of his natural feelings.

But how can systematic doubt lend itself to any activity other than instinctive animal behavior, which from the viewpoint of specifically human activity is equivalently a state of passivity? If the skeptic is not to be condemned to a life of rational in-activity, which is the very negation of human life itself, what alternative has he other than the equally irrational *il faut parier* of the skeptically minded Pascal? Pascal tried to compensate for his skepticism and its consequent lack of motivation by his fideism. But even this avenue of escape from the doom of moral inertia is closed off for the Greek skeptic, for whom belief of any kind is anathema. If he is to act at all as a human being, his choice of activity will have to be a continuous, frustrating gamble, a pragmatic experiment of trial and error.

Sextus seems acutely conscious of this classical objection to skepticism (sections 21-24). He tries to evade the difficulty by taking refuge in the phenomenalism which is the last resort of the skeptic. Human activity, he admits, requires some kind of norm but not necessarily a theoretical, metempirical criterion based on the unknowable nature of the real. Disillusioned by what appears to him to be the inevitable failure of the philosophical sects to attain certitude, the skeptic finds "as if by chance" that mental quietude follows upon the suspension of his assent concerning the intrinsic nature of reality, "even as a shadow follows its substance" (section 29).

As far as our *practical* activity is concerned, he argues, we can rest content with the empirical sequence of phenomena and regulate our actions accordingly. To attain that imperturbability of soul which is the essence of happiness, all we need do, he contends, is to conform our conduct to those "feelings which are the necessary results of sense impressions" (section 13), dismissing as hopelessly vain and as the occasion of endless mental anguish the academic inquiries and rash solutions of the theorists and dogmatists. Those who think that the skeptic is condemned to a life of inactivity, he replies, "fail to see that the skeptic does not frame his life as a *man* according to the doctrine which he professes as a *philosopher*. So far as he adheres to that, he does not act at all. Only, noticing in an unphilosophic way how things go, he is able to choose some things and shun others" (*Adv. Math.*, XI, 162-166). Hence, when hungry, we eat, when thirsty, we drink.

Yet, because our past experience has taught us that, to insure our happiness, we must "moderate our affections," we also try to conform our lives to the conventional customs and laws of our social environment and to contribute to its culture by exercising ourselves to the best of our ability in its arts (sections 23-24). "Adhering, then, to appearances, we live in accordance with the normal rules of life, undogmatically, seeing that we cannot remain wholly inactive."

This is not to imply that the skeptic claims complete imperturbability of soul in his practical life (sections 29-30). His refusal to posit an intellectual assent in no way mitigates the natural discomfort that follows upon his phenomenalistic experience of cold and thirst. These inevitable pains he accepts fatalistically, but his studied indifference has definite advantages, in his eyes, over that of the Stoic. For the latter adds to his natural discomfort by his dogmatic rashness in judging these natural experiences to be "evil by nature," whereas the skeptic views them with not only practical but also theoretical indifference.

The greater part of Book I of the *Outlines* (sections 31-186) consists of a detailed exposition of the stereotyped series of arguments called Modes or Tropes, by which the Greek skeptic strives to defend his thesis that the only reasonable (*sic*) philosophical attitude as regards truth and its attainability is to suspend one's assent. Though he eschews all dogmatism as to what transcends the phenomenal, the skeptic, be it noted, is by no means averse to appealing to reason to support his anti-rationalistic thesis.

Herein, let us remark, lies one of the basic inconsistencies of Greek skepticism. The rational, of its very nature, transcends the purely phenomenal or empirical. Hence a recourse to the principles of reason to justify an intellectual suspension of assent or to refute the pretensions of the dogmatists implies necessarily a dogmatic avowal of the metempirical validity of those principles. The classical argument of the skeptic has been the endless diversity and conflict of philosophical systems. But does not the possibility of such a doctrinal antinomy presuppose that at least the principle of contradiction, not to mention other logical principles, has an objective validity that transcends the datum of phenomenal experience? How can any doctrine be said to diverge from the truth or to conflict with another doctrine save in the tacit dogmatic hypothesis that there is a transcendental absolute truth, which can serve as the criterion of such divergence or conflict?

A case in point is furnished by the ten Tropes of Aeneside-mus (sections 36-163), who seems to have been the first to sys-tematize the arguments of the skeptic and to reduce them to a standard dialectical form. They are tediously elaborated for us by Sextus and overlaid with a profusion of illustration and detail solely for the purpose of their polemical effect.

Sextus' exposition of the ten Tropes has little to recommend it over the proposal of the same arguments by the Sophists and members of the New Academy, which intervened between the early skeptics and Aenesidemus. It marks little or no advance either as to originality of content, logical cogency or systematic arrangement. No effort is made either to synthesize the argu-ments or to disguise their repetitiousness. All the Tropes are based on the antithetical character of reason and sensation, and all conclude to the relativity of human knowledge by contend-ing that our phenomenal experiences cannot *of themselves,* because of their evident relativity and opposition both among themselves and with reason, reveal to us the intrinsic nature of the noumenal objects that occasion them.

This contention, needless to say, no rationalist or intellectu-alist would ever gainsay. Hence all the Tropes are based throughout on the gratuitous postulate of all empiricism that our sense impressions are the ultimate criteria of truth. The whole critique of Sextus is also vitiated at its source by the more basic surreptitious assumption, overtly denied by his antidog-matic pretensions, that the principles of reason have any objec-tive validity. For the gist of his argument is that the opposition between phenomena and ideas (sections 31-34) can afford no *reasonable* basis for a *rational* judgment about the nature of reality.

The skepticism of Sextus Empiricus is postulated on a glar-ing inconsistency, the absurd assumption that tranquility of soul can be attained by the frustration of its most inexorable natural tendency, the desire to know. Imperturbability of mind is utterly meaningless if it does not mean contentment in the discharge of the mind's natural function. Yet the Greek skeptic persists in the assumption that the mind's essential tendency to truth can be satisfied by its very negation, the systematic atti-tude of doubt. He then proceeds to compound this initial absurdity by the further pretension that, while remaining a systematic skeptic, *as such* he is one who "keeps on searching" for the truth (section 4).

This is "the pathos, the inner tragedy which lies at the heart of skepticism." The skeptic begins his quest for peace of soul by actively seeking that which alone can give it to him, the vital possession of truth. In the course of his search, however, he pretends to discover that tranquility of soul "by a stroke of luck" follows on his suspension of assent (sections 26-27). This is tantamount to saying that the mind, which by definition is the faculty of knowledge, can find its satisfaction and repose in a state of uncertainty or, practically speaking, in nescience. But any such artificially contrived peace or quiescence of soul must be short-lived, because it is basically contrary to nature. It can be achieved only by the unnatural intervention of the will, arbitrarily substituting for objective truth the supposed equipollence of contrary opinions, and by the thinly camouflaged dogmatism of practical expediency which, in the final analysis, is nothing more in effect than the naturalistic and quite unphilosophical dictate of so-called "common sense."

But there can be no surrogate, even in the practical order, for truth itself as a relief or as a palliative for the natural inquietude of the soul that wells from its innate desire to know. It is small consolation for one in pain not to know positively that his pain, or rather its cause, is objectively evil. Sextus argues (section 30) that such theoretical knowledge would only add mental anguish to his phenomenalistic torment of soul. Yet, on the other hand, the sufferer can have no hope of assuaging his natural pain except in the positive knowledge that the pain itself or its cause is *not* evil. A pragmatic conformism to convention liberates the skeptic from the exigencies of dogma only to enslave him to the more exacting, precisely because it is the more irrational and therefore the more frustrating, tyranny of natural prejudice, superstition and senseless habit.

The skeptic is an escapist, in terms of modern psychology, an intellectual psychotic who refuses to face the challenge of objective reality. To compensate for his intellectual *abulia* he tries to substitute the world of purely sensible phenomena and the amoral dreamland of conventional social conformism for the objective world of reality and the ethical demands of reason. Lacking the intellectual hardihood to dominate the confusing diversity and opposition of such philosophical systems as Megarism, Cyrenaicism, Atomism, Epicureanism, Stoicism, Platonism and Peripateticism and, as a consequence, bereft of the moral stamina necessary to cope with the ethical and political cynicism of his age, he seeks an escape from his naïve intellectual disillusionment in a veritable schizophrenic dichotomization of the theoretical and the practical.

Herein, as we have already noted, lies the second great antinomy inherent in Greek skepticism. The skeptic perforce admits that human happiness can be achieved only through activity; on principle, however, he is condemned to absolute moral inertia. His principle of equipollence precludes any rational basis for acting one way rather than another or, in ethical terms, for one course of action being right and another wrong.

What about a purely pragmatic criterion, such as success? Even this norm would entail enough concessions to theory and to practical certitude to force the skeptic to deny it on principle. As the modern pragmatists will avow, whatever has been proved experimentally to be a motive for successful activity in the past cannot serve as an effective guide for future action, save in the hypothesis that success is the measure of truth. (As a matter of fact, Pragmatism never seems to have occurred to the Greek skeptic as a possible means of escaping his dilemma; or, if it did, perhaps he was aware, as the modern pragmatist is not, that it would be a vain subterfuge. For mere success cannot be an ultimate criterion of truth even in the practical order, seeing that it requires a further theoretical norm to determine what it is that constitutes the successful.) Carneades sensed this fundamental inconsistency in the skeptical position and accordingly amended the skepticism of the New Academy by his theory of probabilism, which was so severely criticized by Sextus (sections 220-235).

Is human activity, then, to be dictated solely by irrational inclinations and instinctive tendencies? Even the skeptic shied from this implicit brutalization of man and recognized the need of "moderating" his natural appetites, if genuine tranquility of soul was to be achieved. Moderation of "feelings," however, presupposes some norm or "mean" transcending the purely phenomenal or experimental.

For all the subtleties of Sextus there is no way out of his dilemma. He must choose either for intellectual nihilism and inactivity or for peace of mind and at least an implicit dogmatism. To propose a general rule of life, however pragmatic, or to formulate maxims of conduct, however simple and empirical, as the later skeptics attempted to do, necessarily implies a *theory* of action and therefore a compromise with the hated enemy, dogmatism. Sextus tries to evade the issue by protesting that in outlining his plan for happiness he does not formulate or affirm anything positively or theoretically. The only "doctrinal rule" which he admits to is that "procedure which, in accordance with appearances, follows a certain line of reasoning, that reasoning indicating how it is possible to seem to live rightly" (section 17).

But what he refuses to assent to speculatively and orally, he affirms in an even more positive way by his action. The belief that translates itself into action is just as affirmative as, if not more so than, one that is content to remain purely theoretical. Hence the Greek skeptic is actually a positivist in disguise. Viewed existentially, his phenomenalism implies a confused latent dogmatism. On the one hand, his refusal to base any theoretical judgments on phenomena is an implicit denial that phenomena reveal or represent the real; on the other hand, for all practical purposes, he attributes to the purely phenomenal an objectivity which on systematic grounds he denies.

All skepticism, whether ancient or modern, is phenomenalistic. It beguiles itself into believing that by uttering the open-sesame "phenomenon" it can have its epistemological cake and eat it. It disregards the fact that, even if sensible impressions are not exact replicas of what obtains in reality, they can be termed phenomena or appearances only in the hypothesis that the reality they purport to represent in some way "appears." In other words, phenomena, *as such*, imply some correlation with objective reality. If a so-called phenomenon in no way represents reality but actually misrepresents it, by what right can it be assumed to be an "appearance" of any object or, for that matter, to be even occasioned by one? If it is argued that the "phenomenon" is wholly subjective (a later idealistic refinement that no Greek philosopher ever suspected, and rightly so, since the subjective as such is meaningless, save in the hypothesis that there is an objective), what possible grounds can there be for such an assumption?

The Greek skeptic, as we have pointed out, is just as uncritically realistic as any other Greek philosopher, but on systematic grounds he refuses to affirm his realism and seeks a refuge in an inconsistent agnostic phenomenalism. He repudiates any knowledge transcending the phenomenal; yet he does not hesitate to gainsay the claims of reason and of metaphysics by invoking reason itself and by taking advantage of its privileged instruments—the principle of contradiction and the laws of logical consistency. He bases his refusal to assent to any proposition on the equipollence of its reasons pro and con, in apparently complete disregard of the fact that any such equipollence presupposes some norm of truth accessible to reason by which the mind can determine the equal probability or approximation to truth of conflicting opinions.

The skeptic's favorite argument, exploited by latter-day skeptics, such as Montaigne, and his final resort to justify his suspension of assent, is the diversity and opposition of the philosophical sects. Though he will refuse to affirm it positively, he draws the conclusion from the fact of philosophical sectarianism either that there is no truth or that it is unattainable by the human mind. He blandly ignores the assumption implicit in this inference that such opposition and diversity of doctrine on the one hand presupposes some rational norm by which they can be judged to be such and, on the other hand, does not preclude the possibility of a future agreement of minds, once the basic causes of philosophical prejudice and error have been uncovered and eliminated and reason finally comes into her own.

JAMES I. CONWAY

SELECTED BIBLIOGRAPHY

BURY, R. G., *Sextus Empiricus, with an English Translation,* Vol. I. Loeb Classical Library.
BROCHARD, Victor, *Les Sceptiques Grecs.* Paris, Vrin.
BEVAN, Edwyn, *Stoics and Sceptics.* Oxford.

Robin, Léon, *Pyrrhon et le Scepticisme Grec.* Presses Universitaires de France.

Hicks, R. D., *Stoic and Epicurean* (chaps. 8 and 10). Scribners.

Cauchy, Venant, "The Nature and Genesis of the Sceptic Attitude." *The Modern Schoolman,* March and May, 1950.

Sextus Empiricus, *Outlines of Pyrrhonism,* Book I. Regnery.

St. Augustine: Confessions, *Books IX-XIII*

FOR THE PURPOSE of this series, the thirteen books of St. Augustine's *Confessions* are treated as two volumes, the first ending with Augustine's conversion to Christianity, in Book VIII. Most of what was written in the Introduction to that volume is just as relevant to this, and the reader should get hold of it. For those who cannot, a few words in repetition are necessary.

Augustine was born in North Africa in 354. It was only forty years since the Emperor Constantine had had the vision or dream which brought him over to the Christian side; paganism and Christianity were still struggling for possession of the Roman Empire, and the struggle was not to be settled for another thirty years. Augustine's father, Patricius, was a pagan; his mother, Monica, a Christian, so that the struggle was in some sense waged in his own soul. He was a little boy when the last pagan Emperor, Julian the Apostate, made his effort to destroy Christianity and restore the old gods. His last years saw the inrush of the barbarians from beyond the Rhine and the Danube. He died in 430, with the Vandals besieging the city of which he was bishop. He lived, practically throughout his life, in a chaos of catastrophes and upheavals.

In the earlier Introduction some idea is given of his own unique role in producing the order which did at last emerge. No single man has had a more profound influence upon the making of the Western World. Let me repeat here the witness of two great scholars. "Augustine was," says the Catholic historian Christopher Dawson, "to a far greater degree than any emperor or barbarian warlord, a maker of history and a builder of the bridge which was to lead from the old world to the new." "It would seem," says the German Harnack, a liberal Protestant, "that the miserable existence of the Roman Empire in the

West was prolonged only to permit Augustine's influence to be exercised in universal history."

It is in point to mention the vast historical significance of Augustine here, because in the *Confessions* there is no hint of it. He is concentrated upon God and his own soul's relation to God—the movement away, the long hesitation, the slow return, the rush at the end, the joy of possession and the excitement of deepening vision—concentrated upon it so totally that one could hardly guess from the book when it was written, or in what condition of the world, or even by whom. His own name is never mentioned. Only a couple of casual phrases would inform the reader that the writer was a priest. There is nothing at all to tell that he was a bishop. Nothing at all that does not bear upon God and the soul and his own soul's movement to God and life in God. He warned us in the *Soliloquies,* written just after his conversion, that he saw nothing else as really important. "I desire to know God and the soul. Nothing more? Nothing, absolutely nothing." Life as he had to live it was too distracting for a program so concentrated: he had to busy himself, in act and speech and the written word, with a thousand things.

But in the *Confessions,* written twelve years after his conversion, nothing else is allowed to intervene. Public matters are not allowed to intrude, though at the time of writing he was occupied day and night with the Donatist heretics. He waged one of the greatest propaganda campaigns of all history against them, and they tried to murder him: it is marvelous that he found time to write the *Confessions* at all, and miraculous that no faintest echo of so stirring a matter is heard in their pages. Not even the people he knew best are allowed to intrude, save when they impinge directly upon his main theme: the son he has had for fifteen years he mentions for the first time after his conversion, because the son was converted with him; his brother, Navigius, he mentions for the first time at his mother's deathbed; his sister, Perpetua, who became a nun, is never mentioned at all. This is the book of a man who knows how to keep to the point.

Note the important dates. Augustine was born, as we have noted, in 354. He was converted in September 386. At Easter 387 he was baptized by St. Ambrose. In 391, back in Africa, he

was ordained priest. In 396, most reluctantly, he was conse-
crated Bishop of Hippo. In 399 he wrote the *Confessions*.

In length, the two parts into which the *Confessions* have
been broken for the purpose of this series are roughly equal;
but the second is far more difficult to handle in an introductory
note. The eight books of the first part tell the story of his life
and his mental and moral problems in straightforward chronological order: all is of a piece. But the second part, which is my
subject here, falls into two divisions which seem to have no
connection.

Its two opening books, IX and X, continue Augustine's autobiography. The last three are not autobiographical at all. They
are a spiritual commentary on the first chapter of Genesis. One's
first impression is that they have been included by mistake—
a secretary, perhaps, finding them on the table along with the
ten books of the *Confessions,* simply pinned them on at the end
and sent them forth to make their way through the centuries.
But this can be no more than passing fancy. Whatever the reason, the last three books are there; and as one slowly absorbs
their teaching, one is glad that they are: for, if they add nothing to the story of Augustine's conversion, they do, with the
profundity of their discussion of the nature of God and of Creation, of Time and Eternity, of Spirit and Matter, show the
movement of his mind now that he is no longer searching for
God but possesses Him. His heart is at rest, but his intellect is
not stagnant. On the contrary, it is more vigorously in action
now that he has found God than it ever was in the search.

In the Introduction to the first part, we noted the enormous
impetus that has carried Augustine's writing so far and saw that
some, at least, of its secret lay in the combination of philosophy
with passion. The dilemma of his young manhood lay in the
strife between philosophy and bodily passion: what made that
strife so anguishing was that philosophy was a passion too, and
so it was to remain all through his life. Note his cry to God
when he is trying to get at the meaning of Time (Book XI,
section 22): "My mind burns to solve this complicated enigma,
O Lord my God, O good Father, for Christ's sake I beseech thee

do not shut off these obscure familiar problems from my longing."

His philosophy goes to, or comes from, the very roots of his personality. One facet of this is that he writes the strongest objectivity with profoundly felt and brilliantly analyzed subjective reaction: he tells both the reality as he sees it and the effect upon himself of the reality thus seen. A second facet is that he does not abstract or in any way isolate the truth from the living experience in which he came to see it, but gives us both together. So that the book contains, in a pattern for which all antiquity has no parallel, the universal truths that have illumined his mind and the personal experiences that have wrung his heart. He does not simply give us the truth: he gives us himself with the truth adhering.

In Books IX and X we get the chance to see him as father, and as son, and as sinner. As father, first. It gives the reader something of a start to learn (Book IX, section 6) that Augustine has a son, Adeodatus, a boy of fifteen. We have noted that Augustine is quite liable to make no mention at all of the people nearest and dearest to him, unless his theme requires them. So it was with Adeodatus. But once he is mentioned, the father shows his heart unmistakably. "His great intelligence filled me with a kind of awe." When one remembers what Augustine's own intelligence was—one of the most powerful ever given to man—one wonders what kind of prodigy the son must have been to reduce such a father to awe—the prodigy, of course, lies not in the boy's intelligence but in the father's love.

The description in Book IX of his mother's last months on earth, casting back to her childhood and the early years of her married life with Patricius, belongs to the world's literature. If her love for her son runs through all the first eight books, his for her is concentrated here: her tears for him had won him the gift of faith, and now his tears ran for her—"I let them flow as they would, making them a pillow for my heart."

There is self-revelation in what he has to say of his son and his mother: but others have done as much (though not often inweaving it into the profoundest philosophical and theological discussion). What is hardly to be paralleled—not, certainly, in the writing of bishops!—is Augustine's examination of himself as sinner (Book X, sections 30-41)—not with respect to sins he

used to commit and has now given up, but his here-and-now
spiritual stocktaking. Read it closely. It helps us to know Augustine. It may even help us to know ourselves. It is an interesting
piece of self-examination, both for what it omits (he does not
accuse himself of temper, for instance, or conceit) and for one
element that it contains. He finds sin in what to most people
would seem the legitimate pleasures of the senses.

There is not one simple reason for this but a tangle of reasons. There is his own nature, sensitive far beyond the average
to color and sound and scent, so that these things do represent
an unusual degree at once of pleasure and distraction for him.
There is the long struggle—a struggle that did not cease with
his victory but lasted on into old age—to conquer his body's
passions: he must have known himself well enough to know that
his at least was one body that must, like St. Paul's, be castigated
and brought into subjection. But there were also the philosophies he had held on his way to the Faith. The Manichean attitude to the body as wholly corrupting he might well have lived
down, for Manicheanism he had totally disowned. But the
neo-Platonism he has described in Book VII—a philosophy of
spirit, with the body despised as a worthless encumbrance—is
a different matter, for it had helped him into the Church, and it
was not immediately obvious to him that the Christian primacy
of spirit over matter is a comparison of greater with lesser
worth, *not* a contrast of valuable and worthless. There is no
doubt that in his early years in the Church he saw many things
through neo-Platonic eyes: by the time he came to write the
Confessions, he had purified his theology of any such relics of
past error: but to the body as a threat to the spirit's dominion,
he never lost his special sensitiveness.

The last three books, the puzzling postscript to the *Confessions,* are, as we have noted, a spiritual commentary on the first
chapters of Genesis. You will not find here a full exposition of
his view of the Creation story. For that, you must read his book
De Genesi ad Litteram, which he began writing a year or two
after this. It is a surprising book. Written fifteen hundred
years ago, it would give small comfort to today's fundamental-
ist. It may be worth a quick glance here. Augustine writes his
book in the consciousness that we know very little of the actual

facts about the beginning of the universe, and that what Moses writes is too obscure to make any one interpretation certain. Science has its own methods: reason and experiment are valid means of reaching truth in the material order: we must be prepared to drop our own interpretation of Genesis if it is established that the truth is different.

With all this by way of proviso, Augustine sets down his own view: first, that all that is described in Genesis I happened in a single instant—the narrative is divided up into six days to help minds incapable of grasping the notion of creation all at once; second, that while all things were created in one act, they were created not in their completed development but in their "seminal reasons"—that is, all things were there in the seed or germ, so that, with God's cooperation, they would develop into the genera we know. As part of this view, he holds that the creation of man described in Chapter I is creation in this sense—in the "seminal reason"—and that the production of man as we know him is described in Chapter II.

To return to the *Confessions*. What he gives in Books XI-XIII is written with the emphasis on the spiritual and the universal: this was his tendency by nature, and neo-Platonism had made it second nature, so that it was the permanent cast of his mind. He does not deny that Genesis gives an account of what happened in the material order (though even there we must not be deceived by the surface meaning), but he cannot feel that all these material happenings are of the first importance in themselves. They are most useful to men if men make use of them as analogies or material symbolizings of greater things in the spiritual order. And it is to bring these to light that he writes his commentary. Thus, the phrase "Let the waters be gathered together into one place and let the dry land appear" reminds us that "the society of peoples spoiled with bitterness—represented as *the sea*" must be distinguished from "the zeal of pious souls represented by *dry land*"—and when this dry land, this earth, "brings forth fruit," we must think of the souls of good men bringing forth works of mercy. And so on.

And if what thing came before what is of no importance compared with the laws that govern the souls of men, so he has no desire to know at what time it all happened. The story of creation sets him asking *not* "at what time" but "What is time"; not "When did it happen" but "What does *when* mean." That, for Augustine and for us, is a question of really passionate importance: for all our actions seem to be conditioned by time, are rolled along by time, are all but drowned in time: what *is* time?

St. Augustine's answer, given in sections 10 to 31 of Book XI, is one of the most famous pieces of philosophical thinking in existence. His half-comic phrase early in the discussion—"What is time? If no one asks me, I know; if I want to explain it, I do not know"—is a beautiful piece of practical psychology. But the whole section is a masterpiece. The centuries have done nothing to outmode it. So modern a thinker as Bertrand Russell can write of it, in his *History of Western Philosophy*, as "a very admirable relativistic theory of time . . . a very able theory, deserving to be seriously considered . . . a great advance on anything to be found on the subject in Greek philosophy . . . a better and clearer statement than Kant's on the subjective theory of time." One might add a little explanatory comment on the word "subjective," but there is no space for that here: Russell's excellent word is "clearer." Augustine has produced a masterpiece of clarity on a fiercely difficult subject. The unphilosophical reader can have the luxury of reading a famous piece of philosophical writing and understanding every word of it.

One gets the most out of any book by reading it with the same mind with which the author wrote it. As far as possible we should see reality as a whole, things in general, as Augustine saw them. If we cannot manage that, at least let us know how he did see them: if we cannot share his vision, at least let us know what his vision was. To get the most out of the *Confessions,* we must know how Augustine saw God, the soul and the body. If we can manage to see them the same way, so much the better: in any event let us see how he saw them. "In seeking You, my God, it is happiness that I am seeking. I shall seek You that my soul may live. *For my body lives by my soul and my soul lives by You.*"

For the neo-Platonist, the primary distinction was between Spirit and Matter. But Augustine now knows that the primary distinction is between Absolute and Dependent, Creator and things created. Within the created there is distinction between Spirit and Matter: but in comparison with the Absolute, created spirit and created matter scarcely *are* at all.

God made all things—matter and spirit alike—of nothing. They have no being but what He wills to give them, no hold upon being save that He holds them in being. They exist, and they are good; but their existence and their goodness are not only dependent—upon His will to create them—but limited: for no one of them possesses all the perfections of existence; they possess only some of them (and even these not in their fullness but only more or less), and no one of them has permanence in existence of its own right but only if God chooses to maintain it in being. But God possesses the fullness of existence in His own right: there is no perfection that He lacks, nor any that He can lose. As Augustine writes (Book XI, section 4):

We look upon the heavens and the earth and they cry aloud that they were made. . . . It was You, Lord, who made them: for You are beautiful and they are beautiful: You are good, and they are good: You are, and they are. But they neither are beautiful nor are good nor simply are, as You their Creator: compared with You they are not beautiful and are not good and are not.

Note how this same distinction recurs in Augustine's treatment of *eternity,* which is God's duration, and *time,* which is ours. It is a mark of his mental advance, as a result of neo-Platonism plus Christianity that, whereas, earlier his main difficulty was the comparatively trifling one of how God could transcend, while acting in, space, now he is fascinated by the far profounder problem of God's transcending, while acting in, time.

Because God alone is abiding fullness of being, to make God the object of one's life is only common sense. Nor does this mean a reduced, joyless, inhuman or impoverished life compared with the concentration most of us make upon created things: for created things have all their reality from God, so that whatever of value is in them is in Him in a far higher, far more *real,* way. For a most moving statement of the joy of life in God, see Book X, section 7, which is an answer and counterpicture to what he has said earlier (Book IX, section 4) of those who "find their joy in . . . the things that are seen and the things of time, and in their starved minds lick shadows."

This intense awareness does not mean that created things cease to have being and the distinctions among them cease to have importance. Created reality is poor enough in comparison with God, but dazzlingly glorious compared with nothingness: and, within created being, the spirit is dazzlingly glorious compared with matter. To these created things we may give our attention once the mind is firmly grounded in the absolute. We are now back at what was noted earlier, that Augustine combines strong objectivity with brilliant analysis of his own subjective reactions. He puts all the powers of his mind into seeing God as He is, and then into seeing what it means to his mind to see God as He is. Augustine is the first great psychologist. The long discussion of Memory (Book X, sections 8-25) should, of course, be carefully read. And it is not simply a matter of such passages of explicit psychology: psychological analysis is woven into the texture of the whole book—note particularly the famous *amor meus pondus meum*—"my love is my weight"—of section 9 in Book XIII. But, great psychologist as he is, his interest is not in knowledge of the human soul as such or for its own sake, but because the soul is made in God's image, and because by the soul man possesses God or loses Him.

It is this vision of a Reality in which God gives life to the soul and the soul gives life to the body which enables Augustine to gaze upon the ocean of catastrophes mounting around him and his world, serene in the knowledge that there is that—not only in God but in men too—which cannot be engulfed. Absolute Spirit abides eternal and immutable, and the soul of man by God's gift has its own permanence.

If, by chance, one is tempted to smile at all this as unreal, impractical talk, let it be remembered that the man who held it was "to a far greater degree than any emperor or barbarian warlord, a maker of history"—which is more than a lot of practical and realistic men now living are at all likely to be.

FRANK SHEED

SELECTED BIBLIOGRAPHY

D'ARCY, M. C., S.J., and others, *A Monument to St. Augustine*. Sheed & Ward.
PRZYWARA, Erich, S.J., *An Augustine Synthesis*. Sheed & Ward.
DAWSON, Christopher, *The Making of Europe*. Sheed & Ward.

HUGHES, Philip. *A History of the Church*, Vol. II. Sheed & Ward.
ST. AUGUSTINE, *Confessions*, translated by F. J. Sheed. Sheed & Ward.
ST. AUGUSTINE, *Confessions*. Dutton (Everyman's Library).
ST. AUGUSTINE, *Confessions*, Books IX-XIII. Regnery.

Genesis, *Chapters I and II*

THIS BRIEF SELECTION from the first book of the Pentateuch seems to have been made to serve as a companion piece for the reading from St. Augustine's *Confessions* where these two chapters are discussed. The first Chapter of Genesis, which should include the first three verses of Chapter II, is introductory to all that follows, while the rest of Chapter II is the beginning of the first main section of the book; this main section sketches the history of early man from his initial happiness in Eden up to the birth of Abraham.

Even if the reader stops at the close of this second chapter, he will have a fair introduction to the spirit of the Bible. God reigns supreme, and He manifests His wisdom and power by bringing into existence this marvelous universe, with its awesome vastness and its limitless intricacy, while over it all shines the divine goodness, imparting perfections to these various grades of being and crowning it all with man, God's most perfect work in the visible order. The rest of the Bible, even down to the close of the Apocalypse, simply carries on the history of God's dealings with man and of man's response, a response that is marked only too often by perversity and rebellion.

The beginning of man's failure to live according to the divine plan is narrated in Chapter III, when the first sin is committed. But already in Chapter II a note of warning is sounded in the command laid upon Adam with the ominous threat of death for breaking it. When he does break it, he is banished from Eden, but is comforted with the promise of a Redeemer. This first sin is followed by the murder of Abel, and then the sad tale of evil passions unrestrained begins to unfold. In the Flood and in the call of Abraham, God intervenes directly to keep man in proper relationship with Himself.

The promises made to Abraham are renewed to his descendants Isaac and Jacob, the latter in his old age removing with his large family from Canaan to join his son Joseph in Egypt. There, in Egypt, Genesis leaves them at the start of their long sojourning far from the Promised Land. In this way it opens the way for their subsequent history to be carried on in the book of Exodus, when they enter more actively on their mission as God's chosen race and the custodians of His revelations.

Since Genesis, especially in its opening chapters, answers fundamental questions about the origin of man and his destiny and records the earliest history of the human race and of the Jewish religion, it is not surprising to find it attacked today from almost every conceivable angle. These attacks are one of the marks of modern criticism. Most of the critics have lost the true idea of God and resort to all sorts of explanations in their efforts to discredit the Biblical narratives. Notable among these explanations is the theory that the religious ideas of Genesis are too advanced to have been possible in the time of Moses, some fifteen or thirteen centuries before Christ. This theory led to the attempt to work out a scheme for the gradual evolution of theological thought among the Jews. The scheme would assign the composition of these earliest chapters of Genesis to the learned men of the fourth or fifth century before Christ.

Though masked under the name of scientific investigation, these attempted explanations have been exposed as mere wishful thinking in their main features. Both Jewish and Christian scholars defend the Mosaic origin of these chapters. Yet, even with the late date assigned to these chapters by radical critics, the ideas presented there are still striking proof of the lofty religious spirit that prevailed among the Hebrews centuries before the dawn of Christianity.

In the Great Books series there are two examples of what the Gentile philosophers were able to do when confronted by the puzzle of the universe. Lucretius explained the origin of the world by the collision of atoms falling in space; these vast organizations that we see and these tiny adaptations are all due to mere chance. Marcus Aurelius relies on pantheism; everything is governed by the world soul, which is nothing more than the constant way material things act and react.

Before the time of the Epicureans and the Stoics, those pagans who still believed in the gods conceded that the world was fashioned by these superhuman beings, but they never penetrated to the idea of creation. All that the gods did was to manipulate existing matter. Where this matter came from was beyond the ken of these idol worshipers; they simply assumed that it had always been there. Modern critics have fared no better; chance is the last resort of the despair felt by atheistic thinkers, and it explains nothing.

Quite different, superior and satisfying is the explanation given by Moses. God made all things, even matter itself. There was no matter at all in existence, and God called it into being. At first this matter had an unorganized constitution, called heaven and earth in the first verse of Genesis. Then God gradually reduced it to a state of diversified organization. He proceeded by stages, but each stage was a logical development of the preceding, though it developed only by the power of the Almighty. Life appeared, not because it was already contained in existing inanimate matter but because out of that material God produced the new living matter. The biggest step was the creation of man. First, vegetable life, then animal life, and finally—as a crown to the work—man with a spiritual soul capable of knowing and of loving the good, the true, the beautiful, and worthy in this respect and in comparison to all other creatures to be given supreme dominion over the whole earth.

This supreme dominion is a manifestation and a guarantee of the special dignity of man. Though all things come from God, they have been made for man's benefit, to aid him in the proper conduct of his life. Yet it is emphasized that this is a delegated dominion; man receives it from God, and as a consequence he must exercise it in accordance with the will of the One who has raised him to this lofty height among creatures.

Two ancient misconceptions are here corrected; in one view, man is the cringing plaything of the elements, and to protect himself he must offer worship to such things as the sun or the moon or even to animals; in the other view, man is claimed to be the measure of all things, owing allegiance to no one, master of his fate in the most absolute sense, and free to use all creatures as he wills or as his whims and fancies suggest.

With Moses, the principles of supremacy and of submission are carefully balanced, and to place these principles in needed prominence man is at once laid under an express obligation to refrain from eating a designated fruit. Obedience to God is a prerequisite for man's proper use of the power given him over other creatures. Order reigns throughout, with harmonious subordination of the lower to the higher, man standing midway between lower creatures and God, and by his subjection to God in his use of creatures making those creatures themselves contribute to the glory of the Creator.

When in Chapter III man steps out of his place as subject to God and abuses his liberty to transgress the commandment given him, the rupture of harmony is marked in unmistakable form. Man is ashamed of his nakedness, he is banished from the garden of delight and sent out into a world that in its own way will refuse him obedience as he had refused obedience to God.

A closer look at Chapter I shows it to be a masterful presentation of great truths in terms fitted to the comprehension of simple people. Notable are its logical order, its drastic condensation, and its singular sublimity and serenity. Neither scientific nor fantastic, it is governed by the idea that, after matter had been created in a primitive state, the work of organizing and developing this matter proceeded by successive stages. When this work began, the world had assumed the formation described in the second verse, the earth being still covered with water and deprived of light.

During the first three "days," or in the first three stages of development, this immense mass of material is divided, light from darkness, upper waters from lower, and dry land from these lower waters. On the next three days the regions established by this division are given proper ornamentation: sun, moon and stars in the heavens, birds in the air, fish in the seas, animals and man on the dry land.

The unique dignity of man is shown not only by his being given dominion over the other creatures on earth but also in his being made in the very likeness of God. Throughout, the religious element is foremost. All things, however vast and wonderful, are the creatures of God and are not to be perverted to rivalry with Him. Man is God's agent in governing the earth, and the seventh day of rest is to mark man's knowledge of his dependence and of his duty to set aside that time for special worship of his Creator.

The relation of the account of creation in Chapter II to the preceding has been variously explained. According to some, Moses is here following a separate tradition, oral or written, and he simply adds this part with no reference to the previous section. A better explanation takes this previous section as a general introduction, giving a rapid sketch of the main features of the work of creation, while at verse four in Chapter II the author begins to concentrate on man.

First comes a glance at the condition of the earth as it was before man was created. After the first appearance of the dry land, it lay arid for some time till God sent the moisture needed for the growth of vegetation. Then God laid out a portion of the land as a delightful garden and made that place the habitation of the first man. The creation of the animals before man is merely hinted at when they are brought before him to receive their names. It is expressly stated that none of these animals was a fit helpmate for Adam, and so God by a special act formed Eve from a part of Adam's body, and Adam recognized in her his counterpart and understood the basic idea of marriage.

In the earlier section, man had been given dominion and a general permission to eat from whatever plants he wished, but here this permission is restricted to keep man in mind of his dependence on God and to test his obedience. The narrative in Chapter III shows in what sense the object of this restriction was called the tree of the knowledge of good and evil. By keeping the divine command and refraining from eating the fruit of this tree, man would have come to know how good it is to live in proper subordination to his Creator, but in the event, since he ate from it, he speedily learned how evil it is to act in defiance of the will of God.

The obvious sense of these two chapters excludes evolution in the crude form that would have all things developing from lower material—life from inanimate matter, animals from plants, and man from some irrational animal. But since the narrative is recognized as having been idealized for the purpose of making it intelligible to men of meager knowledge, it contains some expressions that are surely to be taken not literally but in a popularized or metaphorical or anthropomorphic sense. The creation of the sun, for example, must have preceded the succession of day and night and the growth of the plants. The difficulty of applying this distinction has given rise to many varying explanations, but the guiding principle of sane exegesis is that the literal sense must be retained unless there is solid reason for abandoning it.

This principle rules out even that mild form of human evolution according to which God formed the body of man out of the body of some lower animal and breathed into it a spiritual soul. The literal sense is against such an explanation, and the hypothesis of such evolution still remains merely a hypothesis and as such does not give a solid reason for following it in the interpretation of Scripture.

Since there is no limit to the power of God, He certainly could have taken a mere animal's body and prepared it for the reception of the human soul just as easily as, in the words of Moses, He took "the slime of the earth" for that purpose. Scientists have dug up the remains of "primitive men," or of the supposed predecessors of man in the line of evolution, but so far these discoveries have failed to lift the hypothesis to the level of established fact. The familiar rule of logic is applicable here—the possible is distinguished from the actual, and one cannot prove a fact from its mere possibility. Genuine scientists call such hypotheses "true" only in the sense that they provide clues for further investigation; when no longer helpful, they are abandoned.

In seeking the sources from which they would have the creation narratives of Genesis flow, hostile critics have found a fertile field for their fancy, often masquerading under the honored name of scientific research. In general, they think these sources are to be found in the cosmogonies, mythologies or legends of the ancient east or of Egypt. But these sources are dominated by the idea of a multiplicity of gods having human passions and often at war with one another, and they miss entirely the idea of creation since, when they touch on the subject, they presuppose the existence of matter, the body of some conquered god being used to form heaven and earth.

The real sources for Genesis were either direct revelations

made to Moses by God or the traditions handed down to him from his forefathers, these traditions starting with Adam and being passed on by the patriarchs, with increasing clarity, to Moses. Among the Gentiles these traditions became distorted into various fantasies, but for His chosen people God guarded and amplified them and finally inspired Moses to set them down in writing. God's ways are beyond the reach of human reason, and we can get to know them only as far as He reveals them to us. Moses has conveyed to us some such revelations about the larger features of creation, but the manner in which God performed His wondrous work still lies beyond our ken.

WILLIAM A. DOWD

SELECTED BIBLIOGRAPHY

HETZENAUER, Michael, O.C., *Commentarius in Librum Genesis.* Graecii et Viennae, 1910.
STEINMUELLER, John E., and Kathryn Sullivan, R.S.C.J., *A Companion to the Old Testament.* Wagner.
The Confraternity Translation of the Book of Genesis. Paterson, N. J.
POPE, Hugh, O.P., *The Catholic Student's Aids to the Study of the Bible.*

St. Thomas: On Truth and Falsity; On Human Knowledge (Summa Theologica, *Part I, Questions 16, 17, 84-88*)

ONE WHOSE SOLE ACQUAINTANCE with philosophy has been *Phil. 54* (MWF, 2 P.M. Required for all sophomores) is left with the impression that all philosophers are concerned exclusively with the problem of knowledge, that all speculation on the matter is obscure in varying degrees, and alike only in being unsatisfactory. Such a man is inclined to cheer Cowper's:

> Much learned dust
> Involves the combatants, each claiming truth,
> And truth disclaiming both. And thus they spend
> The little wick of life's poor shallow lamp
> In playing tricks with nature . . .

This quite understandable pessimism is reason enough for including St. Thomas's questions on human knowledge in any symposium of Great Books. Here we have a clear and forthright coming to grips with the problem of what truth is, how man knows it and how he comes to a knowledge of the world about him. Nature is not the subject of tricks, but of analysis and understanding.

The problems treated in these selections have occupied philosophers from the beginnings of human thought and occupy men today: the nature of truth, the nature of falsity, what man knows, and how he knows it. St. Thomas's solutions, as represented here, are a marvelous example of intellectual craftsmanship.

In discussing any point of craftsmanship, however, it is

important to know just what is the purpose of the work. A delicately balanced drive shaft is a beautiful thing in itself, but fully to appreciate it one must know whether it is designed for an airplane or a tractor. There will be a vast difference in the material chosen, the stresses anticipated, the parts machined away.

So with the questions chosen from the *Summa Theologica*. It must be kept in mind that we have here not a monograph on human knowledge but a consideration of certain problems presented in a systematic work. Granted that the problems considered in these questions are philosophical ones, Thomas is nevertheless speaking as a theologian. These questions are asked, and answered, because they have arisen in the consideration of God as He is known to us by revelation and by our reasoning on that revelation. Thomas, with his feet firmly planted on earth, is working down from a knowledge of God.

In the plan of the *Summa* as a whole, St. Thomas has been concerned first of all (after establishing the nature of scientific theology in Q. 1) with the existence of God (Q. 2) and with the nature of God as He is in Himself (QQ. 3-13). He then turns to God's operations—to His knowledge first of all: what it is (Q. 14), the function of the divine ideas (Q. 15). Next, since knowledge is of its very nature concerned with truths, one turns to a consideration of truth in general and of its contrary, falsity. It is here that we join Thomas.

Aquinas works, like any true craftsman, economically. There is to be no needless repetition of material in his work, but neither is there to be an anticipation of problems out of due order. The consideration of truth has arisen from the development of the question on the knowledge of God, but truth must be considered in relation to human knowledge as well. The treatment of the question must be sufficiently broad to embrace both sorts of truth.

The eight articles of this sixteenth question are keyed to the first one: Does truth reside only in the intellect? The answer given is that truth lies in things and in the intellect, but in different ways; and that, in every case, when we speak of truth an intellect is in some way involved. Aquinas analyzes the nature of truth under these two considerations, examines several defi-

nitions proposed, and concludes with a crisp definition expressing both aspects of truth: "Truth is the equation of thought
and thing."

Thomas's technique of argument here is interesting. He
uses the parallel: "Truth is to the intellect as good is to the
appetite." He is able to do so because he has previously (QQ.
5 and 6) considered the nature of good and its relation to the
will, divine and human. When he treats of the same question
as to the nature of truth in his *Disputed Questions* (*Quaestiones Disputatae de Veritate*, Q. I, a. 1) he approaches the
solution from the consideration of being in general. He reaches
the same conclusion, but there he is working as a philosopher
treating a particular question in isolation. Here he is writing a
systematic work and can take advantage of matters already
considered.

The basic conclusion arrived at in the sixteenth question is
that truth consists in the relation—indeed, the identity in some
sense—of a thing with the mind that knows it. In the really
fundamental order of essences, the relation *intellect to thing*
is prior to the relation *thing to intellect*. Our first acquaintance
with the concept of truth is drawn from the second sort of
equation, but the truth of things, based on the knowledge concerning them in the mind of God, is the essential and primary
note of truth. (See a. 1, body of article, and Reply to the Third
Objection.) Truth is to be sought first of all in an intellect
causing and measuring an object. On the human level we see
this verified in creative art. A work of art is true just as far as
his work reflects the image in the mind of the artist. Natural
things, objects in the world about us, are true because they reflect the divine ideas, which cause and measure them. Human
(and angelic) knowledge is true as it is measured and caused
by things.

The general principles are laid down in this first article:
Truth is attainable by a created intellect; truth is not confined
by a created intellect, is not, in the modern sense of the term,
subjective. It is firmly tied to being, to something apart from
mind. It is only in God's intellect, with regard to natural
things, that a mind causes and measures truth.

One must note here St. Thomas's analysis of the nature of
truth as we generally conceive it: truth in the human mind.

In the second article of this sixteenth question, Thomas points out that known truth lies in the judgment. Man has truth fully in his knowledge when he weighs the thing in his mind against the reality outside it. The simple intellectual grasp of the nature of a thing has truth, yes; but it is of the order of the truth of things. Truth of knowledge, logical truth, demands a joining or separating, a recognition of conformity between the mind and thing, or a lack of conformity. Truth is found in the created intellect when the intellect begins to have something proper to it, something not found in the thing as it exists outside the mind, but only as it is known. (*Quaestiones Disputatae de Veritate*, Q. 1, a. 3.) This is verified only in the judgment.

Truth, then, in its most commonly used sense of true knowledge, will be the known conformity of a mind to the extramental world. It is not a special operation, not a special faculty, not the result of a Cartesian clear and distinct idea, but the operation, the function, of a faculty ordained of its very nature to seize upon the real world.

The conclusions as to falsity will follow as corollaries to the notions established as to truth. Since the truth of things is absolute as they are measured and caused by the mind of God, there is no falsity, in that ontological sense, in things. Falsity will be found in the knowing intellect, the intellect whose act is determined and measured by things. The intellect will be false not when it grasps the nature of things but as it affirms an identity between the known object and the object outside the mind when no conformity is given, or denies it when it is given.

Our consideration in this symposium on the Great Books turns next to that section of the *Summa* in which St. Thomas treats of the objects, nature and order of man's intellectual knowledge. It cannot be emphasized enough that these problems and solutions must be understood in context. Our study is limited to Questions 84-88 of Part I, but we need at least a glance at the order of the questions immediately preceding these. After concluding the tract on the nature of God and the distinction of Persons in the Trinity, the theologian must next turn to the production of creatures by divine power. The hierarchy of created things embraces a large section of Part I, for Thomas inquires successively about angels and corporeal crea-

tures, and turns to man only at the seventy-fifth question.*
Here he begins by saying: "Now the theologian considers the
nature of man in relation to the soul, but not in relation to the
body except in so far as it has relation to the soul . . . we shall
first treat of what belongs to the essence of the soul (QQ. 75-76);
secondly of what belongs to its powers (QQ. 77-83); thirdly of
what belongs to its operations (QQ. 84-88)."

Many of the answers in the questions under our immediate
consideration may seem brief. Thomas, it must be remembered, has already established a considerable background of
scientific conclusions as to the nature of intellectual knowledge
as seen in God (QQ. 14-18), and in the angels (QQ. 54-58). Just
before we join him once more, he has shown (Q. 79) that the
intellect is a power of the human soul and not the soul itself;
that it is a passive power, that is, a power which is not always
actually understanding. With this background, the theologian can treat clearly and concisely of how the soul knows
bodies which are beneath it; how it understands itself and
things contained in itself; and how it understands immaterial
things which are above it.

The first problem presented concerns man's scientific knowledge of the physical world. Here, precisely, is the problem
which started Kant on his critique of knowledge, and which
still vexes many philosophers and physicists of today. It is the
problem with which Eddington wrestles unsuccessfully in his
Nature of the Physical World and *The Philosophy of Physical
Science*. The problem, most simply stated, is this: How can
man possess scientific knowledge, which must be universal and
necessary, of a world which is made of things which are particular and contingent in nature? The problem is older than
Kant, older than Aristotle. The solution which St. Thomas
presents here is basically Aristotle's, though strengthened

---

* The complete order of matter in the first part is as follows: Q. 1, The
Nature of Theology; QQ. 2-43, The Divine Nature and the Persons in the
Trinity; QQ. 44-46, The Production of Creatures; Q. 47, The Distinction of
Creatures, Considered in General; QQ. 48, 49, The Distinction of Good and
Evil, and the Cause of Evil; QQ. 50-64, The Angels; QQ. 65-74, The Corporeal
World; QQ. 75-89, Man. The eighty-ninth Question is concerned with the
operations of the human soul in its state of separation from the body. From
Q. 90 to Q. 102, Thomas is occupied with the production of man, the state of
Adam before the Fall, and some of the consequences of the Fall for Adam's
posterity. From Q. 103 to Q. 119 (which completes Part I), he considers the
conservation and government of things by divine providence.

against positions assumed between the Stagirite's day and his own.

St. Thomas begins with the development of the truth that the mind can have an intellectual knowledge of bodies. He points out that the ancients (the pre-Socratics) erred in attributing a continual state of flux to things. They envisioned a universe which was entirely material, and hence unknowable in a necessary and universal way. Plato's solution, on the other hand, would place the reality of things in a world apart and leave us with a world of shadows before us. We would know nothing of matter and movement, and natural science would vanish. No, says St. Thomas, we must seek the solution in a knowing faculty which can receive the form of material things in an immaterial way, for matter is the source of the particular and the changeable or contingent, immateriality the source of the universal and the necessary. But the intellect of man is precisely such a knowing faculty.

With the fact of intellectual knowledge of bodies established, one naturally seeks to explain the means by which that knowledge is gained. We run through the solutions proposed. Man cannot know things by examining the essence of his soul, as certain of the ancients taught (and Descartes was later to teach). He cannot know by means of forms, *species*, naturally present in the soul—factory-installed, as it were. This had been Plato's solution and, in part, was to be the solution of Kant. He cannot know material things in the light of divine types, as Bonaventure held, nor see them in the divine ideas, as the devout Malebranche was to teach four centuries later. No, "man's spirit will be flesh-bound when found at best." Man is an intellectual creature, but he knows, he understands, in close conjunction with the body. All his knowledge must have its beginning in some way in the senses, though it rises from there.

This affirmation of the body's role in intellectual knowledge is the conclusion of the sixth article, after the examination and rejection of other solutions proposed. The last two articles of the question are but reaffirmations and applications of that solution: Man knows intellectually only by turning to the product of the internal senses, which, in turn, draw their matter from the exterior senses (a. 7); a fact confirmed by the suspension of intellectual knowledge in sleep (a. 8).

One is struck here by the very down-to-earth approach of St. Thomas. There is no *a priorism*, no twisting of the facts to fit a preconceived theory, no "playing tricks with nature." The history of thought is examined and the great figures with their solutions are passed in review: Heraclitus, Empedocles, Plato, Augustine, Plotinus, Avicenna, Bonaventure. All are weighed against the double standard of metaphysical consistency and experience. All are found wanting in some way or other. We are left with Aristotle's conclusion: Man knows material things intellectually in conjunction with his internal senses.

The next problem suggests itself immediately: How do we know? What is the mechanism, so to speak, of our intellectual knowledge? The fact that our intellectual knowledge originates in the senses has already been shown, how it comes to be remains to be discussed.

The solution given in the first two articles of the eighty-sixth question is of paramount importance in the Thomistic psychology and epistemology. The intellect knows by abstracting, by drawing out, by pulling out, the form of a thing from its presence in the internal senses. So the first article.

The second article underlines the essentially real character of our knowledge. We know, says Thomas here, things, not their representations. The species or likeness of the thing in the mind is the means by which we know; it is not the object of knowledge. Here is the rock on which Ockam was to stumble in the next century, and which was to prove insuperable for Descartes. For the philosophizing geometer, knowledge never becomes the thing, but is confined within the mind. We have ideas or concepts of things apart from us, but our knowledge terminates in the mind, not in the thing. The theory of knowledge was thereby torn loose from its ontological moorings, and at the mercy of every idealistic wind and empiricist tide.

St. Thomas examines the errors of Protagoras and Empedocles and, once more, of Plato. He rejects their opinions that what the mind knows is only its own reactions to external stimuli. The mind must become the thing *by* the species or likeness of the object in the mind, true enough, but *that which* is understood is the thing itself. The species is the means of knowing things, but is itself known only by further examination, by an after-thought.

Once the nature and way of knowing of the intellect are established, the further questions as to the soul's knowledge of itself and its knowledge of things above itself fall into place as corollaries. The eighty-fourth and eighty-fifth questions show that the intellect is a potential faculty whose proper function is to grasp the very form, the "whatness" (*quiddity*, the mediaeval man would have said) of material things.

As to man's knowledge of his own soul, Thomas points out that it cannot know its inner nature simply by contemplating itself. Such self-knowledge is proper to God and the angels. Man's knowledge of his own intellectual part must come, in a sense, from the outside. The metaphysics behind this argumentation is interesting, for it is linked, professedly and verbatim, to the notions of act and potency developed in Book IX of Aristotle's *Metaphysics*. Only things in act are knowable, the reasoning runs. But as a potential faculty, the soul is knowable only when it is performing its own proper function of knowing the essences of material things, for only then is it in act (Q. 87).

Since the knowledge of ourselves is thus indirect and through the essences of material things, *a fortiori* our knowledge of the angels and of God Himself must be in this indirect way (Q. 88). Indeed, there is no proportion between these objects and our knowing faculty. We *can* come to a knowledge of God, but only by reasoning from the effects of His power in the world.

God-centered reasoner though he is, Thomas shows in these questions on human knowledge the truer humanism. He avoids the angelic error of Descartes, which would make of man's intelligence an all-seeing intuitive faculty; and the stifling limitation of the empiricists, who would leave man's knowledge but little above that of the brute. Man's spirit, in Aquinas's view, is embedded in blood and bone, but unencumbered by them. Man is placed here in his true position in the hierarchy of beings.

WILLIAM B. MAHONEY

SELECTED BIBLIOGRAPHY

ARISTOTLE, *On the Soul*, in *The Basic Works of Aristotle*. Random House.
ARISTOTLE, *De Anima*, with the *Commentary of St. Thomas Aquinas*, translated

by Kenelm Foster, O.P., and Sylvester Humphries, O.P. London, Routledge & Kegan Paul.

BRENNAN, Robert, O.P., *Thomistic Psychology.* Macmillan.

FARRELL, Walter, O.P., *Companion to the Summa,* Vol. I, chap. xv. Sheed & Ward.

GILSON, Étienne, *The Unity of Philosophical Experience.* Scribners.

ST. THOMAS, *The Summa Theologica of St. Thomas Aquinas.* Benziger.

ST. THOMAS, *The Soul, a Translation of St. Thomas Aquinas's* De Anima, by John D. Rowan. Herder.

ST. THOMAS, *On Truth and Falsity; On Human Knowledge,* Part I, Questions 16, 17, 84-88. Regnery.

Montaigne: Apology for
Raimond de Sebonde

MORE THAN THREE CENTURIES after his death—but still very
modern, still widely read and the subject of numerous scholarly
studies—Michel de Montaigne (1533-1592) appears as the
author who, of his contemporaries, has most successfully with-
stood the test of time. He represents excellently the second
phase of the Renaissance in France in its literary and philosophic achievements. The Renaissance, brought from Italy by
the armies of Francis I, burst forth, with the vigor, the enthusiasm, the indiscriminate eagerness for learning and the lack of
reflection and criticism which characterize youth, in the early
humanists and in Rabelais, who wrote in the first half of the
century.

With Montaigne, the movement acquired maturity. It began to distinguish, among the ancients, the mediocre from
the excellent. No longer did the thinkers of the period accept
ideas solely on the authority of Greek or Latin texts; they tested
the validity of ideas against experience and reason. The work
of selecting the most satisfactory models, their assimilation into
a more personal and national trend which would lead ultimately, through further purification of the language and of
philosophical thought, to the glorious era of French classicism,
was already slowly beginning.

Montaigne belonged to the first generation to have been educated by the Renaissance. His masters were learned men who
had just broken away from medieval pedagogical principles.
His enlightened father made him learn Latin even before his
native tongue. Michel was sent to the famous Collège de Guy-
enne, headed by the Portuguese scholar Andréa de Gouvéan
and numbering among its professors Muret, Guérente and

Buchanan. He afterward studied law at the University of Toulouse and became counselor to the parliament of that city. Montaigne, however, had little inclination for the intricacies of legal procedure. He soon resigned his charge and, in 1573, withdrew to his estate. There, in the solitude of his library, on the top floor of a tower, surrounded by a rich collection of books, Montaigne set about to study himself.

From that painless and dispassionate search, conducted without order and in whatever direction the events of the day or a chance reading of some Latin text led him, were born the *Essays*. The first edition, comprising two books, appeared in 1580, but the work occupied Montaigne for the rest of his life. His short sojourns in Paris, his extended trip throughout Italy in 1580-1581, his scarcely exacting functions as mayor of Bordeaux, did not distract the author from that task but rather provided him with new material incorporated into later editions. A fifth edition of the *Essays*, augmented by a third book, was published in 1888, and a still more enlarged edition prepared by Montaigne was published posthumously in 1595 by the author's adopted daughter, Mlle. de Gournay. The *Essays*, then, represent the observations, the experiences, the reflections, the readings of a lifetime. It is not only the portrait of Montaigne which is given in them, according to the purpose set forth in the preface, but truly the portrait of man beyond the frontiers of nations and the barriers of time.

The "Apology for Raimond de Sebonde" expresses Montaigne's profound and extended thought on the nature of man as it was revealed to him throughout the pages of history and in the works of the moralists. With the essay "On the Education of Children," the "Apology" is undoubtedly the most important chapter of the *Essays*, and also the lengthiest, filling 219 pages of the modern Garnier edition. While the first essay contains an aspect of what we might call Montaigne's practical philosophy, or the principles which, almost without relation to his theoretical philosophy, directed his ordinary behavior, the "Apology" is the most complete exposé of that theoretical philosophy.

Raimond de Sebonde (also called Sebond) was a professor of medicine at Toulouse in the fourteenth century and the author of a little-known book entitled *Theologia naturalis, sive liber creaturarum, magistri Raymondi de Sebonde.* In this the author endeavored to demonstrate that all the articles of the Christian faith could be proved by reason. The book had been given to Montaigne's father by one of his friends, Pierre Bunel, a man of great reputation for learning. On inquiring from the renowned Turnebus (philologist and humanist) the nature of the philosophy underlying the *Theologia naturalis,* Montaigne was told that it was an adaptation of the philosophy of St. Thomas Aquinas. Professing a complete ignorance of philosophy, Montaigne was hesitant when his father, a short time before his death, asked him to translate the book into French. But since he had enough leisure and because he could not refuse anything to "the best father that ever lived," he accepted the task. There was also another, and perhaps greater, incitement. The Protestants were just then attacking the dogmas of the Catholic Church with a renewed intensity. Montaigne believed that Sebonde's demonstration could well answer the objections of that "new religion" (*une nouvelleté*) which is under his pen a term of scorn. The book was published in Paris by Gabriel Buon in 1569.

The "Apologia" is, then, supposedly a defense of the ideas and of the procedure of the *Theologia naturalis.* But soon, following his constant practice, Montaigne seems to lose sight of his main purpose. He wanders along byways, loses himself in long digressions, remembers occasionally that he is discussing Raimond de Sebonde, then succumbs again to the lure of an attractive idea to relate an anecdote or to confide to his readers his own likes and dislikes. Montaigne prefaces his study by declaring that the *Theologia naturalis* is unequaled in proving by human and natural reasoning, against the atheists, all the dogmas of the Christian religion. But since two objections have been leveled against the book, he will attempt to answer them.

The first objection, arising, says Montaigne, from an excess of piety, is that Christians err in trying to establish by rational arguments beliefs which can be gained only through faith and divine grace. That objection, he declares, is without foundation. It is true that purely human means are incapable by themselves of giving the faith; otherwise many excellent minds among the Ancients would have been able to discover revealed truths. But reason has also a role in this process because our faith is often weak. It is frequently deterred by external pressure, by new theories (Montaigne here has Protestantism in mind), by coercion from public powers, by the temporal success of a different religion.

There follows a long digression on the same subject proposing to show that Christians, on account of the imperfect practice of their faith, do not distinguish themselves from members of other religions, except in their language. Their moral behavior is no better than that of heretics or pagans. In the religious wars then raging, there have been excesses in both camps. There is, of course, justice in the Catholic cause, but none in Catholic hearts. Religion has been a shield and a pretext for giving free rein to passions and for satisfying private grievances. Montaigne here develops extensively not the shortcomings of the Catholic religion, but the scandals attached to a religion utilized for personal motives to encourage hatred and cruelty. A real faith would make us love God above everything. But while we fear to outrage a friend, a relative, a master, we do not hesitate to offend God. Likewise, if we truly believed in eternal life, we should not fear death. It appears that we have received our religion as we have received our nationality, that is, passively. We are Christian as we are French or German. Therefore, reason is needed, as Sebonde proposed, to strengthen our faith or to prepare for faith. Sebonde's arguments, says Montaigne, are only the *matter* of faith, to which divine grace will give the form.

The second objection is more serious. Sebonde has been accused of using weak arguments, which do not succeed in proving what they intend to prove. Sebonde's critics claim that they can advance opposing demonstrations which will invalidate those of the *Theologia naturalis*. Montaigne reserves for this objection his most detailed answer, which is also the most notable and the best-known part of the "Apology." To confound Sebonde's adversaries, he will simply show, by a wealth of examples taken from the history of philosophy, the history of nations and his own observations, the nothingness and vanity of man and the vagaries of his reasoning. This particular exposé will be, incidentally, the source, not always correctly understood, of innumerable judgments on Montaigne's presumed skepticism.

It is, however, essential to note that Montaigne here considers specifically man deprived of divine grace and left to his own resources. He starts with a dramatic contrast (later borrowed by Pascal in the *Pensées*) between the immensity of the universe and the smallness of man. He wants to crush man's pride and reduce him to his proper stature. How can man believe himself to be the master of a universe of which he knows practically nothing? There follows the famous comparison between man and animal, which is all to the advantage of the latter. Animals have all the qualities of which man boasts and which he wants to deny to them. They have means of communication among themselves and even with animals of other species. They have a social organization more orderly than that of man. They also possess prudence, discernment, thought, knowledge of an end and of a purpose. They exhibit all the signs of intelligence and of the power of reasoning. Man is superior to animals only by his imagination, and that is a gift for which he pays dearly, since that faculty is the source of fears, illness, despair.

On the other hand, man is decidedly inferior to many animals in physical strength, and even lesser and despicable animals have been known to cause man's downfall. "The heart and the life of a mighty emperor is but the breakfast of a worm." As for moral qualities, animals are more faithful, more grateful than man. Their science is superior to that of man, even though we ignore its sources. Some animals, like the tuna, need evidently a knowledge of astronomy, geometry, mathematics. In short, animals enjoy peace, rest, security, innocence, health, truly the finest gifts of nature. Man has for his part inconstancy, irresolution, uncertitude, sorrow, superstition, worry over the future, ambition, avarice, jealousy, disorderly desires, lies, disloyalty, wars.

Man is inordinately proud of his reason. Montaigne shows, through historical proofs, that reason has often been harmful to man. Reason has not brought happiness to the great philosophers, nor have they been freed of human frailty. Happiness is more likely to be found among simple, ignorant people. Montaigne, who had been brought up among peasants and had continued to frequent their company, had seen hundreds of them happier and wiser than rectors of universities. The inhabitants of newly discovered Brazil, to whom Montaigne makes several important references throughout the *Essays* and particularly in "On Cannibals," die of old age, he says, because they are not troubled by the passions of civilized people.

To the examples of the New World, Montaigne adds those of the early Romans (subsequently made famous by Bossuet, Montesquieu and Rousseau in their quest for an explanation of the grandeur and decadence of Rome) who "smelled of garlic" but were virtuous. The later Romans, of the Empire, smelling of perfumes, were full of vices and had lost the robustness of their ancestors. Knowledge engenders maliciousness; the desire for knowledge stems from pride, as is shown in the fall of our first parents. Such is, in its general aspects, Montaigne's apology of ignorance, which will leave durable traces in French literature.

Man's limitations are even more pronounced when he attempts to understand the nature of God. All that we know of Him we owe to revelation, and God again has chosen for His witnesses the most ignorant people. Man's ignorance extends also to nature, its possibilities and occult qualities. He does not know the composition of celestial bodies, and even his own body is a mystery to him. The nature of the soul and its location in the body have been the object of endless and inconclusive discussions. No one had been able to prove whether the soul was mortal or immortal. The senses, from which comes all our knowledge, are themselves the source of continual errors. Finally, our language is also the cause of constant difficulties and obscurities.

In the course of this discussion, Montaigne examines the position of the various philosophical schools in relation to the possibility of attaining truth. Everywhere he finds contradictions and absurdities. There is not a single philosophical proposition which does not need defending against a hundred contrary opinions. He rails at the dogmatic philosophers, among them Aristotle, "the prince of dogmatists"; at the peripatetics, Epicureans and Stoics, who pretend to have found the truth. But neither does he approve of the philosophers of the Academy, who despair of ever embracing a firmly established truth because it is, according to their belief, beyond our reach. These philosophers are still too dogmatic, too assured in their denial.

Montaigne seems to adopt the position of the Pyrrhonists, who teach a universal metaphysical doubt, though in the proposition "I doubt," he sees a certitude as to the existence of that very doubt. Montaigne's attitude will then be more properly expressed in the interrogative and dubitative *Que sais-je?* ("What do I know?"), which rejects even the positive statement of a doubt. In summary, Montaigne spurns all the traditional criteria of truth: the authority of philosophers (for philosophy is just *un tintamarre de cervelles,* "a clatter of brains"), the principles of metaphysics, reason, science, universal consensus. Nothing stands of the edifice so painfully built for centuries, nothing except the unimpaired authority of the faith.

There would seem to be a considerable confusion and even several contradictions in Montaigne's "Apology," and Montaigne would surely be the last to deny it. He did not pretend to write an orderly and dogmatic demonstration. The answers to the second objection could rightly be considered as invalidating completely Sebonde's own thesis. Montaigne wanted merely to write down, in his own leisurely and homely fashion, the various reflections which occurred to him in connection with the *Theologia naturalis.* Yet, some general propositions may easily be drawn from this essay.

First, in all metaphysical questions Montaigne is a pure skeptic. He denies to reason any ability to reach the truth. But once faith confirms the findings of reason, that faculty becomes a valid instrument of inquiry. It provides both an approach to, and a preparation for, the truths of faith. Montaigne, then, far from being a skeptic in matters of faith, is dogmatic or, more precisely, a fideist. He is prepared to admit that he would believe even the "truths" of faith which reason might prove to be impossible and absurd.

This strange attitude, fundamentally illogical, will be better understood in the light of several currents of thought prevalent during the sixteenth century. Montaigne has not escaped a form of anti-Aristotelian rationalism, originating with the Arab philosopher Averroes in the fourteenth century, which sought to reconcile either the Koran or the Bible with philosophy. The conciliation was generally not effected, but those who attempted it kept intact their beliefs in religious truths and their conviction that these are irrational. Thus Montaigne, who is essentially a disciple of the Stoic philosophers, can be a good Christian as well, because the first adherence is in the nature of a theoretical and intellectual acceptance, the other in the practical and ethical domain. The life of the intellect and the life of faith are then completely separated and evolve, one might say, in different channels.

This difficulty accounts for the various and contradictory opinions among the critics who have studied Montaigne's "Apology" and the philosophy of the *Essays*. He is held by some to be a rationalist, and they attribute to prudence or to fear his many declarations of respect for Catholic dogmas. For others, notably the Abbé Dréano (*The Religion of Montaigne*), Montaigne is a sincere, even devout, Christian who profoundly believed the teaching of his faith and practiced his religion earnestly. Montaigne's skepticism does not extend to the truths of faith. It does not apply, either, to the practical and moral problems of life. He has frequently, and in this very "Apology," taken a position on many questions of his time and condemned Protestantism on grounds other than those of faith. He preaches the respect of customs, obedience to the law and to the princes.

The "Apology" offers also many proofs of Montaigne's erudition. It is replete with quotations from the Latin authors, from Lucretius principally (who had been the most influential in the formation of Montaigne's thought as well as of that of his century), from Cicero (not the orator but the philosopher of *De Finibus* and *De Natura Deorum*), from Seneca, Plutarch and Horace (here considered also as a philosopher more than as a poet), from Virgil and Ovid. He borrows philosophical conclusions and also many an anecdote from the historians Herodotus, Livy, Tacitus and Sallust. But he counterbalances the pagan authors with several quotations from St. Paul, St. Augustine, Tertullian. He quotes occasionally also the Italian authors Dante, Tasso (whom Montaigne saw insane in Ferrara in 1580) and the *Orlando Furioso* of Ariosto.

The influence of the "Apology" has been tremendous and lasting. The seventeenth century, which despised Rabelais for his vulgarity, read Montaigne faithfully. Pascal, who condemned Montaigne's skepticism in his *Entretiens avec M. de Sacy sur Epictète et sur Montaigne,* owes to the "Apology" many arguments and perhaps an important part of what was to become an apologia of the Christian Religion, his *Pensées.* The famous Pascalian contrast between the immensity of the universe and the powerlessness of man is, as has been seen, in the "Apology of Raimond de Sebonde." There, also, may be found the condemnation of reason and yet its utilization as a preparation for and an adjuvant to the faith; and the reflection on the vagaries of laws, varying with times and nations, which was expressed later by Pascal in the famous words: "Truth on this side of the Pyrenees; error on the other side."

The eighteenth century took from Montaigne several fundamental points of its rationalistic philosophy. Leaving aside here Rousseau's many borrowings from the essay "On the Education of Children," which found their place in the pedagogical principles of *Émile,* Rousseau discovered in the "Apology" the praise of ignorance and simplicity, the vanity of science and even the contrast between the early and later Romans, which are the substance of his *First Discourse.* Many articles of the *Philosophic Dictionary* of Voltaire appear almost textually in the "Apology." Such are the contradictions of philosophers on essential truths, the disdain of metaphysics, the incertitudes on the nature of God and on the nature and immortality of the soul, the errors of the senses, and even specifically a criticism of Aristotle.

When Montaigne visited Rome in 1580, he carried with him a copy of the first edition of the *Essays.* These were examined by ecclesiastical authorities of the papal court and returned to him with only minor criticisms, bearing notably on his frequent use of the word "Fortune," which had a pagan connotation and appeared to deny Providence. Montaigne was simply asked to make some changes in the next edition of his book. Yet the *Essays* were put on the Index in the seventeenth century and the reasons should be obvious. By denying in the "Apology" the power of reason to prove some truths which are also revealed truths, he deprives faith of a potent support. He goes counter to the teaching of scholastic philosophy and even to the official teaching, since 1870, of the Church, which proclaimed in the Council of the Vatican that faith is not a blind and sentimental adherence to revealed truths but an act of the intellect founded on the authority of a revealing God. Furthermore, the condemnation of Bautain for fideism implied also a condemnation of the "Apology of Raimond de Sebonde."

FERNAND VIAL

SELECTED BIBLIOGRAPHY

PARADOL, Prévost, *Les Moralistes Français*. Paris, Hachette.
BONNEFON, Paul, *Montaigne, l'Homme et l'Oeuvre*. Paris, Colin.
STAPFER, Paul, *Montaigne*. Paris, Collection des Grands Écrivains Français.
VILLEY, Pierre, *Les Sources et l'Évolution des Essais de Montaigne*. Paris, Hachette.
DRÉANO, Abbé, *La Religion de Montaigne*. Paris, Beauchesne.
MONTAIGNE, Michel de, *Essays*. Random House (The Modern Library).
MONTAIGNE, Michel de, *Apology for Raimond de Sebonde*. Regnery.

Rabelais: Gargantua and Pantagruel,
Books I and II

IN ALL THE HISTORY of literature there is probably no man who has been so thoroughly maligned and distorted by the legend that has grown around his name as has François Rabelais. To most of us he represents the perfect picture of an overstuffed, besotted and debauched friar. On the other hand, grave critics and historians speak of him as a moralist, a thinker, an atheist, or as an early adherent of the Protestant revolt against the Church. So religious a man as Samuel Taylor Coleridge was able to say of him that "I could write a treatise in praise of the moral elevation of Rabelais's work which would make the church stare and the conventicle groan, and yet would be truth, and nothing but the truth."

As is usual in such cases, the individual whose reputation before posterity is so cavalierly treated and mistreated has some grounds for complaint, but also at least a partial responsibility for the confusion. No matter how pure and grave a man's life may be, when he deliberately sets about to write a best seller he must expect that his character in the public eye will stand or fall with his book, however unfair to the whole man such a state of affairs may be.

If, as I think, Rabelais was neither an atheist nor a Protestant, he never made clear, throughout the four (or possibly five) volumes of his *Gargantua and Pantagruel*—in the course of which he touched upon everything under the sun—just what he did think on matters of religious faith. The error and unfairness of blaming him for this, or of pressing his book too hard for a statement of systematic belief or disbelief will become apparent if we try to imagine what conception we would form of the mind and faith of St. Thomas More, if all we knew of him was his *Utopia.*

Not, of course, that Rabelais may be compared to Thomas More, but, *mutatis mutandis,* the case is not dissimilar, for *Gargantua and Pantagruel,* like *Utopia,* is a half-facetious, half-serious, intellectual and imaginative work written as a diverting but thoughtful pastime. Although they both express in an amusing and fantastic framework many of the very serious ideas of their authors, they do not express, and never were intended to expound, the whole of their philosophic and religious concepts. No man, after all, is obliged to put all of himself into any one book or even into the sum total of his writings.

Rabelais, one Catholic critic has written, may not have been an atheist, but his religion was at best that of a deistic pagan. Such a conclusion may indeed be drawn from certain passages of his works and certain facts of his life, but in the final analysis and after careful reflection it seems decidedly temerarious. He was indeed a runaway monk, a man in Holy Orders who had an illegitimate child, but neither of these facts was so shocking and so damaging in the public opinion of the early sixteenth century as it would be today. In the society of Rabelais's time, men and women with no religious vocation whatsoever were only too often led or even forced to enter convents or the priesthood, sometimes at a very early age. Under these circumstances, it is no wonder there were scandals.

In Rabelais's case, at any rate, the lack of religious vocation is quite evident. Still, when he left the Franciscan monastery of Fontenay-le-Comte, it was in order to be transferred to the Benedictine Abbey of Maillezais, which was under the more enlightened authority of his protector, Geoffroy d'Estissac, Bishop of Maillezais. We do not know under what circumstances he left his Benedictine life, but we do know that he was on intimate terms of association and friendship with serious and highly placed men of religion, statesmanship and scholarship, such as the Bishop of Paris, Jean (later Cardinal) du Bellay, Guillaume Budé, Guillaume du Bellay (the governor of Piedmont), Cardinal de Guise and others. His canonical situation was regularized by a special pontifical dispensation, and he was granted two curacies. He was present at the meeting of Francis I and Charles V at Aigues Mortes in 1538. He enjoyed the highest reputation for his humanistic scholarship and his medical skill, having received his medical degrees from the University of Montpellier, and appointments as physician at the hospitals of Lyons and of Metz.

Such a man could not well have been the overstuffed, dissolute reprobate of legend. This is not to say, of course, that he was a model of piety, wisdom and decorum. The truth, as usual, lies somewhere between these two extremes; he was a human being of flesh and blood, compounded of good and bad like the rest of us, but perhaps of rather more blood than most of us. If his name and legend are so very much alive today, however, it is not because of his scholarship or his irregularities—these were all too common in his day—but solely because of his *Gargantua and Pantagruel*. As the author of this work, he was quite unlike most of us, a man not only of enormous learning and energy, but of monstrous verve, enthusiasm, humor, imagination, verbosity and crudity, a giant of a man, like his protagonists.

There is today very lively debate over the religious and philosophical ideas expressed in *Gargantua and Pantagruel,* and even over the very nature of the work itself. For some, it is essentially a philosophical book, a bearer of an audacious and unorthodox doctrine more or less hidden under the phantasmagoric fiction. For others, it is merely a vulgar and obscene attempt to pander to the lowest tastes of the lowest stratum of the book-buying populace; and for still others it is simply the jovial, harmless, if quite crude, pastime of a learned scholar and physician, written for his own amusement and recreation and for those of his friends. In reality, I think, it may be said with considerable justification that it is all of these things, but that it is no one of them exclusively. As a matter of fact, *Gargantua and Pantagruel* is not a book at all; it is rather several books, written over a long period of years and quite different from one another.

The initial fiction is not of Rabelais's invention. The huge, beneficent and comic giant Gargantua is the descendant of a long line of such giants popular in late medieval fiction. While the lords and ladies of the courts were entertaining themselves with high-flown artificial romances of love and knightly ad-

venture, like those that finished addling poor Don Quixote's
pate, and with the even more artificial and pedantic "poetry"
of the *Grands Rhétoriqueurs,* the mass of the uneducated and
semi-educated third estate was amusing itself with crude tales
combined from the traditional stories of kings, warriors, giants
and magicians, with an added dose of new and frequently
scurvy inventions and burlesquing. With the rapid spread of
printing, these tales were made available in inexpensive little
books that were hawked about and sold principally at the great
periodic fairs which were the life of commerce in those days.

Among the most important of these fairs were those of Lyons,
then one of the great business centers of the world. In that
city, in the year 1532, the learned physician François Rabelais
published an annotated edition of the text of the great Greek
medical authorities, Hippocrates and Galen; simultaneously,
at the August fair there was offered for sale an anonymous little
book, certainly not by Rabelais, called the *Great and Inestimable Chronicles of the Hugh Giant Gargantua.* Like many
a learned author today, Rabelais no doubt reflected somewhat
bitterly on the vastly superior sales of the inferior book. At any
rate, he tells us in the Prolog of *Pantagruel* that "the printers
have sold more of them (the *Chronicles*) in two months' time
than there will be bought of Bibles in nine years."

And so, at the November fair in Lyons in the same year there
appeared on the stalls a sequel to the *Great and Inestimable
Chronicles of the Huge Giant Gargantua,* which purported to
relate the adventures of the latter's son, under the title of
*The Horrible and Dreadful Feats and Prowesses of the Most
Renowned Pantagruel,* and signed by one Alcofrybas Nasier.
This anagram of François Rabelais was no doubt transparent
enough to Rabelais's intimates, but he probably hoped it
wouldn't be noticed by the authorities of the great hospital at
Lyons at which, just a few days previously, he had been ap-
pointed physician, a position of great dignity and importance.

This first published portion of Rabelais's work was obviously written to exploit and emulate the commercial success
of the Gargantuan *Chronicle,* but with an enormous difference.
Whereas the earlier, anonymous work was a traditional, comic,
unoriginal and rather flat piece of popular fiction, the *Pantagruel* was the explosive product of a writer of enormous gifts of

creative and comic imagination, of tremendous erudition and strong emotions, and of great independence of mind and spirit. With all its outrageous crudity and obscenity, the book is obviously the expression of a very uncommon mind. With its wealth of creative imagery, its superbly sumptuous flow of language, its often delightful satire, as well as its completely unrestrained crudity, its lack of organization and unity, its sometimes tiresome display of learning and inexhaustible wealth of linguistic invention, with its great qualities and its enormous defects, the whole book springs from the totally unbridled imagination, loves, hates and unparalleled sheer gusto of its author.

It would, then, be a mistake to interpret the book as primarily a reasoned expression of Rabelais's thought. It is that, of course, but only in a very fragmentary and facetious way. It is primarily a work of amusement and hilarious entertainment. Being the man he was, Rabelais naturally made his fun in his own way, the way of a scholar, a disgruntled friar, a man intoxicated with the new humanism, and perhaps profoundly disappointed by his own religious and moral experiences, by his society and by himself. One may wonder whether his incessant harping on disgusting digestive pleasantries and his apparent relish for the comedy of excrement and filth is not at least partially a catharsis of his own guilt feelings, like Villon's harping on the theme of old age and death, and his haunted description of the agonies of death and hanging.

For Rabelais, like Villon, despite all his sins, enormous though they may have been, had a profoundly Christian mind. His gross obscenity does not spring from a total absence of any sense of decency. Indeed there cannot be any real obscenity except as an outrage to decency. Rabelais's crudity is not the natural freedom of the untutored pagan; it is a highly sophisticated and deliberate assault on a real sense of propriety, his own as well as other people's.

The success of this *Pantagruel* was enormous and instantaneous, and the book was reprinted and reedited several times very shortly after publication. This tremendous success no doubt inspired the author to continue on the path he had chosen, and in 1534 he published his *Gargantua,* which was not a mere reworking of the original anonymous *Chronicle,* but an entirely new story incorporating only a few of its features. With this second book (it is now called the first book, since it has been placed in the chronological order, before the *Pantagruel,* which relates the adventures of Gargantua's son), Rabelais knew more what he was doing. He was apparently in a little less of a rush, and the book shows rather more reflection and a somewhat greater coherence. There are more chapters of serious intent and even style, such as those of Gargantua's education and on the Abbey of Thélème. In the latter chapter, Rabelais, like most of his humanistic contemporaries, shows his distaste for the monastic life as it was then widely practised, and portrayed its counterpart in a sort of naturally good community of honorable, well-born and well-educated young men and women living in a Utopian community whose motto was "Do what thou wilt." He makes it perfectly clear, however, that such a society is not for all, but only for a natural and social élite. He is no naïve Rousseau or modern demagogue, exalting the imaginary and wholly unblemished virtue of the Noble Savage or the Common Man. His Abbey is peopled only by young gentlemen and ladies well endowed by nature with ideal physical and moral traits of health, beauty and virtue, and well-nurtured and educated in mind and character.

In describing this imaginary and obviously impossible ideal "Abbey," Rabelais goes into minutest detail as to the construction of its magnificent palace and its members' way of living and sumptuous costume. He gives evidence of a very keen sense of propriety and decorum in his account of the ladies' headdress, which was "in summer, of the fashion of Tuscany, except only upon the holidays and Sundays, at which time they were accoutred in the French mode, because they accounted it more honourable, and better befitting the garb of a matronal pudicity." The French headdress, indeed, consisted at that time of a tight-fitting cap, descending fairly low on the forehead, and surmounted by a long veil, whereas the Italian was composed mainly of jewels and feathers worked through the long hair and braids.

The Third Book was not published until 1546, some twelve years after the *Gargantua,* and the Fourth Book appeared from 1548 to 1552. They are rather more bitter and satirical than the first two books, but despite all the thinly veiled attacks on the follies and cupidity of fanatics and unworthy venal prelates, it is the folly and the venality he is attacking, just as he lampoons superstition and hypocrisy, not religion, and the stupidities and corruption of lawyers and judges, not the administration of true justice. No one could maintain that his satire is always just and prudent, and it is certainly never moderate. He is surely no model for imitation today, but on the other hand, neither can he be read according to the standards and conditions of today.

Rabelais makes it quite clear, for instance, that it is violence, tyranny and bellicosity which are ridiculous and odious in a ruler, not the wise and legitimate exercise of his princely authority. He is, accordingly, careful to oppose the absurd and criminal Picrochole with the pacific, sage, and benevolent ruler as typified by Grandgousier and Gargantua. One should always be on guard against falling into the error of taking Rabelais's heroes, particularly Friar Jean des Entommeures and Panurge, for Rabelais's ideal. They are amusing figures after his own heart, to be sure, but he endows them with vices which it is clear he reproves, such as laziness, lack of studiousness, dishonesty, and so on. When Rabelais speaks seriously of education and character, it is obvious that his sights are high, whatever he may say when he is riding his jokes hard. For Rabelais, like many of us, is frequently carried away by his own loquacity, and he goes to any lengths for a good, boisterous laugh. And readers familiar with the period know that tastes then were very much less squeamish or modest than they are now.

Those who claim that Rabelais was an atheist, or at best a proponent of a natural, pagan morality, lay great stress on his "rationalism" and his "naturalism." These terms, however, are often deceptive abstractions, which must be used with great caution, particularly in dealing with men who lived before Bacon, Descartes, Locke and the French Encyclopedists. Rabelais certainly placed emphasis on the essential goodness of nature and on the validity of human reason, but this was to a very great extent simply his violent reaction to the current scorn and ignorance of nature and the misuse and even disuse of natural reason. Who, moreover, can claim that it is obligatory upon a Christian to scorn God's creation and His gift of human reason? Rationalism and naturalism become anti-Christian only when they deny the realm of faith and divine grace, and that, despite certain arguments based on a biased inter-

pretation of isolated passages, Rabelais never did. Although his
pen and his imagination very frequently outstripped his better
judgment, and led him to extremes of coarseness and violence
of satire, he never overtly or by inference attacked the fundamentals of the existence of God, the divine inspiration of the
Scriptures, or the divine institution of the Church. On the
contrary, his heroes are brought up to worship God, to pray to
Him, and render thanks to Him, and to read the Bible and
meditate upon it regularly. His Abbey of Thélème is not
merely a temple of natural religion, for, although he set upon
the Great Gate of the Abbey an inscription beginning

> Here enter not, religious boobies, sots,
> Imposters, snivelling hypocrites, bigots . . .

yet the inscription continues:

> Here enter you, pure, honest, faithful, true,
> Expounders of the Scriptures, old and new . . .

It should be clear that although Rabelais does not speak
here of the Mass, the devotion to the Blessed Virgin and the
saints, and other specific features of Catholic practice, this is
not to be taken as an indication of Protestant belief, as it sometimes has. In the first place he was not writing a book on religion, and in the midst of his enormous crudities we are grateful
for the omission of detailed reference to pure Christian belief
and worship. He was the intimate of bishops and cardinals, and
persona grata at Catholic courts, but anathema to the Protestant capital of Geneva and to the "demoniacal Calvin," as Rabelais calls him. He was not an atheist or a pagan, neither was
he a Protestant. He was essentially a man of his own time and
background, a man of the early sixteenth century, who recognized, as did all thinking men, that religious reform was sadly
needed, and the movement toward reform within the Church
was well on its way with men like Erasmus, Lefèvre d'Etaples,
and Briçonnet, the Bishop of Meaux, exercising a very strong,
if not always entirely sound, influence in that direction.

Living in a time of great disorder within the Church, Rabelais was a man of enormous common sense, vitality and passion, writing with the greatest possible gusto about everything
that came into his head, and frequently dashing bull-like about
the ideological china shop of European Christendom. He was

most probably a sincere Catholic, like many men of his time, who held firmly to the essential Christian spirit of love of God and of his fellow man, but was rather confused on points of doctrine and discipline which had not yet been defined and clarified by the labors of the Council of Trent and the Catholic Reformation.

If his theology was weak, it should be remembered that he was no theologian and never pretended to be. It is a serious error to take his book as basically a veiled exposition of a system of heretical thought. It is rather a highly disparate series of imaginative writings which are sometimes sheer buffoonery, sometimes political and semiofficial pamphleteering (as when Rabelais espouses the politics of Henry II against those of the bellicose Pope Julius II), and sometimes social satire, but it is first and foremost entertainment produced by an artist of tremendous, uninhibited and undisciplined genius.

JEAN MISRAHI

SELECTED BIBLIOGRAPHY

Rabelais: readings selected by W. F. Smith. Cambridge University.
PLATTARD, Jean, *The Life of François Rabelais.* Knopf.
TILLEY, Arthur, *Studies in the French Renaissance.* Cambridge University.
RABELAIS, François, *Gargantua and Pantagruel.* Random House (The Modern Library).
RABELAIS, François, *Gargantua and Pantagruel,* Books I-II. Regnery.

Descartes: Discourse on Method

SOMETIMES a man's best contribution to the welfare of the people is to fail in his chosen task. The failure of a great man will never be total, and its by-product can be positive. Somehow that is the summation of the life and work of René Descartes (1596-1650). He was a remarkable figure in the history of the West, and he deserves a special place and high esteem. His intentions were always excellent and his talent was exceptionally rich. Too many speak of him with condescension or dismiss him because he did not quite bring his project to the happy consummation that he desired. Yet the West never had a nobler soul to represent it.

Descartes lived in a time of troubles. By the time he was born, Christendom as a political and cultural unity had already gasped its last, and by the time he died it had lost the capacity of resurrection. The new nationalisms had been consolidated, and in place of one Europe there existed a Europe divided politically and religiously. Germany was in the throes of wars which did not give her the time or the environment to build up a world view. Spain's star was descending, and France was rising as the new luminary of the continent. There was too much fighting going on all over to permit many men to take academic philosophies very seriously, though there were philosophies implicit in all that was going on. Yet, in spite of a background of wars, Galileo had actually produced a revolution in thought, with the result that science and mathematics had made progress in the sixteenth century and were making greater advances in the seventeenth.

René Descartes, younger son of a well-to-do French family of the lesser nobility, and of frail health, was not greatly interested in the political agitations of Europe. He liked thought and thinking. His early years at La Flèche, the best school in France, were happy ones. His weak constitution excused him from many of the hardships of a French boarding school, and the excellence of the instruction filled his mind with ideas. Mathematics pleased him very much, but the revived Scholasticism taught him by his Jesuit masters did not satisfy him at all. It was too polemical against other philosophies that were equally polemical. It gave him no calm security. Yet the subject interested him deeply.

Once out of school, he dedicated himself exclusively to thought. He did not find any attraction in the more obvious lures of Paris. He looked for men who engaged in the spiritual problems of the time, problems that had taken on a new color in the light of the sciences that were flourishing mightily. His own interest in mathematics now became pervasive and intense; it lasted all his life. The result was fruitful, for he became the father of the new mathematical branch now called analytic geometry. But his interest was not restricted to mathematics; he was anxious to solve the philosophic problem. He was looking for a first knowledge that could be solidly constructed into a validly deductive scheme which would meet the approval of all men without controversy, just as happened in mathematics. In 1619 he had a deep insight, not unlike a mystical experience, in which he saw the nucleus of the new philosophy, and in a flash he discovered the method whereby it could be constructed. And it was the *method* that he was searching for; given the right *modus procedendi,* the rest would be easy.

Descartes was a creator, but such an epithet when applied to a creature of history has a meaning far different from the philosophical concept of creation. The French thinker was really anxious to produce something without using the materials left behind by others, but of course in this desire he was frustrated. He unwittingly took a great deal that was predigested. The most interesting phenomenon in the life of Descartes was his loyalty to the Catholic faith, producing a devotion to and a dependence on numerous priests, many of whom were Jesuits. This was the initial commitment from which he could not and would not divorce himself. It naturally influenced all that he thought and wrote.

Secondly, Descartes was a lover of meditation rather than of reading and research. He read, of course, and he made scientific observations, but he was not passionately given to personal positive investigations. Construction on idea-bases suited his temperament more. In this, we see an immaturity in the great philosopher. He was a perpetual adolescent, and like an adolescent he olympically dismissed all that had already been said or done, in the optimistic hope that he could answer all the questions of life by means of an inward gaze.

Thirdly, mathematical method bewitched Descartes. He understood it better than most mathematicians and he loved it. Unconsciously, he wished to build a geometry of truth and of reality. Analysis and deduction, therefore, would be his rationale, and he was subjectively incapable of criticizing this urge in himself. The most important of Descartes's works are his studies on method, and in consequence his famous *Discourse on Method* is an excellent medium through which we can see the workings of the Cartesian mind. It was published in 1637 but was begun years before, and was a belated fruit of his vision in 1619. This little work will show what he thought philosophy should be and how it should be constructed.

It is a pleasing essay, personal without being egoistic, and even if the reader is not eager to derive from it a picture of philosophy, it will still give him a picture of the philosopher who wrote it. It is full of excellent observations concerning life and men, so that even if it were not a philosophical classic, it would still be worth reading for its keen recognition of human virtues and foibles.

Though there is much that is attractive in the Cartesian essay, yet a modern reader with a slight knowledge of the history of philosophy will wonder why it was ever considered such a startling innovation. That it was a new departure, Macaulay's schoolboy knows. As a fruit of Descartes's thinking, the Scholastic tradition not only lost its predominance over the thought of Europe, but plunged dully to its death. Francis Bacon (1561-1626) had written more ambitious works with a view to reforming philosophy, but he did not really bring it off, whereas Descartes in a humbler essay succeeded where Bacon had failed.

The Cartesian triumph was due to various elements. First of all, Descartes was a Continental, and his influence was immediately felt in the philosophic centers of Europe, especially in France, then exercising the hegemony of thought, while England at the moment was only something peripheral. Second,

Descartes was a Catholic, and the Catholics were still the vast majority in western intellectual life. Third, Baconian empiricism was too abrupt a shift from the rationalism which was the air that Scholasticism had blown over European thinking for centuries, and Europe could not breathe freely in the heavier air of Bacon. Fourth, Bacon, who admired the new science, was himself no scientist, though he understood the spirit of the new method quite well. Descartes, on the other hand, was a scientist, and although he did not quite comprehend the dynamism of the new discipline, he had a grasp of it derived from familiarity and the sure touch that comes of knowledge from within.

Perhaps the first novelty in the work of Descartes that attracted the attention of the intellectuals was the simple fact that it was not written in Latin. Bacon still reflected the awe of the English people for Latin as rediscovered by the Renaissance, and he considered it the only vehicle proper to elevated discourse, but Descartes had seen the difficulty inherent in the use of this medium as an expression of new thought:

And if I write in French, which is the language of my country, in preference to Latin, which is that of my preceptors, it is because I expect that those who make use of their unprejudiced natural reason will be better judges of my opinions than those who give heed to the writings of the ancients only; and as for those who unite good sense with the habits of study, whom alone I desire for judges, they will not, I feel assured, be so partial to Latin as to refuse to listen to my reasonings merely because I expound them in the vulgar tongue. [*Discourse,* part VI, *ad finem.*]

What is the essential novelty of Cartesian philosophy? Certainly not the fact that it was written in French. Nor is it any one thesis nor even a complex of theses. Descartes's much-criticised dualism was just as typical of Plato. His rationalism can be found in Aristotle and the Scholastics. His mechanism would have pleased Democritus and Lucretius. His intuitionism is better explained in Plato. His proofs for the existence of God can be found in St. Anselm and his mathematicism was at once Pythagorean and Platonic. The novelty of Cartesianism consists in making these theses the necessary conclusions of a new method of philosophy. He is an innovator in philosophy because he reconstructed it with a boldness that had not been equaled since classical times. Bacon's novelties were not really so novel, for he was only the logical final expression of the nominalism of the fifteenth century. Descartes did not continue a prevailing philosophy. He established a new starting point, making his doctrine really new, not in its theses but in its dynamism.

Descartes was fully aware of this novelty and he takes great pains to justify it. However, his justification is really that of an adolescent. No young man feels himself bound by the thought of the present or the past. For a young man, especially a talented young man, to whom doubt comes as spontaneously as the first hairs of his moustache, an appeal to authority, which is really an appeal to the accumulated wisdom of the past, is quite irrelevant. He wants to see the truth itself without the intrusions and censorship of guides, and the exulting powers within him never suggest that he is not capable of fathoming the unfiltered real in all its depths, nor does he think that he himself is thoroughly imbued with tacit prejudgments acquired during his growth in a determined environment. A young man believes himself singularly free from prejudices, which is as totally false as any error that can be conceived. It is more than false; it is killing, because the youth is not even aware of the prejudices that are operative in him. Only time and rough encounters with reality in every shape and form finally tame the innocent arrogance of adolescence.

Descartes was a very young man when he made his first philosophic discoveries. He had sufficient money to keep himself out of the hustle and bustle of life, and he used it effectively to create for himself an atmosphere of serenity and calm. He kept as far away from life as possible. He was a thinker, but there was little in vital experience that had much contact with his thought. His sensitivity to cold made him even do much of his meditating in bed. He was, if there ever was one, an isolated thinker, who paradoxically joined the army to be alone.

Consequently it is not unintelligible that he begins his philosophy with doubt. This of itself is not necessarily a new thing. In fact, it is in some sense inevitable, for philosophy deals with problems, and all problems indicate doubt. The history of philosophy is full of doubt, not merely as a fact but as a principle of procedure. The Sophists doubted, but theirs was a doubt of cynical indifference. Pyrrho and Sextus Empiricus were doubters, but their doubt was born of metaphysical despair. Thomas

Aquinas prefaced every article in his *Summa* with a question, and that means a doubt, but his doubt was more of a pedagogical device than a reality, and in so far as it was real, it merely proposed a hitherto unexplained and thus doubtful proposition to be explained by principles concerning which there was no doubt.

The most surprising thing in the Cartesian doubt is that it was no doubt at all. It was the stubborn rejection of everything that had been said, even by himself, and the resolute demand that affirmations which were quite firm and unquestioned be driven back to their ultimate bases in thought. Descartes never once doubted that such bases were indubitable, nor did he ever doubt that he could see the truth, but he wished to see it in itself and not merely in the refracted reflections projected on man and history by this initially intuited truth.

Hence, the first proposition which bases Cartesianism, *cogito ergo sum* ("I think, therefore I am"), was not meant to be a proof of anything. The great philosopher certainly did not fall into the egregious fallacy which even a tyro in philosophy could detect, namely that, given an activity, there is given a subject. What Descartes said was that, given thought, there is reality, for any proposition implicitly affirms the reality, since it either explicitly posits "is" as the illuminating principle that connects subject and predicate or it supposes it on the principle that *agere sequitur esse* ("action follows being"). When Descartes said, "I think, therefore I am," all the terms are meaningless except two; thinking and being, and his celebrated aphorism really boils down to the following: thinking is an undeniably experienced instance of reality. In that instance he saw reality, the intelligible object meaningful to the mind alone and the basis of all meaning.

Reality immediately raised a question which the acute and profound Descartes saw clearly, and which his valiant honesty could not refuse to meet. Reality is not resolvable into other notions. It is the first and the last notion, and therefore reality is absolute, the ground of thinker, thinking and the thought. All has to be referred to it, and it need not be referred to anything. This original ground of the all was known only in its meaning, "isness," which cannot be defined but only intuited. There are no limits to it, for it includes all and excludes only the unreal. Infinity, therefore, is the necessary glory of the real, for it is meaningless without it. Therefore, given the real, God is given too.

On this point we meet with some very superficial objections hurled at Descartes by men who do not possess more than a fraction of the Frenchman's genius. We are told that the Cartesian reasoning is a sheer repetition of the invalid Anselmic argument. This is no place to discuss Anselm, but certainly Descartes never said that because God cannot be conceived without conceiving Him as existent, therefore He exists. It can be seriously doubted if that is a just formulation of the mind of Anselm. What Descartes said was that reality cannot be affirmed without affirming God, but reality is affirmed in the perception of thought, and therefore God exists.

This is no illicit leap from the conceptual to the actual but rather a forthright recognition of the implicits contained in the affirmation of the real. This kind of careful analysis of thought with the brave readiness to accept the consequences is work most distasteful to many thinkers in our day. They do what Descartes shrank from doing, for without a doubting criticism they identify the real with experience. On such a postulate Descartes's thinking is just meaningless—but so is experience, for the same reason. A little bit more of Cartesian depth and boldness in current thinking would make Existentialism and Logical Positivism vanish into very thin smoke.

The reader must be constantly reminded that Descartes did not rely on the teachings of others in coming to his stands. He sat back and reflected until he had driven all affirmation to its last implicit. He then saw what was really being affirmed. He was faithful and docile to the data. There was no *a priori* postulate to limit or deform his findings.

However, Descartes moved too rapidly forward after his slow and valid thinking back. He saw that in his original affirmation, "I think, therefore I am," the "I" was really only thinking, for in no other sense is the proposition undeniable. Thought was affirmed but not a subject. Hence the substantial meaning of "I" is thought. But thought points to objects which are not thought, and these can be reduced to realities spread out in space and subject to mechanical movement. Hence all reality can be divided up into two classes: thought and mechanical quantities, quite irreducible one to the other. That the thought of quantities was really a perception of reality, he accepted willingly because of the reflection that thought is by its reality perceptive, but reality is ultimately God, and therefore a perception that does not perceive is a lying or ungodly thing, which is nonsense, for all reality is godly since God is the basis of reality.

This last line of argument has been attacked by critics who show too narrow an understanding of Descartes's line of thinking. We are told by the little books that here Descartes committed that unpardonable sin in a philosopher, the vicious circle. However, there is nothing vicious or circular in the Cartesian argument. It is not true that the thinker knows God by quantities given him by thought, and then knows that they are real quantities because God gave him that knowledge. Descartes knows that God exists because he has perceived reality *in se,* not merely quantified reality. Because certain phases of reality are quantified in thought, they must be quantified objectively, for thought is only a reality-grasping product of a truthful God.

The failure of the Cartesian enterprise lies in the fact that Descartes did not delay on the meaning which founds his whole system—being or reality. If he had done so, he would have developed a fuller metaphysic which would have orientated him more successfully in his other investigations. As it is, except for an initial glance at being, he dwelt no more on it. Of course, he had no interest in metaphysics and was led to deal with it at all because it was the first step toward a valid entry into fields that were his more immediate concern. He was more anxious to deal with physics and physiology, for these new sciences were opening up rich vistas for investigation. Descartes never knew the distinction between philosophy and science.

In that, he seems to be too modern, but there is all the difference in the world between his fusion and the current fusion or confusion. Descartes, like all his contemporaries, thought that science was a branch of philosophy, while so many of our contemporaries think that philosophy is a branch of science. Such concepts, whether sponsored by Descartes or modern Naturalists, bring forth no good. It might be profitable to see where the confusion leads.

In Descartes the fundamental difficulty was how to bring quantity and thought together. He was not anxious to deny one or the other. He was not desirous of reducing one to the other. He was dedicated to the task of making thought and matter more intimately one without confounding them. Even if it had occurred to him, he would not have dared to reach the conclusion of his disciple Benedict Spinoza (1632-1677), who united the two realities by making them two aspects, but only aspects, of the one absolute reality perceived in Cartesian reflections. Descartes's absolute was a personal deity, who was transcendent, while Spinozan immanence makes reality pantheistic and God impersonal, ideas quite repugnant to the pious Descartes. He had to look for another way out, but he never found it, and in consequence Cartesianism failed.

Descartes perceived the reality of thought in itself through thought, but he perceived the reality of matter not in itself but only in thought and as thought—and yet matter itself was utterly different and removed from thinking. He was quite willing to admit that the mind was influenced by matter, but there is the tragedy; by his principles he could not show how matter could contact mind nor how mind could inspire matter. Leibnitz (1646-1716) later found a non-Spinozan answer to the Cartesian riddle: God made mind and matter, and filled mind with ideas about matter. In order to keep the two in step, He produced a perfect parallelism of mind-history and matter-history flowing along together in preestablished harmony. The French mathematician never got so far as the German mathematician, but he would probably have been forced along the same road if he had lived longer.

In the philosophy of Descartes, though knowledge through material experience is not denied but rather admitted and defended, yet it has no place nor intelligibility. The Naturalists of today have the same difficulty but inversely. They take their stand on experience, and though they do not wish to deny thought but rather are anxious to defend it, yet thought is unintelligible in their system. They are forced to reduce it to experience or, as Descartes would say, to quantity.

The Naturalists of today are related to Descartes, because Cartesianism influenced all subsequent philosophies. It is intriguing to see how this influence worked out, for, as we have seen, Descartes failed in the task he proposed to himself, and failed utterly. He did not construct a philosophy that would be accepted by all without controversy. His attempt to make of philosophy a mathematics resulted neither in mathematics nor in good philosophy. His desire to justify solidly the values which he found in the West of his time weakened them because he destroyed the unity of being. His dualism had disastrous results, for the world of quantity, subject to mechanical movement, became totally segregated from the world of the spirit. It could be investigated without reference to the spirit, and the result was that science, which followed this road, perforce became materialistic.

Kant, like a true philosopher, was dissatisfied with Cartesian dualism and tried to achieve an intelligible unity of experience and thought by reducing thought to the level of an organizational principle of experience. The Idealists, on the other hand, recognizing the unshakable rock in Descartes's process, reduced dualism to a monism of thinking. Positivism, more inspired by the Bacon-Locke-Hume tradition, identified, as Descartes did, philosophy, mathematics and science, after rejecting the heuristic pretensions of thought.

In spite of his good intentions, the French genius did us a disservice because he refused to deal adequately with the basic notion of true philosophy, being. Instead of leaving us one world more intimately bound together than ever, he gave us two worlds, separate and distinct. We have tried to live in these worlds ever since, but it is an existence of tension and schizophrenia. The link which Descartes used to keep the worlds together, God, is no longer thought of as real but as either a signal of the upsurges of a wishful heart or the ultimate mathematical matrix for the universe, more appropriately called Space-Time.

One short supplement can be tacked to these reflections. Even though Descartes failed in his self-appointed task, yet he did succeed in something else. He showed, as few have done, the efficacy and power of deductive thought. Modern science was in its infancy in the seventeenth century, yet Descartes, without the aid of countless subsequent experiments, did anticipate many of the later theses founded on experiment. He discovered the circulation of the blood independently of Harvey. He was vaguely aware of Newton's universal law of gravitation, for he keenly saw the complete interrelationship of all things material, so that, given one situation, by necessity other determined situations had to follow in all the universe. He was deeply convinced of the basic uniformity of all material things, intelligible in terms of a mathematical insight. He saw clearly that matter was not only inert quantity but actually in motion. He could not explain the origin of motion, but the fact was for him patent. He also saw that matter in motion was energy, which is a basic principle of quantum physics. He proved conclusively the validity and fruitfulness of a mathematical investigation of nature, which in our time has led to such triumphant revelations.

In fact, the name of Descartes will forever suggest the idea that thought rather than experience, and almost without experience, can best describe natural structures and foretell future events. Whether the suggestion is good or not, at least Descartes's life was dedicated to it, for it was never because he had empirical proof for his theses that he affirmed them but rather because his assertions had to be so by reason of analysis, or because of a resolution to a few first principles, accepted on their own evidence in the purview of a thinking mind.

The incidental success of Descartes points to a philosophy quite different from his own. The Cartesian point of departure is perfectly valid, but once established, he went off on a tangent. The next question was not whether thinking was the "I," but rather, what is thought? If Descartes had faced that question he might have come to this conclusion: thought is the thinker's grasp of the real, because thought by its inner structure must reveal reality, all reality, even reality beyond thought, because the structure of thought is its dynamic adjustment to the real, of which it is man's first instance. Such a proposition would have formed a philosophy quite different from Cartesianism, but it would not be altogether arbitrary to think that it would have been a better vision of God and the world, of man and time.

GUSTAVE WEIGEL

SELECTED BIBLIOGRAPHY

GIBSON, A. B., The Philosophy of Descartes. Methuen.
GILSON, É., René Descartes. Discours de la Méthode. Texte et commentaire. Paris, Vrin.

KEELING, S. V., *Descartes*. Oxford.
MAHAFFY, J. P., *Descartes*. Blackwood & Sons.
MARITAIN, J., *The Dream of Descartes*, translated by M. L. Andison. Philosophical
    Library.
DESCARTES, René, *Discourse on Method*. Regnery.

Bacon: Novum Organum, *Book I*

In 1620, a time when the direction of modern thought was being charted out, Francis Bacon (1561-1626) published a great book, *Novum Organum*. As with many other books, its greatness lies in catching the spirit of an age and in summing up the new trends that were replacing an old order. If modern philosophy has been tending more and more to become nothing but logic, a clear and somewhat prophetic glimpse of this tendency can be found in Bacon's book.

The old *organon*, of course, was Aristotle's logic. Bacon's was to be a new *organon*, a new logic, a fresh and fertile instrument for thought and learning, a summons to the empiricism awakening in seventeenth-century Europe. The new Baconian logic typified the rising tide of interest among philosophers in problems of method.

Novum Organum lays down a program for an inductive approach to nature. Taken literally, this program failed, as even the champions of Bacon today admit. But it did express and urge on the interest of modern thought in induction and experiment. Bacon's method died with the man, but his enthusiasm for an empirical study of nature has survived down to our own day. He neither set the stage for the drama of modern science nor did he direct the writing of the script that physical and biological researchers were to follow in their laboratories. But as a rhetorician urging men to induction, Bacon did attract the actors and the audience for the empiricism of modern Anglo-American philosophy. Therein lies the greatness of Bacon and of his book.

Bacon's book may be summarized as a polemic against Aristotle's logic for being a game of words, a mere play of ideas with no practical test and no material results for the betterment of life. Bacon feels that the old logic does not allow enough factual checks. In place of this old *organon,* he proposes a highly empirical method, where induction prevails over the syllogism and where experiment is glorified as a test of truth.

The times were ripe for such a book.

The Renaissance by the year 1620 had cut deeply into the great respect which Scholasticism had built up for speculative reason, searching after truth for its own sake. In the Europe of 1620 the new mercantile economy and the beginnings of nationalism were loosing a flood of interest in the practical order, and the discovery of distant lands and new routes of travel and trade had opened new horizons to dazzle the fancies of men. During a long career in government which lifted him at last to the lofty post of Lord Chancellor and to the peerage, Bacon could feel the pulse of political, geographical and economic expansion in England, and he saw in his program for the human mind implications that we would today term nationalistic.

By the year 1620, Descartes was twenty-four years old; in 1637, he was to publish a book, *Discourse on Method,* that in name and content was to be a companion volume to Bacon's *Organum.* A decade previous to 1620, Galileo had built the telescope that was destined to read the heavens in a Copernican language. By the close of the seventeenth century Gilbert, Harvey and Boyle had lived, and Newton had done his major work. This was the century when modern science, however it may have been born in the late Middle Ages, finally attained the use of its own reason and wandered away from philosophy. As a champion of this new science, Bacon is best remembered today.

Novum Organum sets forth a method for the advancement of science, and during and after Bacon's lifetime, science rode onward to victory after victory. Bacon's ambitions, set against the progress of empirical knowledge in his century, have sometimes prompted the view that he is "the philosopher of science" and even "the father of modern science." Actually, the method which brought experimental knowledge to its signal triumphs in modern times was not and is not the method which Bacon urged. The empiriological disciplines, to borrow Jacques Maritain's term, owe to Bacon only the general encouragement he gave to empirical, practical, inductive research. He was out of touch with the techniques which even his contemporary experimentalists were exploiting. Hence, *Novum Organum* is more of a shadow than a light, more of a symptom than a cause. It reflects in a general and rhetorical way the new attitude toward the study of nature, an attitude that was to grow into the pragmatic, positivistic, operational philosophies of a later date.

Akin to the spirit of the Renaissance then closing on the European continent, Bacon was a man of vast ambitions—grandly projected, solemnly announced, and then only partially fulfilled. Here was a man—something of a novelty in European philosophy—who regarded himself as a kind of Messiah writing for the ages. As a reformer, he was keenly aware of rhetoric, and it is as a rhetorician of the learning he championed rather than as its architect that Bacon had a great influence and wrote a great book.

Novum Organum was first published in Latin as the second part of a six-volume venture called *Instauratio Magna,* a careful program for the total reform of human knowledge. Critical of the state of learning in his own age, Bacon writes: "There was but one course left, therefore,—to try the whole thing anew upon a better plan, and to commence a total reconstruction of the sciences, arts, and all human knowledge, raised upon the proper foundations." *Novum Organum* is the most important part of the *Instauratio.* Of the five other parts, only the first, *The Advancement of Learning,* reached completion.

Novum Organum carries the alternate title *True Directions Concerning the Interpretation of Nature.* It consists of two books of "aphorisms," one book assailing the methods of the old sciences and the other proposing Bacon's own method for interpreting nature. The first book hacks away at ancient and medieval learning for being without practical fruit or, as the twentieth-century naturalist would later say, without a pragmatic test; the second book stands for an historical, experimental, inductive and even naturalistic approach to reality.

In the first book, Bacon claims to "have purged and swept and leveled the floor of the mind . . . ;" in the second book, after outlining his own method, Bacon boasts that he can "hand over to men their fortunes, now that their understanding is emancipated and come as it were of age. . . ."

Bacon's assault on Aristotle reads in many ways like that of a twentieth-century anti-Aristotelian, say John Dewey or Count

Alfred Korzybski, author of the widely read tome *Science and Sanity*. Thus, Bacon charges Aristotle with having "made his natural philosophy a mere bondservant to his logic, thereby rendering it contentious and well nigh useless." Aristotle is classed among "sophistical" philosophers. He is accused of

fashioning the world out of categories; assigning to the human soul, the noblest of substances, a genus from words of the second intention; doing the business of density and rarity (which is to make bodies of greater or less dimensions, that is, occupy greater or less spaces), by the frigid distinction of act and power; asserting that single bodies have each a single and proper motion, and that if they participate in any other, then this results from an external cause; and imposing countless other arbitrary restrictions on the nature of things; being always more solicitous to provide an answer to the question and affirm something positive in words, than about the inner truth of things; a failing best shown when his philosophy is compared with other systems of note among the Greeks.

Bacon must have based such an attack on Aristotle upon Aristotelians in the fifteenth and sixteenth centuries. No one who read Aristotle himself could find evidence to support these charges. The late Scholastics had prostituted logic until philosophy had become nominalistic. It was not the real Aristotle but the nominalism of the late Scholastics that could merit Bacon's charges of turning philosophy into a play on words.

"The syllogism," says Bacon, "consists of propositions, propositions consist of words, words are symbols of notions. Therefore, if the notions themselves (which is the root of the matter) are confused and overhastily abstracted from the facts, there can be no firmness in the superstructure."

Aristotle, as a matter of fact, recognized the weaknesses and dangers of syllogistic reasoning and insisted in his *Topics* on what Bacon declares he overlooked, namely, clear definitions. Aristotle would concur in Bacon's view that the premises of the syllogism must be established inductively, but he would not agree that the Baconian induction (through enumeration) is the only induction that there can be.

Bacon sums up his case against the prevailing logic by calling it an "anticipation of nature" as opposed to the "interpretation of nature." What Bacon means to say is that the Aristotelians make "rash and premature" generalizations about matter and insist that nature conforms to such abstract universals. Bacon proposes instead "a very diligent dissection and anatomy of the world." He intends, as he implies, to make no decisions in advance about the results of induction and experiment; he will let his mind be a *tabula rasa,* to register the secrets of nature as they are revealed by nature rather than by his own prejudice.

Perhaps the most famous and in many ways most valuable of all topics treated in the first book of *Novum Organum* is Bacon's doctrine of the "idols" or "false notions which are now in possession of the understanding, and have taken deep root therein. . . ." There are idols of the tribe, idols of the cave, idols of the marketplace, and idols of the theater.

The idols of the tribe have as their victims the whole human race, Bacon feels. They come from our common tendency to let will and emotion dominate our judgments, and from the infirmity of our senses.

The idols of the cave are produced by the peculiar condition, physical or mental, of each individual. Everyone is somehow influenced by education and habit and, according to Bacon, these accidents of birth and surroundings tend to shape our thoughts and our judgments even in matters of science.

The idols of the marketplace arise from words and names, as they influence our understanding and distract it from things as they are. Finally, the idols of the theater are those which come from the mind's desire for perfect organization of its knowledge. We tend to systematize reality on the basis of paltry data and to complete the system in ways that anticipate nature but fail to interpret her.

There is much that is sound in Bacon's doctrine of the idols. It is this doctrine that is most frequently mentioned as a positive contribution to the fund of perennial philosophy.

The second and positive theme of *Novum Organum* is Bacon's doctrine of induction. He envisioned his method as supplying the senses with helps: "for I do not take away the authority of the senses but supply them with helps; I do not slight the understanding but govern it."

Yet there is more to Bacon's ambition than this. He wants to give man power over nature. As religion and faith redeem the spirit of fallen man, so Bacon's program, he tells us, will repair to some extent man's loss of his dominion over matter after the

Fall. Bacon, therefore, proposes a program to equip man with physical power. He laments the "dearth and barrenness of arts and inventions." He is interested in commanding nature and, reasoning that nature to be commanded must first be obeyed, he sets forth a method to analyze the physical universe.

To interpret nature, there are three facts, Bacon says, that the mind must grasp: "form," "latent process" and "latent configuration." Although he refers to the form of a thing as its "specific difference," he really gives to this term a new and quite non-Aristotelian sense. Here are some of his synonyms for "form," as he conceived it: "nature-engendering nature," "source of emanation," "a fixed law," and "determination of absolute actuality." The form of heat is the law of heat, and that of light the law of light.

From such vague references, it is not surprising that the notion of form should be the most debated part of Bacon's thought. There is hardly any agreement among critics about what Bacon meant. Perhaps his most enlightening remark on the point is this: "The true form is such that it deduces the given nature from some source of being which is inherent in more natures, and which is better known in the natural order of things than the form itself."

Bacon appears to identify a thing by its activities and to mean nothing more by the form of a nature than the measurable properties characteristic of the nature. Philosophy was on the way to defining a nature in terms of quantity alone, an identity that Descartes was soon to announce in emphatic fashion.

Forms, for Bacon, exist only in simple natures. The latent process, as he calls it, can be found only in compound bodies, and it seems to mean nothing more than the process of their development. Latent configuration is Bacon's term for anatomy or, in the case of minerals, physico-chemical structure.

Bacon assigns the study of forms to metaphysics, and the study of the latent process and latent configuration to physics. It is significant, too, that Bacon, in *The Advancement of Learning*, removed final causes from the subject matter of physics and anticipated Descartes by making physics the study of efficient and material causes alone.

The final part of *Novum Organum* is concerned with the method for getting at the forms of things which determine everything in nature. There are three stages of this method: Natural and Experimental History; Tables and Arrangements of Instances, and Induction.

Bacon stood for an historical approach to the study of matter. In analyzing a phenomenon like heat, for instance, he would urge an experimenter to make an exhaustive catalog of all the cases of heat in the world. Such a history was conceived to be not merely a description of nature but an inventory also of human art in the production of material things. For, like a typical twentieth-century physicist, Bacon felt that nature, under human coercion, would yield up her innermost secrets.

After this first and historical stage of analysis, the next phase of Bacon's method is one of arranging the instances. For this purpose, there are three tables: the Table of Essence and Presence; the Table of Deviation, or of Absence in Proximity, and the Table of Degrees, or of Comparison. In these tables, Bacon makes use of the principle which Aristotle set down at least twice to be a rule of logic, that nothing can be a cause of any phenomenon, e.g., heat, unless it is present when the phenomenon, e.g., heat, is present, absent when the phenomenon is absent, and more or less intense according as the phenomenon is greater or less.

Finally, at the inductive stage of Bacon's method, there is a sorting of instances by the mind on the basis of the tables. Induction proceeds by rejecting and excluding false answers to an experimental problem. As Bacon puts it,

> The first work therefore of true induction (as far as regards the discovery of Forms) is the rejection or exclusion of the several natures which are not found in some instance where the given nature is present, or are found in some instance where the given nature is absent, or are found to increase in some instance where the given nature decreases, or to decrease when the given nature increases. Then indeed after the rejection and exclusion has been duly made, there will remain at the bottom, all light opinions vanishing into smoke, a Form affirmative. . . .

As the second stage of Bacon's analytic has analogy to an Aristotelian idea, so this third phase should be compared to Plato's method of arriving at definitions, for instance at definitions of virtue in the *Meno*.

Novum Organum concludes with a long inventory of various

kinds of instances of phenomena, so as to help the mind in its work of rejecting and excluding, which is eventually to bring about positive knowledge of phenomena. It is hard to draw a line in Bacon's logic where the method of exclusion changes into an affirmative mood, and on purely sensistic premises it would be harder to hold that line even if it could be found.

For better or for worse, Bacon's method was ignored by scientists from his own day down to ours. Harvey accused him of writing philosophy like a Lord Chancellor. Joseph Needham resents the mechanical picture which Bacon gives of how scientists are supposed to think. Augustus de Morgan has pointed out forcefully that Bacon wanted to use fact "to draw theories *from*," whereas the working scientist uses fact "to test theories *by*." Bacon's weakness as a philosopher of science lies in his total neglect of the role which theory and hypothesis have played in the advance of modern knowledge. Contrary to Bacon's idea, the modern researcher does not believe that he can interpret nature and command nature until he has first anticipated her.

No science and no successful scientist has ever employed the exhaustive, historical survey of fact which Bacon proposes in the first phase of his formal method. It is impractical, unnecessary, undesirable. Mill improved on Bacon as a methodologist and, like Hume, developed his own version of Bacon's tables. But even Mill failed to recognize the place of theory in empiriological method. The working scientist does not stop at a catalog of observed fact. He wants to predict and produce. And a theory, as the instrument to predict experimental result, is an essential part of what we call the scientific method.

As a formula for the construction of the sciences, *Novum Organum* failed. What, then, made it a great book?

First of all, it is an expression of the empirical and practical temper that was to dominate learning in post-Renaissance universities, and in this respect the book is important. Bacon was the poet laureate of the scientific movement, urging men to do their learning in laboratories and to attend to sense knowledge only.

Bacon gave impetus to a whole stream of British empiricism in modern philosophy and could claim as his descendants Hobbes, Locke, Hume, Mill and Schiller, all of whom came at least indirectly under his influence. Bacon became a name for experimentalism, a kind of slogan in the history of thought, for induction.

In the second place, Bacon gave a broad urge to the modern interest in discovery as opposed to demonstration. He is not really the competitor of Aristotle that he thought he was. Whatever value his ideas may have, they form a dialectic for discovering fact and not a method for proving principle. Bacon accentuated the importance of invention, of fact finding, of art as opposed to science, and in this respect he has likewise been of influence in the career of modern research.

But Bacon never glimpsed the difference between fact and principle, discovery and proof, induction and the syllogism. As a result, he labored whatever insights he had until they became extreme views that sound reason cannot accept. That is why *Novum Organum* is not a truly great book in the Christian sense.

VINCENT EDWARD SMITH

SELECTED BIBLIOGRAPHY

BACON, Francis, *The Works of Francis Bacon.* Edited by J. Spedding, R. Ellis, and D. Heath. Boston, Taggard and Thompson.
ANDERSON, Fulton, *The Philosophy of Francis Bacon.* University of Chicago Press.
BROAD, C. D., *The Philosophy of Francis Bacon.* Harcourt, Brace.
TAYLOR, A. E., *Philosophical Studies.* Macmillan.
BACON, Francis, *Novum Organum,* Book I. Regnery.

Galileo: Two New Sciences

GREAT BOOKS, like great men, are rarely of uniform excellence throughout. A great physicist like Galileo (1564-1642), can really be very awkward in the conduct of public relations. And a great book, like his *Two New Sciences,* can really be quite mediocre in much of its contents. No apology therefore is required for an essay which, omitting all allusion to Galileo's clumsy controversies with his contemporaries and his random contributions to mechanical engineering, prefers to focus its attention exclusively on those significant factors in physics which make Galileo's *Two New Sciences* the uniquely great book that it indisputably is.

Galileo's purpose, if we take Salviati as his dialog mouthpiece, is "to expound *a very new science* dealing with *a very ancient subject.*" Much of the assured content of this new science is already of fundamental importance, but Galileo admits: "What I regard as *more* important is the fact that there have been opened up to this vast and most excellent science, of which *my work is merely the beginning,* ways and means by which other minds more acute than mine will explore its remote corners." For the *Two New Sciences* is in fact a bridge of successful transition from the ancient physics of observable bodies to the modern physics of molar masses. And no one can appreciate the splendor of that span who does not know the anatomy of the unfamiliar universe of ancient physics whence it came and the main contours of the world of modern physics to which it led.

Take a piece of paper and a pencil. At dead center of the page place a heavy, dark dot and label it C. This will represent the absolutely fixed and immovable center of the large but limited universe of ancient physics. Around this point C describe a circle of rather small diameter. Shade the enclosed area somewhat darkly and inscribe therein the letter *E*, for earth, one of the four basic elements in its undiluted state and *natural habitat*. About the same central point *C*, construct a second circle with twice the diameter of the first. Shade the newly enclosed area a little less darkly than the first and write therein the letter *W*, for water, the second of the four basic elements in its pure state and *connatural home*. With the same point *C* as center, draw a third circle with a diameter three times the dimensions of the first. Shade the newly constructed region still less heavily than the second and imprint therein the letter *A*, for air, the third of the primitive elements, likewise in its pure state and *natural position*. In the same way construct a fourth concentric circle of proportionately larger diameter. Shade the resultant enclosed area ever so lightly and print therein the letter *F*, for fire, fourth and last of the basic terrestrial elements in its naturally pure state and *natural location*.

This is the skeletal blueprint for the conventional world of ancient physics in its *ideal* and static condition. For *all* the globs of earth in the universe, as heaviest of the four elements, *belong* by natural destiny in a dense, homogeneous cluster about the fixed point *C*, in *E*. And *all* the drops of water in the cosmos, as lighter than earth but heavier than air, *belong*, as a continuous three-dimensional blanket of uniform thickness, in *W*, around *E*. And *all* the winds of the world, as lighter than water but heavier than fire, *belong* within the confines of *A*. And *all* the flames of flickering fire in the universe, as lightest of all, *belong* in the superior region *F*.

But the *real* state of the world of experience is vastly different. Large land masses of earth protrude above great ocean depths of water. Disturbances on the ocean floor release explosive bubbles of air which reveal the presence of winds imprisoned beneath its turbid surface. Combustion discloses that both air and fire are contained within wood, as well as earth which reappears in the ashes. And ebullition is proof enough that air was contained in what seemed to have been merely water. The fact is that the four elements of the ancient physics were all mixed up. The physical objects of familiar experience were not masses of elements in their pure state, but variously compounded and distributed in forced exile from their natural locations of existence and rest.

To understand how the *ideal* condition of static and mutually exclusive regions for *E, W, A* and *F* degenerates into the actual heterogeneity of the physical world, revert to the blueprint diagram.

About *C,* construct a fifth circle with a diameter somewhat larger than that for *F.* Upon the surface of its upper hemisphere imprint a heavy, dark dot and label it *Mo* for the moon. Around the same point *C* draw another circle with diameter proportionately larger, and on its upper periphery mark another dark spot, tagged *Me* for the planet Mercury. In the same manner construct five more such concentric circles with progressively enlarged diameters. Dot and label the upper hemisphere of each circumference *V, Su, Ma, J* and *Sa,* respectively and in that ascending order for the planets Venus, Sun, Mars, Jupiter and Saturn. Finally, around the same central point *C* describe the last of the system of concentric circles with proportionately the largest diameter, spangle the upper hemisphere of its circumference with a rather heavy scatter-distribution of distinct dots, and label them in sequence S_1, S_2, S_3 . . . S_n, to represent the fixed stars which, unlike the planets, do not appear to wander in different orbits through the heavens. This static, cross-section design thus completes, for all practical purposes, the conventional blueprint for the total universe known to ancient physics.

But behind and beyond this architectonic system resides in inaccessible transcendence an eternally desiderated Prime Mover which provokes the wheels-within-wheels of the structure, each of which is inhabited by a native Intelligence, into a motion that is perpetually repeated but forever frustrated. Under the influence of this irresistible attraction toward an unattainable objective, the outermost sphere of the fixed stars rotates from East to West at a pace which is calculable from earth observation of the heavens. This motion communicates itself to the *Sa* sphere which it encloses. *Sa* in turn affects *J. J* influences *Ma,* and so on, until all the planetary spheres are rotating in uniform *circular* motion about the fixed point *C* as center. The total effect, moreover, of this interlocking system of upper planetary spheres is to disturb the ideal equilibrium of the *F, A, W* and *E* regions and thus distribute the elements into the mixed state of combination that characterizes the heterogeneous world of physical experience. The dynamism of the science of physics, therefore, is nothing more nor less than the instinctive and spontaneous effort of the displaced elements to return to *the natural levels of rest* from which the smoothly geared rotations of the celestial spheres have forcibly exiled them. This is the meaning of *motion* in ancient mechanics. This is the paramount problem of the ancient science of physics.

In brief, then, there were two irreducible classes of moving objects in the ancient physics: (1) the imperishable celestial bodies above the region of fire; (2) the terrestrial elements and their soluble compounds below the lunary sphere. Both moved. But the motions natural to each were (a) *irreducible* to the other and (b) *unresolvable* into geometrically more simple components.

The *simple* motion characteristic of the celestial bodies was *circular*. It is thus inevitable that the crucial problem of ancient physical astronomy will be to "save the phenomena" of actually observed planetary paths by theoretical constructions of *circular* orbits that fit the facts, as known, and allow successful prediction of future patterns of relative positions in the skies.

The *simple* motion characteristic of the terrestrial elements was *perpendicular* to the plane of the horizon, and either vertically upward from the level of the observer's eye or vertically downward toward *C,* depending upon the natural lightness or relative heaviness of the exiled elements or compounds concerned. It is thus inevitable that the first crucial problem of the ancient terrestrial physics will be to "save the phenomena" of actually observed free fall of heavy objects to the surface of the earth by transposing the theoretical "homing instincts" of dislocated elements in the process of self-repatriation in *E* into a set of successful physico-mathematical equations in units of time, distance, density and velocity that fit the facts, as known, and allow for verifiable predictions of future falls.

But along with these two natural and simple motions in a circle and along the perpendicular, experience also disclosed a *third unnatural and complex* motion along an approximately horizontal plane and in any arbitrary compass direction. It is thus inevitable that the second crucial problem of ancient terrestrial physics will be to "save the phenomena" of the actually observed path of projectiles by adjusting and recombining natural motions into physico-mathematical equations that fit the facts, as known, and allow successful prediction of future trajectories of horizontally directed missiles.

The crucial problem of ancient physical astronomy became progressively more complex by the steady accumulation of observational data concerning what were termed the "progressions," "retrogressions" and "stationary points" in the apparently quite irregular circular paths of the planets. The conventional solution to these critical complications ingeniously developed a geometrically intricate system of dovetailing "circular motions of circular motions" in the form of "equants," "eccentrics" and "epicycles." (It *is* a fact that planetary orbits could theoretically be described and predicted to any required degree of approximation by such a proportionately complex system of interlocking circular motions.)

The first crucial problem of ancient terrestrial physics, concerning the free perpendicular fall of bodies to the surface of the earth, did *not* in fact become progressively more complicated by the steady accumulation of mathematically more precise measurements of experimental data. The contours of the problem actually expanded into critical dimensions under the persistent inquisitive influence of theoretical considerations by successive generations of professional physicists. The conventional solution to the problem, moreover, progressively streamlined and standardized the complex existential situation by abstracting successively from some observed variations in rate of descent, due to random differences in shape, size and physico-chemical constitution. After such partial isolation the relevant factors were restricted to two: (1) *the inherent weight of the object* and (2) *the inherent density of the medium,* both construed as *simple and irreducible constants* of nature.

These considerations congealed into the two following physico-mathematical laws: (1) under standard conditions the velocity of free fall is directly proportional to the weight of the object and inversely proportional to the density of the medium, so that (2) for any two bodies of *unequal* weight but of identical shape and in the same medium the ratio of their velocities is equal to the ratio of their weights. The actual rate of observed acceleration in fall stubbornly escaped accurate measurement but was interpreted as directly proportional to progressive approximation to the natural habitat of rest in *E*. And it *is* a fact that bodies of heavier weight *do* actually fall in air more rapidly than lighter ones of the same shape.

The second crucial problem of ancient terrestrial physics, concerning the path of projectiles along the horizontal, did *not* in point of fact become progressively more complicated by the steady accumulation of mathematically more precise measurements of experimental data. The contours of this problem, too, expanded into critical dimensions under the equally persistent inquisitive influence of theoretical considerations by successive generations of professional physicists. The nub of the problem was to devise a theoretically satisfactory analysis of impetus or momentum. The conventional solutions, moreover, progressively streamlined and standardized the complex existential situation by abstracting successfully from some irrelevant differences. After such partial isolation the pertinent factors were limited to three: (1) *force,* (2) *time* and (3) *weight,* which was once again construed with systematic consistency as a simple and irreducible constant of nature. These considerations issued in the following physico-mathematical law for projectiles in flight through air or in transit over a given surface: the distance traversed varies directly as the product of a given force applied continuously through a given time and inversely as the weight of the object.

Such then is the relevant *content* of the ancient physics. But what is of importance concerning the *method* by which such results were achieved?

Note first that motion and rest are indissoluble correlatives which thus offer two possible alternatives of methodological procedure. Take motion as the primitive datum, and one sets for physics the problem of analyzing the phenomenon of rest. Take rest as primitive, and one assigns to physics the problem of analyzing the phenomenon of motion. The choice is paramount and decisive. For the problem makes the science. The ancient physics, for reasons which it is not difficult to understand, chose the latter alternative and thus set about the scientific task of explaining how motion proceeds from rest.

In the solution to this chosen problem the ancient physics realized clearly that the science must start the construction of its analysis with *simple* motions and *simple* constants of nature. The crux of the matter was to choose all those elements and *only* those elements which are in point of fact *irreducible* to more fundamental factors. For existential reasons, as disclosed in actual concrete experience, the ancient physics selected as the *simple* motions of the science: (1) circular motion about a *fixed* center and (2) rectilinear motion along a perpendicular path of *privileged* direction. As its *simple* constant the ancient physics accepted as irreducible the *inherent* property of weight. With these fundamental simple concepts the ancient physics undertook to work out the problems of motion in the world in terms of the physico-mathematical laws of its behavior.

And at this point it is interesting and instructive to notice the impartial observations of a contemporary Cambridge historian:

In this whole picture of the universe there is more of Aristotle than of Christianity. It was the authority of Aristotle and his successors which was responsible even for those features of this teaching which might seem to us to carry something of an ecclesiastical flavour —the hierarchy of heavens, the revolving spheres, the Intelligences which moved the planets, the grading of the elements in the order of their nobility and the view that the celestial bodies were composed of an incorruptible fifth essence [*The Origins of Modern Science,* H. Butterfield, pp. 21-22].

Thus far, then, for both the content and method of the ancient physics, from which the bridge of Galileo's *Two New Sciences* leads into the new, by means of innovations in methodology that uncover fresh results.

The main *innovations in method* are four: (1) filter out from the confused facts of the complex existential situation *all* those factors and only those factors which can be geometrically neutralized; (2) reduce *all* elements pertinent to the problem, singly and jointly, to their most simple state and then proceed to locate them for purposes of theoretical analysis in the highly unnatural and idealized instances of imaginary limiting-cases where mathematical manipulation is sure to be more easy, lucid, fruitful and secure; (3) in all calculations operate with confidence according to the intuitive principle that of any two theoretically possible solutions to a problem the more simple one is more likely to be the correct one; (4) to insure clarity, solidity, completeness and accuracy in significant detail, construct the theoretical solution according to the rigorously logical hypothetico-deductive system of Euclidian geometry and test selected implications of the theory at significant junctures by recourse to theoretically well-designed experiments. With these four rules of revised procedure directing its program of research and analysis, the new physics will advance at a steady pace toward its contemporary triumphs.

If, then, one desires to grasp the techniques by which Galileo built his bridge of successful transition, notice must be given to passages that explain the process of geometric abstraction:

> . . . Of these properties of weight, of velocity, and also of shape, infinite in number, it is not possible to give any exact description; hence, *in order to handle this matter in a scientific way, it is necessary to cut loose from these difficulties;* and having discovered and demonstrated the theorems in the limiting-case of zero resistance, to use them and apply them with such limitations as experience will reveal. And *the advantage of this method will not be small;* for the material and shape of the projectile may be chosen, as dense and as round as possible, so that it will encounter the least resistance in the medium. Nor will the spaces and velocities in general be so great but that we shall be easily able to correct them with precision.

This process of adequate abstraction, moreover, is precisely what the ancient physics failed to practice in a ruthlessly complete and thorough fashion. For Aristotle, motion-in-a-straight-line was *not* geometrically neutral. It was rectilinear motion, indeed, but along the perpendicular in a *privileged* direction. For Aristotle, circular motion was erroneously construed *en bloc* as unresolvable into geometrically more simple components. And in concluding that distance traversed in forced motion along the horizontal plane varies directly as the product of force and time, the ancient physics did not carry abstractive analysis far enough. For the effect of friction and the resistance of the medium were lumped together in the single and presumably simple factor of inherent weight. The *ideal* case of a body moving without friction in a medium of zero resistance under the pressure of a single constant force was not considered.

There is no passage anywhere in the vast library of ancient physics that even approaches the abstractive isolation of relevant details, characteristic of the following excerpt from the *Two New Sciences:*

Imagine any particle projected along a horizontal plane without friction; then we know . . . that this particle will move along this same plane with a motion which is uniform and perpetual, provided the plane has no limits. But if the plane is limited and elevated, then the moving particle, which we imagine to be a heavy one, will on passing over the edge of the plane acquire, in addition to its previous uniform and perpetual motion, a downward propensity due to its own weight; so that the resulting motion which I call projection, is compounded of one which is uniform and horizontal and of another which is vertical and naturally accelerated. We now proceed to demonstrate some of its properties.

Here *motion* is the primitive datum, not rest. Here one *imagines* a limiting-case rather than confronts directly a complex existential situation. Here one *reduces* friction to a zero value. Here the projectile shrinks to the *ideal* dimensions of a mass-point. Here the abstractive process of analysis, although not perfect, is sufficiently impressive to be instructive and illustrative.

Galileo furthermore is represented by Salviati as saying:

We have already seen that the difference of speed between bodies of different specific gravities is most marked in those media which are the most resistant; thus, in a medium of mercury, gold not merely sinks to the bottom more rapidly than lead but it is the only substance that will descend at all; all other metals and stones rise to the surface and float. On the other hand the variation of speed in air between balls of gold, lead, copper, porphyry, and other heavy materials is so slight that in a fall of 100 cubits a ball of gold would surely not outstrip one of copper by as much as four fingers. *Having observed this, I came to the conclusion that in a medium totally devoid of resistance all bodies would fall with the same speed.*

Altogether unnatural, nonexistent, and purely imaginary limiting-cases are thus more rich in penetrating insights into the factors that make physics than a wholesale dedication to comprehensive observation of *all* the components of a complex existential situation in concrete experience.

Again, Salviati reports Galileo's intuition of the simplicity-criterion as follows:

> When, therefore, I observe a stone initially at rest falling from an elevated position and continually acquiring new increments of speed, why should I not believe that such increases take place *in a manner which is exceedingly simple and rather obvious* to everybody? If now we examine the matter carefully we find no addition or increment more simple than that which repeats itself always in the same manner . . . thus we may picture to our mind a motion as uniformly and continuously accelerated when, during any equal intervals of time whatever, equal increments of speed are given to it.

There is here no pompous attempt to prove or to justify on other grounds the intuitive criterion of simplicity. Its success in practice suffices to vindicate its role in the procedures of scientific decision.

Nor is it possible to overestimate the scientific importance of Galileo's adherence to the logical rigors of the hypothetico-deductive method of theoretical construction. Nowhere in ancient physics, not even in the systematically developed lore of optics, does one find such a careful attention to the elaborate apparatus of definitions, axioms, theorems, corollaries, scholia. Galileo knows "the nature of mathematical definitions which consist merely in the imposition of names, or, if you prefer, abbreviations of speech established and introduced to avoid the tedious drudgery" of the complex locutions of conventional natural languages, not at all designed for the precisions necessary in scientific discourse. Nor does Galileo blush to state in explicit and labored terminology such a trite and obvious axiom as: "In one and the same interval of time the distance traversed at a greater speed is larger than the distance traversed at a less speed." For *only* by such conscious and rigorous formulation does the scientific intelligence master and control the multiple and overlapping factors in a given problem. And when the validity of an axiom is not instantly and intuitively clear, Galileo does not hesitate to accept it conditionally "as a postulate, the absolute truth of which will be established when we find that the inferences from it correspond to and agree perfectly with experiment."

Nor should one think that the new method succeeds merely because it immerses itself with reckless abandon in oceans of

random experimental data. Recourse to experiment is significant as a test if and only if the procedure is carefully designed
according to theoretical considerations. Listen to Galileo's
model report:

A piece of wooden moulding or scantling, about 12 cubits long,
half a cubit wide, and three finger-breadths thick, was taken; on its
edge was cut a channel a little more than one finger in breadth;
having made this groove very straight, smooth, and polished, and
having lined it with parchment, also as smooth and polished as possible, we rolled along it a hard, smooth, and very round ball. Having
placed this board in a sloping position, by lifting one end some one
or two cubits above the other, we rolled the ball, as I was just saying,
along the channel, noting . . . the time required to make the descent. We repeated this experiment more than once in order to measure the time with an accuracy such that the deviation between two
observations never exceeded one-tenth of a pulse-beat; having performed this operation and having assured ourselves of its reliability,
we now rolled the ball only one quarter the length of the channel;
and having measured the time of its descent, we found it precisely
one-half of the former. Next we tried other distances, comparing the
time for the whole length with that for the half, or with that for
two-thirds, or three-fourths, or indeed for any fraction; in such
experiments, repeated a full hundred times, we always found that
the spaces traversed were to each other as the squares of the times,
and this was true for all inclinations of the plane, i. e., of the channel, along which we rolled the ball. We also observed that the times
of descent, for various inclinations of the plane, bore to one another
precisely that ratio . . . predicted and demonstrated for them.

Perhaps nowhere else in scientific literature can one discern
more forcibly the indispensably intimate correlation between
the hypothetico-deductive method of theoretical construction
and procedures for experimental test of implied consequences
than in the above passage, wherein Galileo has to remind himself that in a report from the experimental laboratory it is "the
channel groove" and not exactly the "theoretical plane" which
is pertinent.

These innovations in method, moreover, proved to be rich in
the content of their results. For they led Galileo to discover,
what ancient physics consistently missed, the law of falling bodies: "The spaces described by a body falling from rest with a
uniformly accelerated motion are to each other as the square of
the time-intervals employed in traversing these distances."

And they led Galileo far beyond the inadequate formula-

tions of ancient physics *almost* to the very threshold of Newton's first and second laws of motion. For Galileo declares somewhat incidentally without a full realization of the epochal
significance of his statement:

> . . . we may remark that any velocity once imparted to a moving
> body will be rigidly maintained as long as the external causes of
> acceleration and retardation are removed, a condition which is
> found only on horizontal planes; for in the case of planes which
> slope downwards there is already present a cause of acceleration,
> while on planes sloping upward there is retardation; from this it
> follows that motion along a horizontal plane is perpetual; for, if the
> velocity be uniform, it cannot be diminished or slackened, much
> less destroyed.

Here motion replaces rest as the primitive datum of physics.
Here the principle of inertia comes into view. Only one defect
mars the insight. For Galileo supposes "the horizontal plane
which slopes neither up nor down, to be represented by a
straight line as if each point on this line were equally distant
from the center." So difficult was it for a student of the ancient
physics to divorce his mind cleanly and decisively from the
traditional obsession with *circular* motion and to operate at
ease in the geometrically neutral and altogether direction-
less dimensions of an abstract Euclidian space. The approach
to the second law is more satisfactory: "the horizontal motion
remains uniform, the vertical motion continues to be accelerated downwards in proportion to the square of the time, and
. . . such motions as these combine without altering, disturbing, or hindering each other, so that as the motion proceeds
the path of the projectile does not change into a different
curve."

Thus far, then, the major innovations of method and the
main contributions of insight to modern physics by the *Two
New Sciences*. But Galileo realizes that "the door is now opened
for the first time to a new method fraught with numerous and
wonderful results which in future years will command the attention of other minds." And they did. For in the spirit of the
newer physics Newton will develop these insights into the laws
of motion, link them with Kepler's three laws of planetary orbits, and formulate the *universal* law of gravitation which dis-

sipated forever the persistent prejudice of the ancient physics that there were *two* irreducible classes of moving objects in the universe with connatural motions so fundamentally different as to defy comprehension beneath a single law.

At this stage the ancient physics is far behind us. At this stage modern physics is all around us. And Galileo's *Two New Sciences* is the book that built the one-way bridge between them. And that man surely abandons all *scientific* appreciation of the structure of that span who presumes to think that the passage was closed then, or is closed now, to integral Christians.

Every serious student should secure, if now available, a copy of *Dialogues Concerning Two New Sciences* by Galileo Galilei, translated by Henry Crew and Alfonso de Salvio and published by the Macmillan Company in 1933. This is the text I quote. The translation is good. But it has two defects: (1) the precise transposition of the problems into *modern* terminology sometimes obscures the real genius of Galileo, and (2) the sentence structure is awkward and heavy. The conscientious and capable reader should cover the complete text. Others may find the Henry Regnery Company *Selections* edition suitable for their purposes. If sampling is advisable, do so elsewhere in the text quite liberally but concentrate on large sections of the dialogs of the third and of the fourth day.

For a competent survey of the ancient sciences consult J. L. Heiberg, *Mathematics and Physical Science in Classical Antiquity,* published in London in 1922. Those who desire closer inspection in detail of Aristotle's theory of motion will find it profitable to consult I. E. Drabkin's paper in the *American Journal of Philology* 59 (1938) 60-84. And Edward Rosen, in the *Scientific Monthly* 63 (1946) 213-217, will report for you the vicissitudes, through the years, of the Ptolemaic system of astronomy. For a modern and competent presentation of the main elements in the scientific background of Galileo's age, written in a precise and engaging manner, see *The Origins of Modern Science: 1300-1800,* by H. Butterfield, published in London in 1949. Students who have time for only one piece of collateral reading would do well to take Butterfield as their choice. Read chapters 1, 2, 4, 5 and 8. Omit the others at pleasure of the reader. Or see Philip P. Wisener, "The Tradition behind Galileo's Methodology," *Osiris* 1 (1936) 733-746.

For more about Galileo than the *Two New Sciences* reveals, consult A. Koyre's excellent *Études galiliennes*, published in Paris, 1939-1940. No one should refer to the "leaning tower of Pisa experiment" who has not read Lane Cooper's intriguing study *Aristotle, Galileo and the Tower of Pisa,* published by the Cornell University Press in 1935. And if one cares to revive the issue of Galileo's "condemnation" by ecclesiastical authorities, the article on Galileo in the monumental and authoritative *Dictionnaire de Théologie Catholique* is indispensable reference material.

Readers, finally, who feel the need for more information concerning the hypothetico-deductive method of scientific theory construction in order to appreciate adequately its value and importance, may peruse with profit A. Tarski's *Introduction to Logic and to the Methodology of Deductive Sciences,* Oxford University Press, 1946, as well as the expository articles on the postulational method by L. O. Kattsoff in the *Philosophy of Science* journal 2 (1935) 139-163: 3 (1936) 67-89, 375-417.

JOSEPH T. CLARK

SELECTED BIBLIOGRAPHY

CONANT, James B., *Science and Common Sense.* Yale.
GALILEO, *Two New Sciences.* Dover.
GALILEO, *Two New Sciences,* Selections. Regnery.

Harvey: The Motion of the
Heart and Blood

The *Exercitatio Anatomica De Motu Cordis et Sanguinis in Animalibus* by William Harvey was published by the House of William Fitzeri in Frankfurt in 1628. Known generally by the shorter title "De Motu Cordis," it is one of the great books of the world and without question is one of the world's greatest medical books.

In order to understand fully the impact made by this important work, it is necessary to recall the status of anatomic and physiologic teaching and knowledge, both prior to and contemporary with its publication. This, in turn, calls for some knowledge of the author, for it is through his eyes that we shall view the over-all picture and make our judgments.

William Harvey, son of Thomas Harvey, yeoman, of the town of Folkestone in Kent, was born on April 1, 1578, and after completing the required course at Canterbury Grammar School and having entered his sixteenth year, "was privileged to join the scholars of Caius-Gonvil College Cambridge." In thus honoring the lad with this privilege, the university honored itself, for in time Harvey was to describe the circulation of the blood, modernize the science of physiology, and make his name the greatest in seventeenth-century medicine.

There is little knowledge obtainable regarding Harvey's antecedents and early life, and there is equally little known of his school and university days. The information which is available regarding these days is singularly unexciting; suffice it to say that he gave little promise of the greatness which he was to achieve in later life. It can be postulated, however, that the seeds of his interests in anatomy were sown in his sojourn at Caius College, for that institution (known to Cantabrigians as "Keys College") was founded by the distinguished Dr. John Caius, one-time attending physician to the Queen, and the first to introduce public dissection and the study of practical anatomy into England.

It is of interest to deviate here for a moment to note that Caius, like many other illustrious Englishmen, had completed his medical education in Italy. What is even more interesting is that they were drawn thither by a scientific climate more salubrious for the study of anatomy and physiology and most favorable to the practice of dissection. In fact, Harvey was drawn to Padua because of the fame of the professor of anatomy there, one Hieronymous Fabricius of Aquapendente, a pupil of the great Fallopius.

This deviation is justified in a Christian appraisal of this book, for students for years have been regaled with the statement that science and particularly medicine was delayed in development due to papal prohibitions and ecclesiastic intransigence. Here we see men coming from foreign lands to study anatomy in institutions which were under papal protection, yet apparently there was an ecclesiastical prohibition of dissection. The scholar knows, however, that much of the trouble came from a misinterpretation of the meaning of the Bull of Pope Boniface VIII which dealt with the burial of individuals who had died in foreign lands. (This is the Bull *De Sepulturis* (1300), which can be found in its full Latin text in James J. Walsh's *The Popes and Science,* pp. 413-414; the meaning of the Bull is discussed *ibid.,* pp. 28 ff.)

To return to the story, although Fabricius, whose fame had attracted Harvey, was true to the traditions of Padua in making many valuable scientific contributions, neither he nor his pupil suspected that his greatest claim to fame and the most valuable heritage he would leave to the scientific world was *Gulielmus Harveius Anglus,* whose coat of arms, only recently discovered, adorns the courtyard of the medical school which both of them graced and whose *magnum opus* we discuss here.

Upon acquiring the coveted degree "Doctor of Physic," Harvey returned to London and, after taking a second degree at Cambridge, began his practice. Honors were accorded him at regular and seemly intervals. Not the least of these honors was the appointment as Lumellian lecturer at the Royal College of Physicians, and it was in these lectures, entitled *Praelectiones Anatomicae,* that he set forth, for the first time, his views upon the motion of the heart and blood vessels, twelve years before he was ready to offer them for publication. Later he became physician extraordinary to James I and physician to Charles I, and to the latter he dedicated his monumental work.

Of the personality make-up of the man Harvey we know little, except what we can cull from his writings and a few prolix and tedious biographies, plus some questionable material from one John Aubrey, whom Doctor Harvey met late in life under fortuitous circumstances. Aubrey, a strange and contradictory character, was an admixture of antiquarian, bibliophile, psychopath and seventeenth-century counterpart of a modern gossip columnist. From him we learn that Harvey "was not tall but of the lowest stature, round faced, olivaster complexion (like the wainscot), little eie, round, very black, full of spirit, his haire was black as a raven but quite white 20 years before he dyed." From the same source we learn that Harvey was reserved, uncommunicative, intense and not at all interested in contemporary events. Aubrey adds one characteristic which seems discordant and out of place—that "he wore a dagger which he displayed upon slight provocation."

To orient ourselves as to the time in which the author practiced, experimented and wrote, we need only recall that at the time of his entrance to medical school, Shakespeare's plays were creating their initial furor in London, and when he was graduated in 1602, a new offering called *Hamlet* was being tried on the London stage. Also, the year 1616, which marked the advent of Harvey's Lumellian lectures, was the year of Shakespeare's death.

Peculiarly enough, several of the Bard's lines might lead one to suspect that he was aware of Harvey's teachings on the motion of the heart and blood, though this was probably more by chance than by design. It will be recalled that on one occasion Shakespeare has Brutus say to Portia:

> You are my true and honourable wife,
> As dear to me as are the ruddy drops
> That visit my sad heart.

and again in *Coriolanus:*

I send it through the rivers of your blood
Even to the court—the heart—to the seat of the brain.

While it is probable that Shakespeare had little knowledge of the actual course of the "ruddy drops" in question, it would come as little surprise had he known and had he assimilated Harvey's teachings, for through the centuries dramatists, writers and poets have apparently been far in advance of scientists and physicians in accepting new medical theories, particularly in anything relating psyche to soma.

Before going into detail regarding the volume itself, there are several interesting sidelights connected with it which are worthy of note. One observes particularly the method by which the ideas later to be published were allowed slowly to filter out, in order that any criticism they evoked could be investigated and answered. This is testimony to the wisdom and psychological acumen of the author. It is not unlikely that he was convinced of the soundness of the ideas and dates twenty years before he published them, yet he awaited the opportune time, for he knew that publication of his work would arouse a storm of protest and hostile denunciation from his fellow scientists. It was opposition of his colleagues, which he knew would be vehement, that he feared most, rather than fear of ecclesiastic disapproval, as some writers would have us believe. He had an excellent example of what he might expect in Vesalius, who a century before had met with calumny and abuse for straying from the beaten path of contemporary scientific thought.

At last, when the author was ready to commit himself to print, he further buttressed his offering by presenting it through his "learned friends and colleagues," which was an astute maneuver. After addressing himself to his dear friend Doctor Argent, the excellent and accomplished president of the Royal College of Physicians, he stated: "Were not the work indeed presented through my learned friends, I should scarce hope that it could come out scathless and complete, for you have been faithful witnesses of almost all of the instances from which I have either collected the truth or confuted error." Then he states: "as this book alone declares the blood to course and revolve by a new route very different from the ancient and beaten pathway," he was greatly afraid lest he be charged with presumption should he put it before the public at home or beyond the seas without first proposing it to his colleagues and confirming its conclusion by ocular demonstrations in their presence, answering their doubts and securing the support of the distinguished president.

Previously, Harvey had dedicated his treatise to "The Most Illustrious and Indomitable Prince Charles," as was the custom of the time. In effusive paragraphs he compares the king to the heart, as the sovereign of everything and the source from which all power proceeds. Withal, however, his attachment to the king was probably more on a verbal level than on a political or idealistic one, and it is noteworthy that he was never knighted.

In the introduction to the seventy-two pages by which ultimately he was to change the ideas of physiologists and anatomists throughout the world, Harvey found it imperative first to state "what has been thought of these things by others in their writings and what has been held by the vulgar and by tradition, in order that what is true may be confirmed, and what is false set right by dissection, multiplied experience and accurate observation."

He noted that "almost all anatomists, physicians and philosophers up to the present time have supposed with Galen that the object of the pulse was the same as that of respiration and only differed in one particular, this being conceived to depend upon the animal, the respiration on the vital faculty." He called attention to the fact that Fabricius in his book on respiration affirmed that as the pulsation of the heart and arteries does not suffice for the ventilation and refrigeration of the blood, "therefore were the lungs fashioned to surround the heart." "From this it appears that whatever has hitherto been said upon the systole and diastole, on the motion of the heart and arteries has been said with especial reference to the lungs."

The Alexandrian physician, Erasistratus, had taught that spirits were contained in the arteries, while Realdus Columbus was of the opinion that the lungs could either make or contain spirits, but Galen had written to prove that the arteries contained blood and nothing but blood: neither spirits nor air. Harvey examined these statements, considered the experiments and asked questions of those who believed the motion of the ventricles to be different. He personally had noted that the structure of the ventricles was almost identical and wondered why they should be thought different when the action, motion and pulse of both are the same. Petulantly he asked pertinent questions, for instance: "Wherefore, if the pulmonary vein were destined for the conveyance of air, it has the structure of a blood vessel, for nature had rather need for annular tubes such as those of the bronchia in order that they might always remain open, not have been liable to collapse and that they might continue entirely free from blood, lest the liquid should interfere with the passage of air." Step by step he reviewed contemporary belief and in the end of the chapter concluded that what had heretofore been said was obscure, inconsistent or even impossible and therefore it was necessary then to appeal to vivisection and constant inspection and investigation in order to find the truth.

The task was not to be a simple one and in Chapter One we see what might have happened had the investigator not been a man of perseverance and fortitude. He began this chapter as follows: "When I first gave my mind to vivisection as a means of discovering the motions and uses of the heart and sought to discover these from actual inspection and not from the writing of others, I found the truth so truly arduous, so full of difficulties, that I was almost tempted to think with Fracastorius that the motion of the heart was only to be comprehended by God." He continues then to detail the trials which he underwent, the difficulties he encountered, the criticism he evoked and his reasons for writing.

Chapters Two to Four consider the motions of the heart and arteries as seen in living animals when the chest is laid open and the pericardium, the envelope which surrounds the heart, is slit. Proceeding cautiously but firmly, he disputed with Casper Bauhin and John Riolan, and after paying them tribute as "most learned men and skillful anatomists," he disagreed with their belief that the heart in living animals has four motions distinct in time and in place, two proper to the auricles and two to the ventricles. With due deference to such authority, Harvey stated there are four motions distinct in point of place but not of time, for the two auricles move together and so also do the two ventricles, "and though the places be four the times are only two." He then described these motions of the heart as we know them today.

Step by step he moved carefully, marshaling his facts, and after determining that the one action of the heart is the transmission of the blood and its distribution by means of the arteries to the very extremities of the body, he declared unequivocally that the pulse which we feel in the arteries is nothing more than the impulse of the blood derived from the heart. He stated that the grand course of hesitation and error seemed to be in the intimate connection between the heart and blood vessels—this is where previous observers had gone astray.

As the author proceeds carefully to explain his thesis, his industry, inspiration and resourcefulness become more and more apparent. He stated, "had anatomists only been as conversant with the dissection of lower animals as they are with that of the human body the matters that have hitherto kept them in perplexity of doubt would in my opinion have met them freed from every kind of difficulty." After numerous questionings and strictures as to method, he confirmed the details of the lesser circulation whereby in the warmer adult animals and in man the blood passes from the right ventricle through the pulmonary artery to the lungs and thence by the pulmonary veins into the left auricle and thence to the left ventricle. This circulation had once been described by the ill-fated Spaniard, Michael Servetus of Villanova, but not too much attention had been paid to it. Servetus himself was burned at the stake by John Calvin at Geneva in 1553, for reasons doctrinal rather than anatomical.

Having traced the passage of blood from veins into arteries and followed the manner in which it is transmitted and distributed by the action of the heart, Harvey believed it incumbent upon him to speak of the quantity and the source of the blood, and here his ideas, he said, were of such novel and unheard-of character that he trembled lest he have mankind at large for his enemy. "Still," he says, "the die is cast and my trust is in my love of truth and the candour that inheres in cultivated minds." He began to think what might be the quantity of blood which was transmitted and the time of its passage, and reasoned that mechanically the best possibility was that the blood should somehow find its way from the arteries to the veins and so return to the right side of the heart. "I began to think whether there might be a motion as it were in a circle. Now, this I afterward found to be true."

There remained the proof, however, and Harvey, not one to make assertions without demonstrable foundation, posed several propositions and set about to prove them. He knew the heart could only eject the amount of blood the ventricles contained, so he measured and weighed the capacity of the sheep's ventricles—the capacity of man's ventricles being nearly the same. Next he multiplied the ventricular output by the number of heart beats, roughly 72 per minute, and determined that the output of the heart was about 3½ pounds of blood per minute. By exsanguinating a sheep he found that the total blood volume was but little over 4 pounds. Now, if the output of the heart be 3½ pounds of blood per minute and the total blood volume be only 4 pounds, it is obvious that the same blood must be used over again. Ergo—the blood has to return to the heart for redistribution, and it thus moves in circular fashion.

There remain nine chapters of Harvey's great work in which he details every step of his way, in which he checks and rechecks and seeks to confirm every proposition by some experiment. In generous, thorough, meticulous manner he proved his propositions and left nothing to chance. Always he invoked his trustworthy methods of vivisection and ocular demonstrations. Chapter Fourteen is entitled "The Conclusion of the Demonstration of the Circulation," and we might consider this as final enough, yet it does not satisfy Harvey. Chapter Fifteen confirms it further "by probable reasons," while Chapter Sixteen proves it from "certain consequences," and the like, until almost all conceivable aspects of the problem are covered. One gap only remained in Harvey's hypothesis—he was never able to demonstrate the actual interchange between arterial and venous blood. It remained for Marcello Malpighi to explain this action thirty years later, for he saw through the microscope the blood slowed down into tiny streams and his researches ended in a description of capillary interchange and circulation. Although this final link in the description of circulation was only forged four years after Harvey's death, Harvey had postulated its existence some years before.

Numerous questions have been raised regarding Harvey's priorities and the work of his predecessors. Although the heat has gone out of the controversy, the question of who should get credit for what discovery still recurs at times. Undoubtedly there were many anatomists who were close to the truths which Harvey taught, but usually they either stopped too soon or assumed too much. Claims have been made for priority of Hindu, Chinese, Arab and Egyptian savants, Italian physicians and laymen, Shakespeare, Cesalpinus, Columbus and Servetus, and all have had champions who claimed their part of the laurels which Harvey wore.

Some of these claims have merit; others are ludicrous, and it is obvious that while some investigators saw small segments of the problem, Harvey saw the whole. By careful, patient and astute observation and experiment he demonstrated the truth of his postulates. His book is great not from a literary standpoint but from the importance of the subject matter and its demonstration of a real scientific method.

FRANCIS J. BRACELAND

SELECTED BIBLIOGRAPHY

Exercitatio Anatomica De Motu Cordis et Sanguinis in Animalibus. Francofurti, 1628. Edition published in 1928, the third centenary of its first publication, by R. Lier & Company, Florence. Special limited edition printed for College of Physicians of Philadelphia, Pa.

GARRISON, *History of Medicine,* fourth edition. W. B. Saunders.

ROBINSON, VICTOR, M.D., *The Story of Medicine.* Tudor.

HARVEY, William, *The Motion of the Heart and Blood.* Regnery.

Hume: Enquiry Concerning
Human Understanding

DAVID HUME (1711-1776) has every right of inclusion in the company of writers of Great Books. His mature life covered and reflected the middle decades of the eighteenth century, a crucial period in the formation of the modern European outlook. During this time, the sharp clash between the two prevailing currents of thought, rationalism and empiricism, came to a head. At stake was the ability of reason to demonstrate certain truths, important alike for philosophical theory and practical life.

To specify the exact limits of experience was the exploratory work of Locke and Berkeley. Thus, Locke showed that we can know only the fact of the existence of substance, material and spiritual, but not its intrinsic constitution. Berkeley further narrowed the scope of the understanding by revealing the groundlessness and even contradiction of belief in material substance. The range of knowable reality shrank rapidly with the application of the empirical criterion. The danger was that, in becoming cautious and modest in its claims for the human mind, empiricism was also well on the road to complete skepticism. There seemed to be no end, in principle, to the process of whittling down the mind's field of competence. As Hume wittily put it, in reference to Berkeley: "That all his arguments, though otherwise intended, are, in reality, merely skeptical, appears from this, *that they admit of no answer and produce no conviction.*" Hume's own problem is formulated implicitly in this statement. How can a man remain faithful to the empirical way and still preserve the convictions required for successful living in human society?

This question haunted Hume during his young manhood.

He read widely in, and meditated intensely upon, the works of Bacon, Hobbes, Locke, Berkeley, Hutcheson, Clarke, Butler and the Cartesians (especially Malebranche). He shook himself loose from all formal religious belief, and yet retained a life-long animus against what he customarily referred to as the fanaticism of Presbyterianism and the superstition of Catholicism. He was convinced neither by Berkeley's theistic immaterialism nor by the systems of Continental rationalism. In comparison, the ancient skeptical arguments, recently revived by Bayle, provided an honest purgative. Nevertheless, a man cannot live by purgatives alone. The paramount consideration for Hume was to bring his speculation in line with the demands of the practical order. That is why he spoke indifferently of undertaking a study of human nature and a study of morals. Like Descartes, he was forced to admit that the noble superstructure of ethics was resting on a bed of quicksand. It lacked the solid rock of a reliable theory of the human understanding and its limits.

In reflecting on this problem, Hume was led to "a new scene of thought, which transported me beyond measure, and made me, with an ardour natural to young men, throw up every other pleasure or business to apply entirely to it." It seemed to him in 1729 that modern philosophy was now at last entering upon its Socratic phase, as Bacon had predicted. This consisted in the application of experimental reasoning to psychological and moral subjects. Anticipating Kant in this respect, the young Hume regarded himself as the Newton of the moral world (taking "moral" in the broad sense of whatever falls within the specifically human mode of reality). He entertained high hopes of applying the Newtonian method to the field of human knowledge and action. The great scientist and philosopher of nature had recommended the use of a two-fold procedure: analysis and synthesis. By the former method, the complex phenomena in the natural world are broken down into their constituent elements and widest laws. These elements and laws suggest theories to account for more remote phenomena in a synthetic way. But every hypothesis must pass the test of experience: it is acceptable only if it accords with the actual course of events.

Hume's new prospect was to recognize the fundamental

identity between Newton's method in natural philosophy and that practised by the British analysts and moralists in the sphere of human nature. His enthusiasm for the empirical standpoint rested on the belief that man is accessible to the same kind of reasoning as was so successful in investigating the material world. The elements of mental life had been isolated in their main outlines by Locke and Berkeley, but it was necessary to organize these findings into a comprehensive system through the conscious employment of the scientific method, dedicated now to the ends of practical life. Hume hoped to combine the empirical rigor of his philosophical predecessors, the practical moral bias of Hutcheson, and Newton's uncompromising search after universal principles of explanation.

In the laws of association (the habitual combining of ideas according to resemblance, contiguity in time or place, and cause and effect), Hume felt he had possession of a general formula that would account for mental phenomena just as inclusively as Newton's gravitational principle and laws of motion were held to cover material phenomena. He consistently underplayed his debt to the philosophical tradition, ancient and modern, in this respect. Aristotle and Aquinas, Hobbes and Locke and Malebranche had noted the importance of these psychic tendencies. But it was left for Hume to erect them into universal root causes of our major convictions. His chief warrant for regarding the associative mechanism as a universal force of attraction in the mental order is the analogy with Newton's natural philosophy. This claim also had its strategic value, since it traced our vital beliefs back to the spontaneous, "natural" operation of imagination. This provided a positive substitute for the purely rationalistic interpretation of mental functions. Hume called his position a moderate skepticism, since he placed a halter around the understanding and at the same time allowed for belief, as the product of feeling and sentiment.

Hume's *Treatise of Human Nature* (whose subtitle is "Being an Attempt to Introduce the Experimental Method of Reasoning into Moral Subjects") is the record of his first attempt to construct a science of human nature on this basis. Published in 1739-1740, it combined resilience with frankness in tackling the great problems of human belief and conduct. But in an Appendix to the last volume, Hume confessed his own dissatisfaction with the results. Having analyzed mental phenomena into their atomic units, he was unable to synthesize these units sufficiently to account for personal identity. The unity of the human self proved to be something more than the summation of its supposed components. The elementist hypothesis—that the logically more simple is also unconditionally the more genuine and real—broke down just at the point where it might reasonably be expected to receive direct confirmation. This contretemps suggests both that the Newtonian method breaks down when transferred from the physical world to man and that the principle of association of ideas is not of universal import. Hume placed too great a strain upon the example of Newton and the metaphor of natural attraction.

In the midst of a busy career as companion to a mad marquis and as secretary and aide-de-camp to General St. Clair on military and diplomatic missions, Hume found time to revise his *Treatise*. His reworked version of Book I was published in 1748 under the more unassuming title *An Enquiry Concerning Human Understanding*. Although professional philosophers have concerned themselves more with the *Treatise*, still the *Enquiry* has held its own position. Without being a mere piece of vulgarization, it has always attracted readers by its skilful union of the "easy" and the "accurate" modes of thinking. It is Hume's mature appraisal of his own projects, his effort to sift out the chaff from the wheat.

The one feature about the *Treatise* which he unqualifiedly repudiates is its cocksure tone, which betrayed him into affirming more than his premises warranted. Furthermore, the broad claims for associationism are somewhat toned down in the *Enquiry*. Belief in the external world, for instance, is accepted as an irreducible conviction rather than as a product of associative bonds. In addition, he remains silent about awareness of the self as an identical person and about the immateriality of the human soul. These topics are avoided not (as some critics suppose) because Hume's skeptical conclusions would shock the wider public but because they could not be made to follow with rigor from his principles. His philosophy is better represented as a questioning attitude, rich in problems and hints, than as a comprehensive doctrinal system. Many central concerns of men are left dangling or unmentioned.

Despite several modifications, the *Enquiry* retains the central structure of the *Treatise*. This point must be underlined if the reader is to come to critical grips with Hume's line of argument. The comparison with Newton is still suggested, at least as an ideal at which to aim. The associationist mechanism is still hailed as the "cement of the universe," the "universal principle, which had an equal influence on all mankind." It is appealed to at crucial phases in the discussion, because Hume has ruled out beforehand an independent source of mental connections. In the all-important case of causal inference, there is complete reliance on this hypothesis.

Above all, the Locke-Berkeley theory of knowledge continues to supply the presuppositions of Hume's reasoning. His refinements and corrections do not disturb the major theses, which are incorporated just as uncritically into the *Enquiry* as into the *Treatise*. But in the former work, they seem more unobtrusive, partly because there is no extensive discussion of belief in the continued existence of the external world and partly on account of the expert use of examples having a realistic tenor. Listening to Hume's appeal to fire, salt, earthquakes, organs of the body and the like, one is inclined to forget that he is quite noncommittal about the extramental reality of such entities. He follows unquestioningly the view that the mind is directly aware only of its own perceptions and that some of these perceptions are "faint copies" of others.

Hence the term "object" properly signifies the impression or idea present in the mind, although Hume does not eliminate the possibility of beings existing independently of consciousness. But the understanding has as its objects the perceptions which constitute its experience. Again, the term "impression" remains neutral with respect to the ultimate source from which the mental state derives. As far as empirical significance is concerned, the entire emphasis is laid upon the impressions and ideas as such. They do not figure primarily as intentional means for knowing independent beings, as Thomistic realism suggests.

Sections IV-VII, on cause and effect, comprise the core of the

Enquiry. In answer to the critics of his theory of causality, Hume protested that he did not deny—but then, neither did he affirm—the independent reality of the causal process. He often spoke as though there were causes operative in material nature and in the human mind. Despite some dogmatic assertions on what the real causes of certain phenomena are and are not, he wished to restrict his investigation to a study of our alleged *knowledge* of causal process. His conclusion is that an empirical analysis does not support this allegation if it pretends that man can become acquainted with the operation of powers beyond the phenomenal order of objects. The necessary connection between what we term cause and effect is supplied by imagination and custom rather than by some independent source. A customary link of association is established between a certain present impression and a past sequence of events. Once the new impression is presented to sense or memory, the mind so habituated is placed under a natural compulsion to recall the past series and to expect in a lively way that the future course of events will be of a similar sort. The certainty of belief in this causal inference is due to the force of habit or customary association rather than to insight into instances of dependence for being.

In examining Hume's theory, it will be convenient to follow the catechetical scheme furnished by himself in Section IV. He asks three basic questions and summarizes his replies in a laconic way: (1) What is the nature of all our reasonings concerning matter of fact? The relation of cause and effect. (2) What is the foundation of all our reasonings and conclusions concerning that relation? Experience. (3) What is the foundation of all conclusions from experience? Custom.

Our critical remarks will be gathered under these same three headings.

(1) Hume prejudices the discussion at once with his strategic distinction between demonstrative and moral reasoning. He proposes an airtight set of definitions in order to exclude causal inference from the sphere of strict demonstration. The exclusion is made, however, only in virtue of an arbitrary designation of the relation between ideas as the sole subject matter of demonstration. Mathematics is taken as the representative demonstrative science, because it determines nothing beyond the ideal connections among numbers and figures. No other type of

demonstration is allowed, and hence an easy case is made for assigning causal inference to the side of moral reasoning, which never attains more than probability. This is an example of how Hume often settles an issue with the aid of a prescribed definition, which begins as an hypothesis and imperceptibly acquires the status of an assured truth. He fails to deal adequately with the Aristotelian-Thomistic view that, while mathematical demonstration is easier and clearer for the human mind, it is not the only kind within our reach. Only on condition that all demonstration is *a priori* or *a simultaneo,* is there justification for restricting it to ideal relations.

Hume locates causal reasoning in the "moral" order, since it bears on matters of fact. It is sound instinct, reacting against rationalism, which leads him to stress the existential bearing of causal propositions. The latter cannot be arrived at in a purely mathematical fashion. It is also true that probability attends many of our investigations of matters of fact. But it does not therefore follow that no demonstrations can be made in regard to existential problems.

Hume argues that the contrary of a matter of fact is always possible and cannot be shown to be false. That which exists is contingent: its nonexistence is possible and so is its contrary. But it must be noted that Hume restricts the analysis to causal inference about the future. He fails to meet the claim that *a posteriori* reasoning can infer the cause of a contingent existent now in being. Although this existent need not be, its actual existence does require an actual cause, which it cannot fail to have. This is the drift of the realistic use of the causal principle, which is more significantly employed as an explanation of present matter of fact than as a prediction about the future.

Hume's appeal to the possible is a revival of a favorite argument of Descartes and the rationalists. It glides over the difference between logical and real possibility (which tends to disappear, once perceptions are regarded as the proper object of the mind), transferring the criteria of clarity, distinctness and internal consistency from the ideal order to the existential. In the latter zone, however, the absence of contradiction in a notion is not sufficient to give it standing as an explanation of the actual course of events. The entire experiential situation must be consulted before it carries this weight of probability. Here,

Hume forsakes the advice of Newton. The well-known Newtonian maxim, "I do not frame hypotheses," is intended precisely to distinguish between mere abstract hypotheses and
fruitful theories suggested by the present state of knowledge.
Contrary propositions, which are recommended only by their
internal consistency, should have no unsettling effect and do
not prove that existential reasoning enjoys no more than moral
certitude.

(2) The second decisive contrast is between reason and experience. Instead of reviewing the several historical views of
reason, Hume generalizes the conception adopted by the rationalists and has little difficulty in exposing its flimsy nature.
Indeed, he paints a caricature of reason which even the Cartesians would be unable to recognize as their own doctrine. Reason is supposed to operate in a purely *a priori* fashion, apart
from all experience. It discerns the essential natures and necessary connections among things through a single effortless glance.
Its deliverances are instantaneous, definitive and unalterable.

Obviously, this fantastic claim cannot be sustained. Yet Humean empiricism is not the only philosophy to puncture such
an inflated appraisal of human reason. In one long footnote
(in Part 1 of Section V) and in some occasional remarks, Hume
comes closer than he realizes to the moderate attitude of Thomistic realism. Both philosophies maintain the original dependence of reason upon sense experience, the need for accurate
observation and analysis, and the proper and constant cooperation between the senses and reason. In this spirit, Hume sometimes refers to "experimental reasoning" as the proper instrument of philosophy. His close association of imagination and
the understanding adumbrates a reformed theory of the relation between reason and sense, what Bacon called "a true and
lawful marriage between the empirical and the rational faculty."

But the Humean reformation is not carried out in a thorough
and unambiguous way. The proper function of reason is lost
sight of, in his zeal to affirm the primacy of sense impressions.
This submergence of the rational power of existential judgment, generalization and experiential demonstration is fostered
by the use of what John Dewey has called the weasel word "experience." For all his discussion of experience, Hume leaves the

term in a fundamentally unanalyzed state. His polemical aim of overcoming Cartesian reason at all costs encourages a multifarious appeal to experience, without clarifying and reconciling the various meanings.

Typical of this unsatisfactory situation is the key assertion: "Causes and effects are discoverable, not by reason but by experience." In support of this view, Hume shows that reason *unaided by experience* can never attain to the actual causes. But this is not the same as proving that experience *rather than* reason discovers them. It is only an unduly autonomous and "transcendental" sort of reason that is impotent, when the test is made. Hume fails to specify the sense in which truly human reason works along with the senses, including imagination, in the discovery of the traits and implications of the existent world. Sometimes he refers to experience as though it includes only sensation, observation and memory, joined with the customary influence of imagination. But these factors are not sufficient to account for Hume's own description of experience. There are modes of judgment, acts of reflection, perceptions of similar features or identities, and absolute generalizations about reason and experience as a whole, which can only be performances of an integrated, moderately regarded reason. No case has been made for thinking that apprehension of cause and effect is totally alien to concrete, experiential reason, acting upon evidence in some manner properly apprehended by itself.

(3) Hume's retort is that the understanding is moved by nonrational motives in the case of causal belief. He sets up an opposition between rational assent and belief induced by "natural" habit. Reasoning based on cause and effect is said to be the characteristic means of going "beyond the evidence of our memory and senses." But this is an equivocal statement. Hume makes no clear distinction between a case where sense and memory convey more data than they themselves are able to interpret, and a case where assertions are made without any ground of implication in sense data. If knowledge of causation is of the former sort, then it has a foundation in sensation, but only after reason grasps the further significance of the deliverances of sense. In the latter instance, the mind is simply outrunning the evidence, as far as existential propositions are concerned. By suggesting that causal inference is included under

the second heading, Hume eliminates any other source than a natural compulsion to supply the causal connection. Yet these two manners of going beyond the evidence are quite different, warranting the trial of an hypothesis that is neither Cartesian nor Humean. A real and yet reasonable foundation for causal inference can be allowed without surrendering the truth that reason is dependent for its data upon sensation and sense perception.

In the Humean scheme of things, this realistic path is blocked by some prior commitments, especially by a peculiar theory of distinction. In the *Treatise,* Hume lays it down that:

> Whatever is distinct, is distinguishable; and whatever is distinguishable, is separable by the thought or imagination. All perceptions are distinct. They are, therefore, distinguishable, and separable, and may be conceiv'd as separately existent, and may exist separately, without any contradiction or absurdity.

This is a sheer instance of logicism, in which irreducibility in the order of descriptive analysis and imagination is made synonymous with existential self-sufficiency. The only way in which it can be justified is by interpreting existence as one among other perceptual objects of the mind, but then existence loses distinctive meaning. Hume admits that, in the context of his outlook, the mind cannot attain to any other existential act than that of impressions and ideas. Because the atomic elements of experience can be analyzed in the state of isolated independence, they are regarded as loose and unconnected either with each other or with any "external" mode of existence. These extreme measures are required in order to counteract the import of those existential judgments, the differentiating trait of which is the affirmation of an existential act other than that of perceptions. In order to criticize Hume's phenomenalism, however, it would be necessary to return to his philosophical sources, where the problem of the object of knowledge is still admitted to be a problem. With Hume, the empirical position is a dogma rather than a problem.

Applied to the analysis of cause, this theory of distinction means that each phenomenal event is "distinct and complete" in itself, with no intrinsic connection with anything else. Consequently, an effect can be conceived to come to be (i.e., to enter the zone of perceptual objects) without the intervention of a cause. Similarly, it may be concluded that there is no connection between sense qualities and the so-called secret powers of nature. Natural agencies become occult forces, lurking behind the phenomena, as soon as cognition is restricted to impressions and ideas, the constituents of which enjoy a descriptive distinctness and completeness. Kant's pseudo problem of a noumenal order of things-in-themselves, having reality behind the phenomena and beyond the scientifically accessible evidence, takes its rise here.

Hume is systematically forced to impoverish not only the meaning of the existential judgment but also the function of repetition of events. He sees in the latter only a means for generating habitual associations, not an opportunity for gaining further rational insight into actual relations. Yet, no explanation is forthcoming for those numerous cases where the habit of constant conjunction is established and expectancy aroused, without any resultant causal inference being drawn between the events so associated. Hume's inflexible notion of reason prevents him from admitting growth on its part. Even empirical understanding is more the victim of the associative mechanism, the "slave of custom," than it is a dominant principle within its own proper order. This antithesis between the rational and the "natural" (another unclarified term) stands in the way of Hume's program of a reform of philosophy. It inclines him to be overcomplacent about stopping his analysis at certain boundaries, and arbitrary in designating certain factors as impressions, to which all acceptable ideas must be traced.

The remaining sections (VIII-XII) stand or fall with the critique of causality. The discussion on freedom, for instance, depends upon the assertion that causality always involves a *necessary* connection between cause and effect. No other sort of bond is compatible with the view that causal inference depends upon a compulsive tendency of the understanding. Nor is Hume in a position to distinguish between various kinds of necessity, since he does not permit reasoning from effect to cause to take its place alongside of reasoning from cause to effect. In the former case, the necessity would only be hypothetical, in the sense that if a contingent being or act does exist, it must have an efficient cause. In regard to agents that can act in the future, physical necessity is required only on condition that ability to foretell the particular future event is indispensable to knowing *that* an entity is a cause. Without begging the issue, Hume cannot extend unmodified the procedure in physical investigations to human agents, where at least the claim to self-determination of certain actions has been made and must be considered in its own right. Similarly, the treatment of miracles rests on the following assumptions: miracles are a *violation* of natural law; the course of nature is now surprisingly immutable and demonstratively knowable; empirical phenomena constitute a closed system of nature, so that the divine wisdom and will cannot be reckoned as further circumstances conditioning certain events in a special way. Patently, these points cannot be discussed apart from the underlying notion of causal knowledge.

JAMES COLLINS

SELECTED BIBLIOGRAPHY

GREIG, J., *David Hume*. Oxford.
LAING, B., *David Hume*. London, Benn.
MAUND, C., *Hume's Theory of Knowledge*. Macmillan.
SMITH, N., *The Philosophy of David Hume*. Macmillan.
STERNFELD, R., "The Unity of Hume's Enquiry Concerning Human Understanding." *The Review of Metaphysics*, vol. 3, no. 2, December 1949.
HUME, David, *An Enquiry Concerning Human Understanding*. Regnery.

Voltaire: Philosophical
Dictionary, *Selections*

THE *Philosophical Dictionary* is the most representative work of the Ferney period, which designates in Voltaire's life the years from 1755 to his death in 1778. A long series of misfortunes had compelled the philosopher to seek refuge in Switzerland. His sojourn in Prussia, begun in 1750 under happy auspices but soon marred by bitter disputes with Frederic II, ended prematurely in 1753. The two erstwhile friends parted irreconcilable enemies. Excluded from the kingdom of France by the hostility of Louis XV, Voltaire found himself in a most difficult situation. The republic of Geneva alone seemed willing to receive him. After a few months of unhappy wandering in Alsace and in the east of France, Voltaire finally reached Geneva at the end of 1753. But there also he was denied the peace and tranquility he ardently sought, for the Protestant pastors of Geneva and Lausanne disapproved of the plays he was giving in the small theater of his home. Voltaire had to take some measures to escape that new persecution.

In 1755 Voltaire bought the estate of Ferney located on the boundaries of Geneva and of France; Ferney enjoyed the right of sovereign domain and thus its owner was rendered quite independent of both Geneva and France. Thus started a period of incredible activity, above all philosophical but also literary and even commercial and industrial. A thousand affairs occupy him there, among the most notable being the rehabilitation of Calas, Sirven and La Barre. But what particularly characterizes the second half of Voltaire's life is the intensification of his struggle against the Church. *"Écrasez l'infame"* ("Crush the infamous one") has become truly the leitmotif of his immense production, extending even to his dramatic works and to his huge correspondence.

Voltaire's method has now changed. With the exception of the *Essay on Customs,* begun earlier, he no longer writes extensive books but only pamphlets, brochures of a few pages, which come out of Ferney by the score. Now relatively secure from the threat of condemnation by the Parliament, whereby many authors of forbidden books were sent to the Bastille, Voltaire dares to attack openly the Church and her dogmas, the Bible and the ecclesiastical hierarchy. The *Sermon of the Fifty,* a direct denunciation of the Bible, inaugurates this campaign, followed shortly by such works as *The Bible at Last Explained, Important Examination of Milord Bolingbroke, The Ignorant Philosopher* and *Questions on Miracles.*

The *Philosophical Dictionary* belongs to the same inspiration. In Berlin, in 1751, Voltaire had submitted to Frederic, who had approved it wholeheartedly, the first article of this work, "Abraham." The *Dictionary* appeared only in 1764 in a volume of 344 pages under the imprint of a London publisher. It contained only seventy-three articles. That number was increased considerably in subsequent editions. The editors of Kehl, in 1792, added to the *Dictionary* all the articles written by Voltaire for the *Encyclopedia* and for the *Dictionary* of the French Academy. This treatment defeated Voltaire's original purpose of writing a pocket dictionary, which would escape detection and could be conveniently carried. The title of the first edition was, in fact, *Dictionnaire Philosophique Portatif,* and Voltaire constantly alludes to it in his correspondence as simply *Le Portatif.*

It would obviously be impossible to attempt to give a coherent analysis of a work composed of articles disposed in alphabetical order, of unequal length and interest. Yet the *Dictionary* is one of the most significant works to come from Voltaire's facile pen. Less dogmatic and dry than the *Treatise on Metaphysics,* more original and also less cautious than the *Philosophical Letters,* it is a compendium of all the philosophical ideas scattered and often disguised throughout Voltaire's dramas, short stories, historical works and satirical and lyrical poetry. The *Dictionary* represents also a later and definitive phase of Voltaire's philosophy, which has evolved considerably on some

essential points. Finally, it is the most perfect example of what
has come to be known under the name of "Voltairianism,"
which comprises a body of philosophical teaching, a spirit
and, perhaps more important still, a carefully conceived
method.

The philosophical teaching of Voltaire is composed of few
positive precepts, none of them original. It is a mixture of ideas,
neither organized nor necessarily connected, borrowed indiscriminately from Montaigne, Locke, Condillac, Bayle, Lucretius, Cicero (*De Natura Deorum*) and the English deists. Voltaire follows now the Stoics, particularly Marcus Aurelius and
Seneca, now the Epicureans, both ancient and modern, and
Mandeville, for the elaboration of a very loose code of ethics.
Voltaire's philosophy, which it would be ludicrous to call a system, is essentially a philosophy of reason, not, however, the reasoning reason (*ratio ratiocinans*) of the Scholastics but a rudi-
mentary reason attached only to the sifted evidence of the
senses. It is dominated by a disdain of metaphysics, of authority,
of universal consensus. Like Montaigne, he delights in showing
the vagaries, the contradictions and the obscurities of the teaching of renowned philosophers on questions of major importance. Thus, an almost universal skepticism permeates the
articles of the *Philosophical Dictionary* on all the problems incapable of a simple solution by recourse to ordinary common
sense.

The most fundamental tenet of Voltaire's philosophy, constantly reaffirmed in innumerable passages of his works, is his
belief in the existence of God. This belief, however, is not
founded on the principle of causality arising from the existence
of the world, but rather on a teleological argument based on
the order which reigns in the physical world. (See articles on
"God," "Atheist," "Religion," "Chinese Catechism," etc.) The
existence of God, indeed, is not evident and presents many difficulties, but His nonexistence is an absurd proposition which
is faced with greater difficulties still. The denial of the existence
of God is so repugnant to human reason that there have been
very few authentic atheists in history. Many of those thus accused and condemned for that offense have been innocent victims of an ignorant mob or fanatical magistrates.

But another consideration, and a secondary one, has played

perhaps a decisive role in convincing Voltaire of the necessity
to affirm the existence of God. God is required to maintain the
social order. Belonging by his wealth and his position to the
privileged classes of the eighteenth century, Voltaire feared
that both his wealth and his position would be endangered by
an unruly mob, no longer restrained by the fear of punishment
in the after life. "I would not want to have anything to do with
an atheist prince who would find it to his interest to have me
crushed in a mortar. I am sure that I would be crushed. I would
not want, were I a sovereign, to have anything to do with atheist courtiers whose interest would be to poison me. I would have
to take a counterpoison at random every day. It is then absolutely necessary for the princes and for the people, that the idea
of a supreme Being, creator, governor, who rewards and pun-
ishes, be deeply ingrained in the mind." (Article "Atheist.")
But Voltaire's declaration here, inspired by a social purpose,
goes far beyond what he is prepared to assert on purely metaphysical grounds. For, beyond the mere existence of God, we
know nothing whatever of His nature and His attributes. The
attribute of creator is difficult to reconcile with the eternity of
matter which Voltaire accepts. (Article "Eternity.") God can
hardly be called "governor," except so far as the purely physical
world is concerned, when Voltaire insists on the disorder and
evil of the moral world. (Article "Good.") The function of
rewarding and punishing attributed to God presumes the immortality of soul which Voltaire generally denies. (Article
"Soul.")

Voltaire's theory of knowledge follows closely, here as elsewhere in his works, Locke's *Essay on Human Understanding*.
The article "Sensation," however, owes more than one argument to Condillac's *Treatise on Sensations*, which appeared in
1757. Rejecting scornfully the Cartesian teaching on innate
ideas, Voltaire is an outright sensationalist. All ideas, even
metaphysical, come from the senses (Article "Sensations and
Dreams.") The apparent spiritual nature of ideas does not require a spiritual soul because God, in his omnipotence, may
have given matter the power to think. (Article "Chinese Catechism.") This is the famous theory of the "thinking matter,"
likewise inherited from Locke, which occurs also in the *Treatise
on Metaphysics*. Having thus excluded the necessity of a spirit-

ual soul, Voltaire will call on the testimony of philosophers to show that their teaching on that point is full of confusion. (Article "Soul.") Again, the existence of a spiritual and immortal soul is a matter of faith, not of philosophy. Voltaire proffers also another argument, namely that the constant intervention of God for the creation of each individual soul is undignified and unnecessary.

Perhaps no other philosophical problem puzzled the eighteenth century as much as the problem of good and evil. The optimistic solution exposed in the *Theodicea* of Leibnitz was held in Germany by Wolff, in England by Shaftesbury, Bolingbroke and Pope, and in France by Rousseau. Voltaire himself had first adopted the theories of optimism in the *Treatise on Metaphysics,* the *Discourse in Verse on Man* and possibly, although this is debatable, in *Zadig.* But since the years 1740-1749, he had progressively evolved toward pessimism, which is the philosophy of the *Poem on the Disaster of the City of Lisbon* and of *Candide.* The *Dictionary* restates that position. In the article "Good," he repeats the arguments of the Epicureans: the existence of evil on earth belies either God's goodness or His omnipotence. As for the existence of evil both in the physical and the moral world, Voltaire proves it by the same demonstration so amusingly and wittily used in *Candide,* that is, a realistic description of the injustices and absurdities of man and the sickness to which he falls victim.

The question of free will has also occupied Voltaire, and he shows in the treatment of the problems it involves the same variations and the same levity. He had defended free will in his correspondence with the Prince Royal of Prussia (1735), who attacked it. But he denies it in *The Ignorant Philosopher* and in the articles "Free Will" and "Destiny" in the *Philosophical Dictionary.* Everything happens as a result of immutable laws. The laws of necessity which rule the physical world extend also to the moral world.

Voltaire's ethics, as exposed in the *Dictionary,* consist entirely in his assertion, common to most eighteenth-century philosophers, that virtue has a social foundation and can exist only in a social relationship. "What is virtue?" asks Voltaire. "Kindness toward one's neighbors." (Article "Virtue.") What will become then of theological and cardinal virtues? They will remain in the theological schools. Voltaire excludes thereby individual virtue and religious duties. For, although it is fitting that we should offer God prayers of homage and gratitude, God does not need our prayers, and prayers of petition cannot have any effect. (Article "Glory.")

Such are the most important aspects of Voltaire's philosophy. But Voltairianism means more than that, and it has properly become attached to Voltaire's war against Christianity and all revealed religions. He starts from the principle, already stated in his first drama, *Œdipus* (1718), that all religions owe their origin to the ignorance of the people and to frauds perpetrated upon them by priests. The power of the state, the tyranny of custom have perpetuated them and prevented timid souls from shaking off the shackles. (Articles "Prejudices" and "Idols.") The Christian religion is even more absurd than the others, and Voltaire endeavors to destroy the traditional proofs of its divine origin. He tries to discredit the Bible, and his well-known anti-Semitism is only a means to that end. The Jews were the most abominable, the most ignorant, the most cruel and the poorest people on earth.

A score of articles, either directly or indirectly, on the flimsiest pretexts, repeat these declarations, often mixed with scurrilous comments. (Articles "Anthropophagi," "Circumcision," "Chinese Catechism," "Hell," "Government.") The Jews inherited all their dogmas from the Babylonians or the Egyptians. Moses did not teach the immortality of the soul, which was unknown to the Jews. The Gospels are no more respectable than the Old Testament. (Article "Christianity.") The miracles they relate are not believable and not different from those which are said to have occurred in the pagan religions. (Article "Miracle.") The Prophecies proved to be untrue or are so confused that anything can be read into them. (Article "Messiah.") The testimony of the martyrs is valueless, because there were very few martyrs and most of them were put to death not for their faith but because they defied the legitimate authority of the emperors.

The organization of the Church, her dogmas, discipline, her history are the object of constant and ironical attacks. Most of the arguments developed in the *Essay on Customs* appear in a more concise form in the *Philosophical Dictionary*. Voltaire denies the primacy of Peter and that this apostle ever went to Rome. (Article "Christianity.") Christ never instituted the sacraments, which are an invention of the Church, nor the ecclesiastical hierarchy. The early Fathers took the dogmas from pagan religions or philosophical systems, notably from Platonism. Finally, religious faith, particularly among the Christians, has always been the source of fanaticism, intolerance and superstition.

Voltaire is, then, the authentic precursor of Renan and of the German rationalists of the nineteenth century. Yet, even in his time, there was nothing new in these arguments. They could be found in the *Dictionary* of Bayle, in Fontenelle, Collins, Tindal and Warburton. Voltaire has simply animated these ideas, expressed them in a lively, witty form, in books which could be easily circulated. He has brought exegesis to the level of the common people by excessive and faulty simplifications. A spirit of disrespect, which is the dominant mark of Voltairianism, inspires all his demonstrations.

But Voltaire owes his success even more to the extremely clever and carefully conceived method that he has followed throughout the *Dictionary* as well as in the *Essay on Customs*. He chooses in the Bible some examples of cruelty or immorality, some expressions or images shocking to occidental ears, a realistic passage of Ezechiel, and then he generalizes, and by constant repetition characterizes the Holy Books by these isolated traits. He selects in the history of the Church an immoral or domineering Pope and some unusual example of holiness on the part of a saint and implies, or even declares, that all the Popes have been like Alexander VI and all the saints insane. He brings forcefully to the attention of his readers some minor change in the external organization of the Church, like the institution of the Sacred Curia or a modification in her discipline, such as the requirement of celibacy for her clergy, or even a mere modification in her liturgy, like the substitution of baptism by aspersion for baptism by immersion.

It is then easy to prove that Christ did not create any cardinal, that St. Peter was married, that Christ was baptized in the river Jordan, and to conclude indignantly that the Church has been unfaithful to the teaching of her Founder. He knowingly exaggerates the severity of some precept of the Church and he sentences to hell "a poor man, starved, who will have eaten a piece of salt pork on Friday" or another who will have worked on Sunday to save his harvest. He confuses the dogmatic teaching of the Church with popular beliefs or practices, particularly during the Middle Ages, which may well have smacked of superstition. Such ridiculous arguments, presented with an appearance of great sincerity, and again constantly repeated, are bound to create either a conviction or at least a suspicion that the Church has not been spared any human frailty and cannot be divinely founded.

Voltaire put all the qualities of his mind and imagination to the service of the cause he had embraced. His wit is sparkling and his irony biting. He is indeed the "genius of mockery." Nothing is sacred to him, and his sarcasm spares no man and no belief. The following example of his method is an enlightening one. Explaining the promises of God to the descendants of Ismael, he says: "The fact is that the race of Ismael has been more favored by God than the race of Jacob. Both have indeed produced thieves; but the Arab thieves have been prodigiously superior to the Jewish thieves. (Article "Abraham.") Sometimes he feigns a complete and humble submissiveness to the decisions of the Church: "Sacred consultors of modern Rome, illustrious and infallible theologians, no one has more respect than I have for your divine decisions." (Article "Glory.") Then he will proceed to demonstrate the absurdities of the theological teaching—which he accepts, nevertheless, with reverence. He assumes occasionally the role of a defender of the faith. He then puts in the mouth of his supposed opponents a recital of the so-called contradictions—"enormous errors of geography, chronology, physics and even common sense"—of the Bible and answers piously that the Bible has not been given us to teach us history but only faith and humility. (Articles "Census" and "Contradictions.")

Voltaire's attacks were not left unanswered, and several serious scholars had the courage to point out the numerous faults of etymology, the false quotations, the unfounded affirmations so frequent in his books and particularly in the *Philosophical Dictionary*. The Abbé Guénée, in a remarkable work entitled *Letters of Some Portuguese, German and Polish Jews to M. de Voltaire,* used Voltaire's weapons of wit and irony combined with a profound science and a thorough knowledge, lacking in Voltaire, of the Hebraic and Greek tongues, to point out the philosopher's innumerable errors. On the Protestant side, the celebrated entomologist Haller opposed the testimony of the early Fathers to Voltaire's declaration that the Gospels were unknown until St. Justin.

The *Philosophical Dictionary*, largely devoted to religious controversy, contains also some articles dealing with philosophical and social subjects or literary criticism. The first are rarely free from antireligious allusions, and they further exemplify Voltaire's general skepticism. His social ideas, however, are the most constructive and reveal a Voltaire generally conservative as far as the fundamental organization of society is concerned, but enlightened and progressive on points of law and customs and intent upon correcting glaring abuses. He does not share Rousseau's illusions that equality among men is natural. (Article "Equality.") He discusses the various forms of government, concluding wisely that they are not equally good for different classes of society. (Articles "States" and "Government.") Above all, he demands liberty of the press in an age when the censor held absolute power, the alleviation of the crushing taxes leveled against the peasants, the improvement of criminal procedure. Voltaire's esthetic principles, which show a considerable evolution since his early adhesion to classical principles, bear also the marks of his relativistic philosophy. There is no supreme beauty in art any more than there is a supreme good in ethics. The notion of beauty is varied and contradictory among nations and, within the same nation, changes with the times. (Article "Beautiful.")

The *Philosophical Dictionary* was condemned by the French Parliament in 1765 to be torn up and publicly burned. It was also condemned by Rome and the Consistory of Geneva. When the book was found in the library of the Chevalier de la Barre, sentenced to death for blasphemy, Voltaire became thoroughly alarmed. He begged his friends, particularly D'Alembert, to deny vehemently that he was the author of that "impious and abominable" book. Voltaire has been reliably informed that this "diabolical" *Dictionary* is from the pen of a M. Dubut, a theological student in Holland! He attributes brazenly one article to Abauzit; another to Polier, a Protestant pastor in

Geneva, the article "Hell" to the Bishop of Gloucester, Warburton. Nobody, of course, believed him, for the indubitable marks of his authorship identified its origin all too clearly.

Thus, the inclusion of the *Philosophical Dictionary* among the Great Books would call for some necessary distinction. A great book, indeed, if judged by its tremendous success during Voltaire's time, throughout the nineteenth century and even into our own period. A great book by its qualities of style, of wit, clarity and simplicity of exposition. But by its decided limitations in historical, philosophical and, even more, theological knowledge; by its disregard for the truth, its total incapacity to appreciate greatness in any form, particularly the greatness of sacrifice and heroism, the *Philosophical Dictionary* hardly deserves to be called great. It has sown the seeds of revolt against ecclesiastical authority and has fathered a generation presumptuous in its conviction that religion is the enemy of reason and of science, a state of mind admirably typified in the unbearable personage created by Flaubert and henceforth known as M. Homais.

FERNAND VIAL

SELECTED BIBLIOGRAPHY

The Portable Voltaire, edited and with an Introduction by Ben Ray Redman. Viking.
DESNOIRETERRES, *Voltaire et la Société Française au XVIIIe Siècle.*
TORREY, Norman, *The Spirit of Voltaire.* Columbia.
VIAL, F., *Voltaire.* Paris, Didier.
VOLTAIRE, François de, *Philosophical Dictionary,* selections. Regnery.

Darwin: The Origin of Species, Chapters 1-6, 15

"THERE IS grandeur in this view of life, with its several powers, having been originally breathed by the Creator into a few forms or into one; and that, whilst this planet has gone cycling on according to the fixed law of gravity, from so simple a beginning endless forms most beautiful and most wonderful have been, and are being evolved." These are the concluding words of one of the most important books published in modern times —*The Origin of Species* by Charles Darwin. (The complete title is *The Origin of Species by means of natural selection or the preservation of favored races in the struggle for life.*) They are moving words and have the flavor of St. Augustine about them. What manner of man was the author?

Charles Darwin was born on February 12, 1809, at Shrewsbury, England. He was the grandson of the physician-natural philosopher, Erasmus Darwin, who had published a speculative tract on evolution entitled *Zoonomia*. His father, Robert, also a physician, was married to Susannah Wedgwood, daughter of the famed porcelain manufacturer.

His early schooling was typically English, with much emphasis on the classical languages. Later he was sent to Edinburgh to study medicine. As he himself admitted, he was bored by lectures in anatomy, and the attendance at surgical operations in those preanesthetic days shocked his sensitive nature. Abruptly, he terminated his medical course.

He then decided to pursue the study of theology at Cambridge and took his B.A. degree in 1831. He considered his formal work at Cambridge tiresome and a waste of time. Fortunately, however, he associated with friends who enjoyed outdoor life and sports, especially hunting. He made various nat-ural-history collections in competition with his friends. In spare moments he learned botany from Professor Henslow, with whom he had struck up an acquaintance. He also assisted Professor Adam Sedgwick on several geologizing expeditions and from this master obtained a thorough grounding in geology.

In 1831, also, he was offered the unpaid position of natural-ist aboard the *Beagle,* a naval vessel scheduled to circumnavi-gate the world on a cartographical voyage. To accept the post meant to postpone his training for the ministry. His father at first refused him permission to go, but through the interven-tion of his uncle, Josiah Wedgwood, the coveted permission was finally obtained.

The voyage of the *Beagle,* which was originally planned to last two years, extended for five. It was without question the turning point of Darwin's life, for it determined his lifelong career and supplied much of the factual material on which *The Origin of Species* is based.

The daily sieges of seasickness, the marvels of nature as revealed in South America, the Galapagos, and in the South Pacific are dramatic stories which cannot be considered here. In passing, however, it should be pointed out that *The Voyage of the Beagle,* by Darwin, is one of the classic travelogs in English. It is one of the volumes in The Harvard Classics. For a more complete understanding of Darwin as a naturalist and observer it is recommended that *The Voyage* be read.

After returning to England, he published some of the scien-tific results of the expedition—contributions which established him as a respected scientist. In 1839 he married his first cousin Emma Wedgwood, and three years later he and his wife moved to Down, Kent. For the rest of his life he suffered ill health. It was only through the loving care and organization of his wife that he continued his works in a relatively secluded atmos-phere.

He had begun gathering data on the problem of species in 1837. For some twenty years he collected and evaluated his notes. In 1858 he was surprised to receive from Alfred Russell Wallace, a professional collector of natural-history objects, a manuscript which developed the identical theory upon which he had been working for so long. Darwin sent the manuscript to Lyell, the high priest of contemporary geology, and suggested its publication. Lyell was familiar with Darwin's work and demanded that he prepare an abstract of Darwin's own findings. Both papers were read at the same meeting of the Linnean Society and were published together in the *Journal of the Linnean Society*, July 1, 1858. The following year Darwin brought out *The Origin of Species*.

He died in 1882 and was buried next to Newton in Westminster Abbey, an indication of the high esteem in which he was held by contemporaries.

In order to understand the profound effect which Darwin's *The Origin of Species* had on the contemporary world, it is essential to feel the pulse of the times. Why did Darwin's theory meet with such overwhelming acclaim, whereas Lamarck's was jeered at and the author branded as a doddering mystic?

Some loose thinkers have suggested that the Church in France opposed Lamarckism and dealt it a death blow. Historical facts deny this supposition. The real answer lies in the romantic natural philosophy of the times. It was not interested in material development and consequently it was indifferent to Lamarckism.

Lamarck assumed that living organisms vary as a result of changes in their "needs" brought about by great changes of the natural environment. He developed his thesis in a work published in 1809 with the elaborate title, translated from the French: *Zoological philosophy or an exposition of considerations bearing on the natural history of animals, on the diversity of their organization and the faculties that they derive from it, on the physical causes that maintain life in them and that give rise to the movements executed by them, and finally, on causes some of which produce feeling and others intelligence, in the case of those endowed with the latter.* Protoplasm, which was infused by the Creator with the tendency to variation, in each generation moves toward greater complexity of structure, largely in response to environmental changes. The use of a structure results in its increase in size and importance, whereas permanent disuse results in eventual disappearance of the organ. All these gains and losses are "preserved by reproduction to the new individuals which arise"; this latter is the concept of the inheritance of acquired characteristics.

The continued neglect of Lamarck through the nineteenth century probably stems from the vitalistic tinge to his theory and from his invoking a Creator. Of course, today, most biologists have no doubts as to the falsity of Lamarck's theory.

The liberalism of the nineteenth century was characterized by belief in the natural goodness of mankind and in the dogma of the greatest happiness for the greatest number as the end of life. This happiness was equated with material welfare, which was assumed to follow if men were left to care for themselves with no direction or regulation. "Human life thus came to be regarded as a dominion of impersonal forces guiding humanity with the necessity of a natural law toward better times, if only they were allowed to operate freely."

Darwin raised evolution to a law which governs all life. It was just the pillar that "intellectuals" of that age were seeking. No wonder the seed which Darwin planted took such deep roots.

Finally, Thomas Robert Malthus (1766-1835) had published his famous *The Principle of Population,* in which he develops the thesis that humankind increases in numbers geometrically while the means of subsistence increase only arithmetically. From this arises a bitter struggle for subsistence; vice, starvation, disease and wars manage to wipe out the poorest in the population, so that the natural increase is restricted. This thesis gave Darwin his basis for the concept of "the struggle for existence."

Hence it is that the failure of Lamarckism left fallow ground which was turned by Malthus and fertilized by nineteenth-century materialism, so that the seedling of Darwin's theory burst into unnatural bloom—more luxuriant than its intrinsic worth merited.

The Origin of Species is one long argument. It can be divided into five logical parts:

(1) The first four chapters, in which artificial selection by man and natural selection through struggle for existence are explained.

(2) The fifth chapter, which describes the laws of variation and represents causes for modifications.

(3) The next five chapters, which present the difficulties in the way of accepting evolution.

(4) The following three chapters (or four, depending on the edition), which give the evidence for evolution.

(5) Recapitulation and summary of the entire work.

The thesis which Darwin develops is simple. Every organism is different from every other. What is the origin of these variations? On the basis of the hypothesis suggested by Malthus, Darwin postulated that for all animals reproductive potentialities are markedly greater than the capacity of this planet to support the individuals produced. Vast numbers of organisms perish. Those with desirable characteristics (the fittest) are selected impersonally by nature (natural selection) to survive. The unfit and many of those with indifferent characters are eliminated from the population, whereas the fit transmit their characters to future generations.

In an attempt to explain the inheritance of variations without becoming wholeheartedly Lamarckian, Darwin turned to the idea of pangenesis.

According to this hypothesis, every unit or cell of the body throws off gemmules or undeveloped atoms, which are transmitted to the offspring of both sexes, and are multiplied by self-division. They may remain undeveloped during successive generations; and their development into units or cells like those from which they were derived, depends on their affinity for, and union with other units or cells previously developed in the due order of growth.

In this connection, it is interesting to note that Aristotle, in his *De Generatione Animalium,* reviewed the general theory of pangenesis and discarded it as not in conformity with the observed facts. Modern researches in the science of genetics leave no room for such an hypothesis. In fact, as Mivart pointed out long ago, it is "almost the explanation of *obscurum per obscurius.*"

Aside from the intrinsic deficiencies of *The Origin,* it did three things which make it one of the milestones along the course of human thought:

(1) In a very persuasive fashion it presented the concept of evolution "as a general principle in the history of life." So force-

ful was the mass of evidence assembled in the book that general acceptance of the principle of evolution followed.

(2) It presented a partial explanation of the mechanism of evolution.

(3) It suggested a theory to explain adaptation in nature— the theory of natural selection.

Was Darwin unable to grasp the meaning of Lamarck? Did he misrepresent him through jealousy or ambition? It is impossible to decide at this late date. In either event, the facts indicate a serious defect of character or mentality in the man whose *The Origin of Species* gave rise to a mystical cult known as Darwinism.

Mivart pointed out in 1870 that there are certain strong difficulties in the way of accepting the theory of evolution as outlined by Darwin. These difficulties still obtain today. He sums them up as follows: Natural Selection does not and cannot explain the origin of incipient stages of useful variations; long before the useful structure can exert a favorable effect on the individual's struggle for life, it is preserved and "selected" before natural selection can conceivably operate. Moreover, there is evidence that some variations appear suddenly and not gradually. The actual data available to Darwin supported only a limited variability to species. The absence of so many transitional fossil forms which might be expected to exist suggests sudden and not gradual variations. These criticisms of the Darwinian theory hold true today.

Interestingly enough, Mivart did not deny the evolution of organic forms; he wrote, "to support the doctrine that these species have been evolved by ordinary *natural laws* (for the most unknown) controlled by the subordinate action of 'Natural Selection,' and at the time to remind some that there is and can be absolutely nothing in physical science which forbids them to regard those natural laws as acting with the Divine concurrence and in obedience to a creative fiat originally imposed on the primeval Cosmos, 'in the beginning, by its Creator, its Upholder, and its Lord.' "

Fair-minded biologists today hold that Darwin's emphasis on natural selection alone was wrong. His masses of evidence did not in truth carry his point. It has been shown by Sewall

Wright that all the effects attributed to natural selection can be brought about in limited population groups through the operation of the laws of probability within a framework of Mendelian inheritance. Today natural selection, as Darwin understood it, is considered only one (and not too important a one either) of many forces operating in the genesis of species. Moreover, modern biology is completely at a loss concerning *how* natural selection works; apparently it does function in evolution, but its mode of operation is one of the major fields of study for modern evolutionary biologists.

The profound influence of Darwin's *The Origin of Species* is most difficult to explain on several counts. Certainly his thesis, as presented, was incorrect. His facts could be and were readily explained by other theories than natural selection of the fittest.

Darwin did not originate the concept of organic evolution, although many of his interpreters have implied as much and too many of the uninitiated are convinced that he did. He is not the first to suggest a theory to explain evolution, but his explanation took hold and stimulated extensive and intensive researches by both those who were *pro* and those *con* natural selection.

Finally, it should be remembered that, when *The Origin* was written, it was necessary to demonstrate that species are mutable. Darwin chose his words and manner of presenting arguments primarily with the view to convincing many doubters of the fact of specific mutability. Such a procedure would not be the most effective for demonstrating the value of natural selection. Consequently, today, when the mutability of species is universally accepted, Darwin's arguments in favor of natural selection appear weaker than they actually are. Moreover, in starting with *species,* Darwin selected one of the most uncertain and confusing concepts in biology. A biological species cannot be defined with any degree of precision; there are probably as many ideas of what constitutes a species as there are biologists. Hence, Darwin chose to show variations in a category of animals the limits of which are still uncertain—a well-nigh impossible task.

The publication of *The Origin of Species* started the growth of a cult of Darwinism which proclaimed its views with religious fervor. The banner bearers for the new cult were so carried away by their enthusiasm that they often failed to respect the facts. The great Huxley, during his controversies with Mivart, misquoted the latter, attributed to him statements never uttered, and used tricks of syntax and punctuation which remind one of present-day Communist apologias. Strangely enough, Darwin, ordinarily a kind man, made no attempt to dissociate himself from this intellectual irresponsibility; and Huxley merely ignored critics who reminded him of his fallacies.

The German zoologist, Haeckel, actually faked scientific illustrations to add support to his recapitulation theory which he hoped would finally clinch the controversy for Darwinism. One wonders at the tolerance with which his misrepresentations were viewed when he was finally exposed.

Darwin himself did not enter the lists but he called upon numerous friends and colleagues to joust for him. His aloofness from the raging controversies has lent a false aura of dignity to the man. To many, his stature would have increased had he admitted his changing views and his debt to Lamarck, and had he called to task those who went beyond the bounds of integrity and good taste in promulgating his theory.

In spite of all this, it must be admitted that Darwin's *The Origin of Species* changed the course of thinking and doing in biology, social studies, economics and cultural activities. In biology, he aroused interest in the geographical distribution of animals; he can probably be called the founder of ecology, for he tried to bring out the fundamental significance of the relation between an organism and its environment. He influenced biologists to look at organisms not as *being* but as *becoming;* he fostered the dynamic rather than the static concept of life.

Before publication of *The Origin of Species* the science of biology was in a rather disorganized state. Darwin's book led biologists to interpret the mass of data on life, then and later available, in terms of an evolutionary concept. Such an interpretation made sense out of the previous chaos and resulted in tremendous advances in basic biology.

In sociology and economics his influence, although profound, was not so fortunate. His emphasis on the struggle for survival gave a semblance of scientific respectability to unlimited exploitation of men and resources. His thesis that the fittest survive was soon amended to equate "fittest" with "best." His sociological interpreters, in wild abandon, pushed forward the view that the best and most desirable win out in any struggle; they thought of evolution primarily in terms of struggle. Since struggle, strife, violence are biologically fundamental to the nature of animals, including man, according to this interpretation, the class warfare of Marxism and the political warfare of Prussianism found apparent justification in the theory proposed by Darwin. Add to this an irrational, cultish fanaticism proclaiming that the best survive, and one is led to the logical outcome, to the horrors of Buchenwald, to genocide.

Karl Marx was a great admirer of Darwin. He never personally met the scientist. His social theories were well developed before he read Darwin's works. Immediately he realized that Darwinian natural selection gave apparent scientific support to his economic system. The followers of Marx still refer to Darwin as scientific authority for their views.

It is quite probably true that Darwin did not foresee the depressing effects of his hypotheses once they were interpreted by men of evil. He did not have a wide-ranging mind and in many ways he was intellectually dull, especially in matters philosophical. One is led to suggest, however, that men who propose theories should also emphasize the boundaries beyond which the theories may not be pushed. Darwin never even hinted that there were limits to his theory in explaining the natural order of things. That neglect marks a serious lack of intellectual responsibility; for men should be held accountable, in part at least, for the damage done by their ideas.

The Origin of Species and the cult of Darwinism have aroused much undue concern for religion among some Christians. As Canon Dorlodot so well points out: "But why, then, has it been possible to exploit Darwinism so successfully against religion, if not because there have not been lacking Catholic authors who have compromised the Christian religion in falsely representing it as irreconcilable with scientific theories?"

Why this situation should be so is not clear, for, says Dorlo-dot, "one cannot find in Holy Scripture, interpreted according to the rules of Catholic exegesis, any convincing argument against the theory of natural evolution—even that of absolute evolution."

Consequently, the Christian appraisal of *The Origin of Species* involves a consideration of the objective truth of the work and an evaluation of the effects of the theory on the course of human thought.

The wealth of data reported by Darwin did much to estab-lish the *fact* of organic evolution; today, all biologists of any importance are convinced that organic evolution is a princi-ple of nature adequately demonstrated. The establishment of this fact is due in large part to Darwin's work. The *mechanism* of evolution is still an open question. Natural selection, as Darwin thought of it, is completely inadequate to explain evolution even at the species level. Today, natural selection is known to be only one of the many factors involved in evolu-tion; the mode of action of selection is by no means clear.

Nordenskiöld sums up the status of Darwin quite satisfac-torily: "To raise the theory of selection, as has often been done, to the rank of a 'natural law' comparable in value with the law of gravity established by Newton is, of course, quite irrational, as time has already shown; Darwin's theory of the origin of species was long ago abandoned. Other facts established by Darwin are all of second-rate value. But if we measure him by his influence on the general cultural development of human-ity, then the proximity of his grave to Newton's is fully justi-fied."

CHARLES G. WILBER

SELECTED BIBLIOGRAPHY

DORLODOT, Canon, *Darwinism and Catholic Thought.* Kenedy.
MORE, L. T., *The Dogma of Evolution.* Princeton University.
NORDENSKIÖLD, E., *The History of Biology.* Tudor.
SEARS, P. B., *Charles Darwin the Naturalist as a Cultural Force.* Scribners.
SIMPSON, G. G., "The Problem of Plan and Purpose in Nature." *The Scientific Monthly,* Vol. 64, pp. 481-495.
SIMPSON, G. G., *The Meaning of Evolution.* Yale University. (Part III, "Evolu-tion, Humanity and Ethics," is of little value; it consists of illogical specula-tions in a field not familiar to the author. Parts I and II, on the other hand, are excellent and well worth reading.)
DARWIN, Charles, *The Origin of Species,* Chapters 1-6, 15. Regnery.

Dostoyevsky: The Brothers Karamazov, *Part II, Book 5, Chapter 5;* *Book 6, Chapters 1-3*

AMONG Fyodor Dostoyevsky's novels, each of which is a masterpiece in its own right, *The Brothers Karamazov* is doubtlessly the most mature. The last fictional work he wrote, it was published in 1879-1880, shortly preceding his death in 1881. The novel was composed at a time when the author's powers as a writer, psychologist and thinker had reached their full development. *The Brothers Karamazov,* moreover, belongs to the flowering years of Russian nineteenth-century literature; thanks to such writers as Dostoyevsky and Tolstoy, this literature not only is representative of the best of Russian culture, but also has become part of the common cultural treasure of the contemporary world.

For all these reasons, *The Brothers Karamazov* is one of the most important books ever written in Russia. And it has even a greater significance, if we consider it from another angle— the religious one; for it can truly be said that Dostoyevsky's fullest religious message is contained in the pages of this work, especially in the selections chosen here for inclusion in the Great Books program.

In order to grasp this message, let us first say a few words about Dostoyevsky's own life and religious experience. He was the son of a petty medical official employed in a poorhouse in Moscow, and his family setting was drab and joyless. Highstrung and oversensitive, the boy experienced personal poverty—due to his miserly and corrupt father—and observed extreme destitution and misery among his father's unfortunate patients. Pity for the "insulted and injured" awoke early in his heart, and it was to them that he dedicated his first novel, *Poor Folk,* published in 1846, when he was twenty-five. This work, though understandably immature, already revealed the qualities of genuine human sympathy, emotion and psychological depth which later grew to form an integral part of Dostoyevsky's creative genius.

Poor Folk brought the young author immediate success and even fame. But this exceptionally brilliant literary debut was followed by disaster. Accused of participating in revolutionary activities (in which actually he was not directly implicated), Dostoyevsky was arrested, imprisoned and condemned to death. He was reprieved at the last moment, as he stood on the scaffold, his sentence having been commuted to hard labor in Siberia. He spent four years as a convict in chains, and when released, was made to serve as a private under strict discipline in a Siberian regiment. Only in 1859, ten years after his arrest, was he allowed to return to his home and resume his literary career.

The four years spent as a convict among other convicts (mostly criminals of common law, robbers and murderers) and the subsequent period of military service, in conditions of great hardships and humiliation, had a deep effect, both physical and moral, on Dostoyevsky. As far back as his youth he had been affected with epilepsy, and he now suffered serious relapses of the disease. He remained a victim of this affliction to the end of his life, and he describes the dread impact of the disorder in his novels: both Prince Myshkine in *The Idiot* and Smerdyakov in *The Brothers Karamazov* are epileptics. Needless to say, life in the Siberian labor camp was fraught with extreme suffering. And Dostoyevsky also witnessed there the suffering of others, such as the ruthless corporal punishment which resulted in mutilation and even death and which he later realistically pictured in *House of the Dead.*

But it was also during these tragic years that Dostoyevsky fully awakened to the reality of spiritual life. He had been religiously inclined in his childhood, but, like most young Russian intellectuals of his generation, he had been assailed by doubts and stirred to rebellion under the influence of atheistic and materialistic teachings. How far these teachings might have led him astray is a matter of speculation. But on his way to the labor camp in Siberia a providential meeting determined his spiritual rebirth. A lady devoted to works of mercy visited the convicts on their weary trek through Siberia and gave Dostoyevsky a tiny volume, which became his constant companion. It was the Gospels. Dostoyevsky read and reread it constantly. It was the only book permitted by prison authorities.

More than that, of course, it was the only book which could relieve him of all the terrors, hopelessness and bitterness of prison life. The French writer André Gide has stressed the important point that the discovery of the Gospels was the main influence in Dostoyevsky's entire existence, infinitely more important than all the outward events recorded in his biography. Through the teaching of Christ, Dostoyevsky not only learned the meaning of his own suffering and accepted it, he learned to understand fully the suffering of others, of which he had already an intuition as reflected in *Poor Folk*. He learned to love his neighbor as himself, to share his neighbor's cross; he learned the meaning of true solidarity, which is Christian brotherhood binding together all men—good and bad, the just and the sinners, the criminal and the innocent—since all are children of the Father, who is One.

Something else which Dostoyevsky learned during his convict years was the supreme value of freedom. Fettered and caged as if he were a dangerous beast, he ardently aspired toward the world that lay beyond his prison bars. After his release, he eloquently described the joy he felt when the prison blacksmith removed the chains from his feet. This physical freedom, which he experienced with all the intensity of his turbulent nature, became the symbol of *spiritual* freedom—the freedom of men who are children of God, liberated through Christ. Spiritual freedom—the dignity of the human person redeemed by the Cross—became in later years one of Dostoyevsky's essential themes. So did human solidarity, born from communion of all men in Christ. Truly speaking, Dostoyevsky was released from the yoke of servitude and hate long before the prison blacksmith broke his chains. This is why these two major notes, freedom in Christ and love in Christ, constantly resound throughout Dostoyevsky's entire work and reach their fullest accord in *The Brothers Karamazov*.

Let us now make a rapid survey of this great book. Ours can

only be a brief commentary, since the novel contains some 900 pages and presents not only an intricate plot but also a complex psychological, philosophical and religious pattern. Human passions flare and human ideologies clash with equal violence, reminding one, as has been often pointed out (for instance by Berdyaev), of a cosmic upheaval. And yet, if we are concerned with the plot alone, we shall note that the entire action of *The Brothers Karamazov* embraces no more than a few days and that the climax is reached in a few hours.

The three brothers Karamazov, Dmitry, Ivan and Alyesha; their father Fyodor Pavlovich, and their half brother Smerdyakov, are among Dostoyevsky's unforgettable characters. Old Fyodor Pavlovich Karamazov, corrupt, cynical, carried away by senile passions, is hated by his two older sons, Dmitry and Ivan (no doubt a reflection of Dostoyevsky's own conflict with his father). Dmitry is reckless, generous, moved by elemental forces and passionately in love with the woman his father courts. Ivan is noble-minded, intellectually inclined, the rationalist—the "Euclidean mind," as Dostoyevsky calls him. Both, for various reasons and guided by different impulses, secretly desire their father's death. Old Karamazov is murdered in mysterious circumstances. Ivan is morally responsible for his death; Dmitry, indicted on circumstantial evidence, is arrested and convicted. Actually, the murder had been perpetrated by Smerdyakov, old Karamazov's illegitimate son, a degenerate and an epileptic, who had been reduced to the status of a servant and who has killed in order to rob the rich and miserly old man.

Thus, Dostoyevsky treats the psychology of murder and parricide both in its most direct and brutal form and in the more subtle, hidden aspects of criminal intentions and aspirations. Smerdyakov hangs himself; Ivan, who alone knows the truth, is the victim of brain fever, which renders him unable to testify. Dmitry, who is innocent, will be the one to expiate. This is indeed a somber ending, reminding us of ancient Greek tragedy or of Shakespeare's final scenes. At the same time *The Brothers Karamazov* contains all the elements of a mystery story, which can be admirably adapted to stage or screen (as has been done by the Moscow Art Theater, and by various motion-picture producers).

But we are here concerned, as pointed out above, with the religious message conveyed by *The Brothers Karamazov*. This religious message is reflected in the words and deeds of the youngest brother, Alyesha, the angelic youth—whom we might call Dostoyevsky's last-born character, the one whom he no doubt loved most, since he gave him the name of his own son who died in early childhood. Alyesha has no part in the family conflict; his "conversation is in heaven." He is a meek and gentle youth, a novice of a nearby monastery. His spiritual director and beloved teacher is the old monk Father Zossima, of whom we shall further speak. Alyesha is a Christlike character and a mystic, and he is at the same time capable of grasping life's realities with direct and supernatural wisdom. He seeks to be a mediator between his two elder brothers and old man Karamazov, and though he does not succeed in preventing the murder, he does much to guide Dmitry and Ivan through the dark night of their tragedy. Alyesha is the incarnation of Dostoyevsky's deepest mystic aspirations.

However, the gentle novice does not alone represent the author's religious philosophy. The proud and rebellious Ivan, who seeks Christ with his reason yet cannot accept Him with his heart, also gives utterance to some of Dostoyevsky's profound views. Thus it is Ivan, conversing with his young brother Alyesha, who raises a series of metaphysical problems of extreme importance; and it is Ivan who relates to the little novice his story of "The Grand Inquisitor," which is one of the chapters chosen for the Great Books discussion.

For the Catholic reader, this chapter may at first glance appear extremely disturbing, since the story presents a Torquemada and is, moreover, told by Ivan, who is prejudiced against Catholicism. Nevertheless, Catholic critics well versed in Dostoyevsky have overcome this initial painful impression to look into the heart of this extraordinary story. Romano Guardini has discussed the "Inquisitor" at length, and Father Henri de Lubac, S.J., in his *Drama of Atheist Humanism*, has called Ivan's story one of the most famous pages in world literature.

"The Grand Inquisitor" is a fantasy, a "poem" (in prose), as Ivan calls it, which actually bears no resemblance to historical *facts*. The "poem" has, however, a historical *setting*, and a most dramatic one, since it is laid in Seville in the days of the Spanish Inquisition. Christ, Ivan tells his brother, chose that time to return among his people. He appears at the Cathedral of Seville; He comes "softly, unobserved," and yet "everyone recognizes Him." The people flock around Him lovingly, and soon His miracles attract the attention of the Grand Inquisitor himself. He, too, of course, recognizes Christ; but instead of bowing before Him, he proudly confronts Him with his own power. The Grand Inquisitor is an old man and has spent many years of his life wielding unbounded authority. Now he feels that this authority will be taken away from him. So he has Christ arrested and thrown into prison. First he wants to burn his victim, but later decides to exile Him, forbidding Him ever to return. Before sending the prisoner away, the Grand Inquisitor visits Him at night in his cell and in a long soliloquy explains his motives.

Ivan Karamazov, relating the story, stresses that the Grand Inquisitor is no hater of humanity; on the very contrary, he seeks to benefit mankind and sincerely believes that he has succeeded in doing so. He has installed a system of slavery, which the masses blindly obey, while a few thousand men have to bear all the responsibilities of power. In this system men live and die peacefully, according to rules drawn out by the "elect." To them is thus insured what seems their bread, both material and spiritual, but they are unaware of the fact that they receive stones instead of bread. They are unaware that they have been deprived of the God-given attribute of free will.

No commentator, no matter to what church he belongs, will seriously believe that "The Grand Inquisitor" is an attack against Catholic doctrine or against the true spirit of the Catholic Church. What Ivan seeks to represent are the distortions and abuses of power which unfortunately exist in all churches, in so far as their purely human institutions are concerned. For that matter, Russian commentators, among them Nicholas Berdyaev, have stressed that "The Grand Inquisitor" was directed in part against Russian Orthodox ecclesiastical authority; in Dostoyevsky's time the Russian Church had been distorted by the fanatical Pobyedonostzev, the Procurator of the Holy Synod. This lay official had become one of the most influential men in the Czar's cabinet; just as does Ivan's Inquisitor, he sincerely believed that he was serving the interests of the Russian people, while stifling their religious freedom.

But even this interpretation of "The Grand Inquisitor" as a disguised attack on Pobyedonostzev would limit the scope of this famous piece to a political and religious situation which now belongs to the irrevocable past. No one except a few aged survivors of the Czarist regime remembers the dread Procurator, and the Russian religious problem presents itself today in an entirely different light. Yet "The Grand Inquisitor" has lost nothing of its impact. On the contrary, the "poem" has grown in significance, and no contemporary religious thinker can pass it by without offering his reflections concerning Ivan's story. This is due to the fact that, beyond all other considerations which moved Dostoyevsky to write "The Grand Inquisitor," there was the ultimate design to raise in these pages the entire problem of spiritual freedom.

It is this problem precisely, and the dramatic way it is presented by Ivan Karamazov, which so deeply moves the contemporary reader. Perhaps we see in these prophetic pages something of our own twentieth-century world. For in the frightful figure of the imposter, "correcting," as he says, "the work of Christ," in this false benefactor of humanity who turns the God-Man out of the city we recognize the totalitarian dictator, the Nazi and the Communist who kills the souls of men in order to make them "happy."

In the three chapters of Book 6, also selected for the Great Books, we issue forth from the Grand Inquisitor's stifling prison (how much is Ivan himself involved in this godless utopia?) into a gentle and radiant world (the free world of Alyesha.) These three chapters are specially dedicated to Alyesha's teacher, Father Zossima, the "Pater Seraphicus," as Ivan half sarcastically, half enviously calls the old religious. This section of the novel is entitled "A Russian Monk"; it represents, one might say, a *summa* of Russian asceticism. We should not, of course, consider these pages of *The Brothers Karamazov* a piece of official Russian Orthodox ascetic teaching. Dostoyevsky, not being an ecclesiastic or, strictly speaking, a Russian Orthodox theologian, was not in conscience bound to expound these official views.

However, the "Pater Seraphicus" is not merely a fruit of the author's imagination; he is entirely true to type and to the highest type of Russian spirituality. This remarkable character was created by Dostoyevsky according to the models offered him by Russian hagiography. Indeed, Dostoyevsky had a special devotion to Saint Tykhon of Zadonsk, a great Russian ascetic of the eighteenth century. He had had, moreover, the opportunity of studying Russian monastic life and had taken a monk of the Optyna Monastery, famous for its spiritual directors, as the direct prototype of Father Zossima. This is why Father Zossima's "exhortations" are true to the deepest spirit of Russian Orthodoxy. They represent the authentic mystic strain which nourished Russian popular piety and was in complete contrast with Pobyedonostzev's State "religion."

Moreover, there is much in these chapters which, as we have said, reflects Dostoyevsky's own religious experience. It was in the prison camp that the future author of *The Brothers Karamazov* first heard the glad tidings of man's liberation through Divine Love. This genuine experience later inspired Zossima's "exhortations."

"Love a man even in his sin," the Russian monk taught on the eve of his death, while Alyesha eagerly listened to his words, "for that is the semblance of Divine Love and is the highest love on earth. . . . There is only one means of salvation, then take yourself and make yourself responsible for all men's sins. . . . As soon as you make yourself sincerely responsible for everything and for all men, you will see at once that it is really so and that you are to blame for everyone and for all things."

Human solidarity, not founded on pride in man's own virtues, but on a communion through and with Christ—such is finally Dostoyevsky's religious message. In these pages, Dostoyevsky writes less as a novelist (although he was a novelist of genius) than as a visionary bringing us out of the purgatory of men's passions, doubts and struggles into the triumphant peace of the Kingdom of God.

HELENE ISWOLSKY

SELECTED BIBLIOGRAPHY

DOSTOYEVSKY, Fyodor, *The Brothers Karamazov,* translated by Constance Garnett. Random House (The Modern Library).

BERDYAEV, Nicholas, *Dostoyeysky,* translated by Donald Attwater. Sheed & Ward.

TROYAT, Henri, *Firebrand* (a life of Dostoyevsky), translated by N. Guterman. Roy.

LUBAC, Henri de, S.J., *The Drama of Atheist Humanism,* translated by Edith M. Riley. Sheed & Ward.

TYKHON, Saint, *His Life and Letters,* translated by Helene Iswolsky in *A Treasury of Russian Spirituality,* edited by G. Fedotov. Sheed & Ward.

DOSTOYEVSKY, Fyodor, *The Brothers Karamazov,* selections. Regnery.

18

Mill: Utilitarianism

FOR A BRIEF but informative biographical summary of J. S. Mill the reader is referred to Volume II of the present series. In his appraisal of *Representative Government,* Father Pacifico Ortiz, S.J., has sketched Mill's background and highlighted those events that had so deep an influence on his work.

Utilitarianism was not invented by Mill, but he does take credit for being the first to bring the word into widespread use. Actually, Utilitarianism has passed through three stages in its development. We find it first defended in Bishop Cumberland's *De Legibus Naturae,* published in 1672. This first stage has been termed "theological" Utilitarianism: God made man a social being; his actions, when they promote the common good, are morally good, when they oppose it they are evil. "Political" Utilitarianism follows, and Mill gives us a brilliant outline of it. It received its initial impetus and direction from Jeremy Bentham, who was particularly interested in legal reform. To circulate his ideas he founded, with James Mill, John's father, the *Westminster Review.* According to the Benthamites, a law is good in so far as it procures the greatest happiness of the greatest number. The third stage has been called "evolutional" Utilitarianism and has been expounded in the works of Darwin and Spencer, especially the latter's *Data of Ethics.* Briefly, egoism is slowly giving way to altruism. As we become more and more sympathetic we discover that unselfishness brings us more satisfaction and happiness than its opposite. The day will come, so these optimists believe, when man will seek only the happiness of his fellow man. Strange as it may seem, contemporary Utilitarians—materialistic evolutionists for the most part—are just as optimistic.

The purpose of this essay of Mill's is obviously a defense of Utilitarianism. But before attempting to prove that the principle of utility is the only workable norm in determining the morality of an act, Mill wisely takes care to explain precisely what he means by this principle, for he is well aware that many of the arguments raised against it are based on a misunderstanding of it.

What is meant by the principle of utility?

The creed which accepts, as the foundation of morals, utility or the greatest-happiness principle, holds that actions are right in proportion as they tend to promote happiness, wrong as they tend to produce the reverse of happiness. By "happiness" is intended pleasure and the absence of pain; by "unhappiness" pain and the privation of pleasure.

The positivism of Mill is quite apparent in this definition of happiness. Happiness is pleasure, and pleasure of a sensible kind, for his positivism forbade him to admit the existence of a higher order.

Nevertheless, we must not understand pleasure in a too restricted sense. Man is superior to the brute beast and has faculties of a nobler kind. Once he is made aware of these faculties, he does not regard anything as happiness which does not include their gratification. But how are we to determine which pleasures are of a higher quality and therefore more valuable? The only source of reliable knowledge for a positivist is experience. In this case we can only rely on the experience of those who have known both kinds, artistic and intellectual as well as coarse sensual pleasures.

It is clear from Mill's theory of ideogenesis that all knowledge is reducible to sense knowledge, and therefore artistic and intellectual enjoyments belong in the sensible order. "Nobler" and "higher" do not mean "spiritual." If they did, there would be a point of contact here between traditional ethics and Utilitarianism.

Pleasure, then, has already been widened in its meaning to include the gratification of the higher faculties. Mill further insists that the principle of utility takes into consideration not only the happiness of the person who is acting but that of his fellow men.

I must again repeat what the assailants of utilitarianism seldom have the justice to acknowledge, that the happiness which forms the utilitarian standard of what is right in conduct is not the agent's own happiness but that of all concerned. As between his own happiness and that of others, utilitarianism requires him to be as strictly impartial as a disinterested and benevolent spectator. In the golden rule of Jesus of Nazareth we read the complete spirit of the ethics of utility. To do as you would be done by and to love your neighbor as yourself, constitute the ideal perfection of utilitarian morality.

There is room for neither hedonism nor selfishness in the utilitarianism of Mill. The point of issue, however, is whether or not happiness (and it should be born in mind we are speaking only of man's happiness here on earth) can be the guiding principle in ethics, the norm of right and wrong.

There is another misapprehension as to the true meaning of Utilitarianism that we must beware of. It has been claimed that it is a godless doctrine and opposed to religion. As a matter of fact, declares Mill, Utilitarianism is more profoundly religious than any other moral code, for does not God desire above all things the happiness of His creatures? Was not this His purpose in creating them? In promoting the general happiness, Utilitarianism is carrying out this purpose.

Bear in mind that the God of Mill (he seems to believe it likely that God exists, but he is not certain) is an inferior kind of god whose goodness has been limited by his impotence. Utilitarianism may not be necessarily a godless doctrine, but its positivistic spirit makes it impossible for it to arrive at a God Who is infinitely perfect—this can only be done through metaphysics or faith. Nor does his god have more than a minor role to play in his code of ethics—this can be seen when he speaks of obligation and sanctions. Mill is ready enough to use God and religion as external sanctions for men of inferior natures who might need them. But the ultimate sanction is a sense of duty, a feeling in our own mind: "a pain more or less intense, attendant on violation of duty, which in properly cultivated moral natures rises, in the more serious cases, into shrinking from it as an impossibility." The conscience which restrains us is, for Mill, only a subjective feeling and in reality is as changeable as any feeling can be. It has no objective foundation. Mill failed to see what Kant, for one, saw very clearly: the absolute character of "I must" and "I must not" cannot be radicated in a sentiment so completely subjective. Despite Mill's best efforts to knock it down, the objection stands. The obligation would cease when the feeling did. Or a person might disregard the feeling when he found it inconvenient, and rid himself of it.

The positivistic spirit of Mill is again evident in the proof he offers for his principle of utility. Recall what this principle is. Whatever promotes the general happiness is good, whatever impedes it is wrong. Unlike other systems, with their involved principles, this one, according to Mill, is simple and workable and easy to demonstrate. We know from experience what happiness is and what makes us happy. We also know from experience that all men always seek happiness. Since each person's happiness is a good to that person, the general happiness is a good to the aggregate of all persons. Now, the end (the *finis*) is the criterion of the morality of an act. Happiness being the sole end of all men's acts, whatever promotes happiness is good.

That all men at all times seek nothing but happiness is not too obvious at a first examination. Men do desire such things as virtue and they do posit acts, out of a sense of duty, that are in no way pleasant. But the Utilitarian doctrine, Mill insists, does not deny that people desire virtue nor that virtue is a thing to be desired, even disinterestedly. However, this admission, he maintains, is not in conflict with the happiness theory. The ingredients of happiness are various and each of them is desirable in itself. Any given pleasure, such as music or painting, is desired in and for itself, for these pleasures are parts of the end as well as being means to the end.

It is true that virtue is in another category, since originally it is not pleasant and thus not a part of the end, happiness. At first there is no ground for desiring it save its conduciveness to pleasure in so far as it protects us from the uncomfortableness of overindulgence. But—and this explains everything for Mill —through the association thus formed it may be felt a good in itself and desired as such with as great intensity as any other good. Thus, in the final analysis nothing is desired except happiness. Human nature is so constituted that it can desire nothing that is not either a part of happiness, such as pleasure, or a means of happiness, such as virtue.

Having demonstrated the principle of utility, at least to his own satisfaction, Mill goes on to insist how simple and practicable it is. He contrasts the ease with which his norm can be applied, with the difficulties involved in using other norms of morality. For is it not easier to determine what promotes greater happiness than what is in accord with man's rational nature, for example, as Scholastic philosophers would have us do? Our knowledge of man's nature is arrived at through a process that is long and full of pitfalls, whereas happiness is experienced and is unmistakable. Moreover, an act that is in accord with man's nature as a whole should make him happy, for such an act should further his perfect development and bring him closer to the end for which he was made and in which he will find his true happiness. Since it is easier to determine what makes man happy than what is in accord with his rational nature, the principle of utility or of greatest happiness would seem to be the best working norm of morality.

The trouble with this principle of utility is that in reality it can be used safely only when the principle it seeks to supplant is tacitly accepted. Try to apply this principle of utility, for instance, to the conduct of the ill-fated inhabitants of Sodom. All have given way to lust in its crudest and grossest forms. Moreover, we can suppose, as Mill himself is ready to admit, that in a relatively short time they reach the point where they become incapable of the nobler pleasures and are satisfied with the sensuality into which they have sunk, for even their consciences have been dulled. In such a situation, according to the principle of utility, all acts of lust are good, for they promote the only happiness these people crave and can achieve. Unless he is willing to admit this, Mill would have to contend that although such acts do promote the only happiness these people seek, they do not promote the *true* happiness of man. But to determine the *true* happiness of man he must first establish the rational nature of man.

Surprisingly enough, Mill comes very close to admitting this when, in a note at the very end of his essay, he inserts a communication he has received from Herbert Spencer. The latter, a Utilitarian like Mill, claims that although happiness is the ultimate end of morality, yet what constitutes happiness is only partially knowable through empirical generalizations from the observed results of conduct and is completely attainable only by deducing, from the laws of life and conditions of existence, what kinds of action necessarily produce happiness. Mill replies:

> With the exception of the word "necessarily" I have no dissent to express from this doctrine; and (omitting that word) I am not aware that any modern advocate of Utilitarianism is of a different opinion. Bentham certainly, to whom in the *Social Statics* Mr. Spencer particularly referred, is, least of all writers, chargeable with unwillingness to deduce the effect of actions on happiness from the laws of human nature and the universal conditions of human life.

It is true that the "human nature" that Mill knows is not quite the same as that of Scholasticism. But it is clear, I think, that he accepts and employs "conformity with human nature as a whole" as a principle of morality. And his happiness principle, to work at all, depends on it.

We do not intend to imply by any means that Mill is really a Scholastic philosopher in a Positivist's clothing. His constancy to the principles of Positivism is most evident in the last chapter of his essay, in which he undertakes to answer the difficulty that every Utilitarian finds very annoying, namely, the essential difference that seems to exist between justice and expediency. Obviously he cannot admit such a difference but must prove that justice can be reduced to expediency.

His analysis of justice reveals but two essential ingredients: the desire to punish a person who has done harm and the knowledge or belief that there is some definite individual to whom harm has been done, whose rights have been violated. He believes that this feeling or desire to punish the wrongdoer is the spontaneous outgrowth from two sentiments—the impulse of self-defense and the feeling of sympathy for the person who has suffered harm. This sentiment taken alone has nothing moral in it. What is moral is the exclusive subordination of it to the social sympathies so as to await and obey their call. This natural feeling would make us resent indiscriminately whatever anyone does that is disagreeable to us, but when moralized by this social feeling it acts only in the directions conformable to the general good.

"To have a right then is, I conceive, to have something which society ought to defend me in the possession of. If the objector goes on to ask me why it ought, I can give him no other reason than general utility." For Mill, justice is expediency plus this peculiar sentiment of resentment, moralized by being made coextensive with the demands of the social good.

Mill's reduction of justice to expediency or general utility is a clever *tour de force* that will satisfy only those who, like him, accept the Positivist's dogma: experience is the only source of certain knowledge. It will not satisfy those who realize that a philosophical question that seeks an ultimate cause cannot be answered by one who remains on the level of sense knowledge. General utility cannot explain the *why* and *wherefore* of inviolable rights. To answer the question: why should society defend my rights?—it is necessary to probe more deeply, to examine the nature of man. Then it will be seen that these rights are radicated in his rationality and spirituality. But we cannot remain in the experimental sciences and hope to attain to a proper knowledge of man's rational nature, for the experimental sciences deal only with proximate causes and answer questions that have to do with such problems as conduction rates in sensation or reflex-action time.

It remains for philosophy to apply the principles of metaphysics to the observable activities of man and thus go beyond these activities to man's powers and eventually to his nature. Only philosophy can tell us what kind of being man is, and until we know, it is pointless to theorize about norms of morality. Philosophy and experimental science are different kinds of knowledge, but each is real knowledge and has its place and purpose. Mill, like so many others in the history of philosophy, made the mistake (in reality his father, James Mill, made it for him in molding his son to his own likeness) of insisting that there was just one kind of knowledge, at least but one source of truly certain knowledge—experience. At times, especially when writing of his experiences of an "ego" that supports his conscious activities, he gives the impression that he would like to break the bonds his father has forged for him and rise above the world of sense. But he succeeds only when he is unfaithful to the tenets of Positivism.

MATTHEW A. ROONEY

SELECTED BIBLIOGRAPHY

BAIN, Alexander, *John Stuart Mill: A Criticism*. Longmans.
MILL, John Stuart, *Autobiography*. Columbia University.
McCOSH, James, *An Examination of John Stuart Mill's Philosophy*. Scribners.
STEPHEN, Leslie, *The English Utilitarians*, 3 vols. Putnam.
GARDINER, Harold C., S.J. (ed.), *The Great Books: A Christian Appraisal*, Vol. II. Devin-Adair.
MILL, John Stuart, *Utilitarianism*. Regnery.

19

James: Pragmatism

No PHILOSOPHICAL WORK can be satisfactorily interpreted until we ascertain the context wherein its meaning may be discerned. It is necessary, therefore, to view every such work in its historical setting, while taking into account whatever can render the thought of the philosopher comprehensible, such as the tendencies and crucial issues of the period under consideration, the state of knowledge and the new intellectual atmosphere in which old problems were set. This method of procedure also calls for a progressive widening of perspective, so as to embrace finally a whole cultural evolution as the proper field wherein the philosopher's work can be objectified and evaluated. Hence we can rightly insist that an illuminating account of William James's thought waits upon a better comprehension of a world of culture which was three thousand years in the making.

The origin of the pragmatic movement in philosophy coincides with the ripening of age-old tendencies and a multiplication of ferments which left no sphere of human activity untouched. The period also witnessed a proliferation of the sciences and, with it, a profusion of perspectives in which man was able to survey reality. As the point of convergence of a potentially infinite number of perspectives, the human mind's interest in itself was enormously intensified, with the result that experience in its widest range assumed a commanding position. But there were other factors contributing to the marked shift of interest in the direction of human subjectivity. For example, the very acceleration of achievement in the economic, political and social fields played its part in the maturation of personal consciousness, creating, as it did, a new hope and expectancy in regard to the future and a pervasive spirit of historical reorientation.

Philosophers reacted in various ways to the dominant trend, and many were the conquests made in the domain of human subjectivity, and at a time which saw much confusion between a psychological and a genuinely philosophical standpoint in regard to the concrete data of experience. Unquestionably, the most fundamental of all the influences redirecting the philosopher's attention to the actual data of experience derived from a truly new element in the intellectual climate of the time, namely, an explicit and proper awareness of the reality of growth and development. With the maturation of the historical sense and the genetic point of view ushered in by evolutionary theories, a respect for the temporal and becoming aspect of things took a firm hold of men's minds. And it became imperative to examine the problem of knowledge afresh, once human experience was viewed in the more all-inclusive relationships of history, and on the developmental plane.

In the quest for a more comprehensive and empirical view of knowledge, the unreality of an overly deductive procedure was evident. Hence arose the widespread hostility to abstract constructions which paid little heed to the growing masses of experience and the necessities made known by the new knowledge. In the general protest, the voice of William James was plainly audible, and while what he said had a distinctively American quality, it drew a quick response from many on the other side of the Atlantic. Indeed, Santayana tells us that "until the return wave of James's reputation reached America from Europe, his pupils and friends were hardly aware that he was such a distinguished man." Like many others, James set out to rethink the problem of knowledge in terms of the larger pattern of life; and, in the wider frame of reference, much came into focus that might otherwise have escaped even his own power of delicate introspective analysis. In general, we might say that he construed experience in a much wider sense than was usually done and was always ready to extend its scope. Then, too, he contrived to show the noetic importance of the conative and affective aspects of human nature, as well as the operational life of man within a real world of time and space, all of which were so often regarded as extraneous to the intellectual process.

It is to be expected that the drive of the philosophers to situate knowledge in the wider context of actual existence should lead, in the initial stage, to certain characteristic confusions. Man has seldom advanced to a more inclusive standpoint without throwing well-tested concepts out of alignment and creating new difficulties for himself. That is why the fuller clarification of the new standpoint is the task of those who come after. With this in mind, we need not be too dismayed by the inconsistencies and metaphysical ambiguity of James, or by the bewildering array of aspects which never seem to get unified. For, if we approach his thought properly, shunning merely external criticism, which is worthless, we shall surely find that James was groping to something more significant than the doctrine popularly attributed to him.

Even if it be conceded that his philosophy contains a nest of metaphysical fallacies, we can still gain much from a study of it, not only because it abounds in insights but also because of the light thrown on a real problem. After all, the warrant for his thought does not lie in its ability to defend itself against all comers, but rather in its power to enlighten us regarding something of importance to all who care to see life in the round.

Not the least of the benefits that can accrue to us in studying James is the intangible but solid gain deriving from contact with the mind of a great human being. For James was a lovable figure whose many wonderful qualities, intellectual and personal, infused his writings and are woven into the very texture of his thought. Indeed, as many discovered, it was quite possible to be thoroughly unfriendly to his ideas, while yet delighting in the man himself and esteeming him highly. Of all the attempts that have been made to sum up his greatness, perhaps the most intriguing, if also the shortest, characterization is that made by A. N. Whitehead when he refers to James as "that adorable genius."

Henri Bergson, well aware of the fact that many pictured pragmatism, *a priori*, as "something that must necessarily be simple," believed it to be one of the most subtle of doctrines, about which one is sure to go wrong if one gives vent to one's opinions without taking care to read James *"as a whole."* Bergson also castigates "the vulgar disparagement of pragmatism as skeptical or utilitarian," while asserting of James that "no one ever loved truth more ardently or sought it more persistently and self-forgetfully." If, then, we follow Bergson's counsel and read James as a whole, we cannot help feeling that a love of truth lay deep in his heart, and that his pragmatism sprang from a real and positive concern with the problem of truth, and not from any desire to evade it.

Turning to the opening words of Lecture I of his "Pragmatism," we find him endorsing the view of G. K. Chesterton that "the most practical and important thing about a man is still his view of the universe." Eulogizing philosophy to his popular audience, he declares that "no one of us can get along without the far-flashing beams of light it sends over the world's perspectives," beams of light accompanied by "the contrast-effects of darkness and mystery." James meant it when he uttered these words, and we do not have to proceed far in our reading to become convinced that he was genuinely concerned with the everlasting problems of philosophy, especially as they touch on moral and religious life. For, back of his thinking lay the burning question of personal destiny, and through the years he meditated on the mystery of life lived in a world of concrete personal experiences, "multitudinous beyond imagination, tangled, muddy, painful and perplexed."

Underlying James's pragmatism is a conception of mind which gives to the purposes or ends which govern thinking a central importance in the cognitional process. Man, he clearly saw, is no mere maker of concepts, for the ordering of his life is dictated by needs and by inner and outer compulsions which play a decisive role in the formation of his convictions. He knew that human personality is roused only by the sharpest needs and by the pressures of life to break through the limitations of any moment of its existence. In short, intellectual activity is seen as an enterprise within life itself, and the triumphs of the intellect are regarded not merely as such but as triumphs of the human spirit seeking fullness of life. Unfortunately, in his desire to satisfy the claims of life, and as a sympathizer with human needs, James seems to emphasize the actual life pattern of the individual to the detriment of the objective character of knowledge. But in pointing to his epistemological and metaphysical deficiencies, we should not overlook the fact that he objectifies for us certain aspects of the intellectual process which had suffered neglect.

It is this purposive view of thought which separated James, so he believed, from the intellectualist who conceives truth as "essentially an inert static relation," that is, a relation which excludes the dynamism of the individual, who lives his life in a real world of time and history and action. Whereas, for the intellectualist, the great truths which thrust themselves at man were regarded as prior to activity, to James they were also its consequences. Because he was concerned with human life in its breadth and depth, and not with any one sector seen in isolation, it seemed to him that, when regarded from an integral standpoint, action took on a significance that might ordinarily escape us. For action has its roots in deep-lying necessities of our nature, such as, for example, the need for an eternal moral order, or the need for a living participation in reality, or the need to project values into actual life. Action thus shows itself to be not merely a consequence but an initiation, through which much that is latent comes to the surface of consciousness.

James was endeavoring to take seriously the fact that reality does not address itself to abstract minds but to living persons inhabiting a real world, to whom it makes known something of its essential quality only as they go out to meet it through action. It is this concrete relation of man and his world, realized in action, which accounts for the fact that our power of affirmation outruns our knowledge, as when we feel or sense the truth before we know it. To James, therefore, pragmatism was a doctrine designed to enlighten the whole of human action and to give meaning to man's irrepressible need to act. While he failed to safeguard the transcendence of truths to which reason has access, his intention was not to debase the theoretical by making it subordinate to the practical, but rather to insist on the intrinsic relation of the two. Like Cardinal Newman, he wanted to survey the problem of knowledge from the point of view of man as "a seeing, feeling, contemplating, acting animal," and to show, moreover, how action may be brought into the realm of self-conscious, reflective, contemplative life.

For the pragmatist, even if an idea be taken as true, there remains this question: What concrete difference does it make in actual life? But it is quite otherwise with the intellectualist, so James tells us, for once he has attained to his true idea, there's an end to the matter, since our thinking destiny has been fulfilled. To James, the intellectualist is merely making a virtue out of necessity, inasmuch as many of his ideas are already imprisoned within an issueless channel. For it seemed to him that true ideas were always generated in life itself and could not be kept away from it. Pressing ever forward into life, "they lead to consistency, stability and flowing human intercourse" and "away from eccentricity and isolation, from foiled and barren thinking."

As James saw it, the entire question of the adequation of mind to reality has to be reopened the moment we perceive that man is no closed system in a state of perfect equipoise in relation to an objective order. The adequation of mind to reality is no static, aimless, unmotivated affair, it is no passive reception on the part of a supposedly neutral intellect, but is rather a vital act involving the whole operative personality, since man always seeks the truth as a good to be embraced. Hence James's query: "Can we then keep the notion of what is better for us, and what is true for us, permanently apart?" It seems to us that if James had not held truth to be a vital good, as "divine and precious and its pursuit a duty," he probably would not even have been tempted to enter upon the path he did in fact choose.

When we view the adequation of mind to reality in a truly contextual manner, the factors of interest and choice assume new importance in the life of thought. We may shun the metaphysical inadequacies of James, but we are nonetheless required to stress the fact that the striving and desiring side of our nature, so far from being merely juxtaposed to intellectual activity, underlies its very dynamism. Accordingly, the compenetration of thinking, willing and acting within the life of each one of us is an inescapable reality, since it is the whole man who thinks and wills, and the whole man who acts toward greater enhancement of life without pause or stop. If we fail to see this compenetration, it is usually because we are viewing man as an abstraction and not in his full human situation, and, therefore, not within the social, historical and cosmic pattern of his existence.

From a proper metaphysical standpoint we should have little difficulty showing that man's deepest needs and exigencies have more than a merely subjective import, being grounded in the finality of the creation and the subjective order of the universe. In brief, without putting the objectivity of knowledge in jeopardy, we can bring the loves and aspirations which constitute our greatest energies into a realistic relation to "cognitional experience," and to the growth of those vital ideas which have motivating power, and with which James was mainly concerned.

There are few doctrines without their historical antecedents, and James was quite right, up to a point, in his belief that his views had roots which could be traced far back into the past. Much in his philosophy strikes us as sheer novelty but only because we are not familiar with our many-sided intellectual tradition as it has taken shape from earliest times. But it is enough to recall here that a new turn in the problem of knowledge resulted from the Christian doctrine of personality, inasmuch as it produced a heightened perception of man as an integral whole, while stressing the multiple aspects and versatility of his nature and the many ties that bind him to reality. The problem of knowledge became much more complex in view of the fact that other powers were given equality with the intellect, and all aspects of human nature were apprehended in a personal synthesis.

Accordingly, even though philosophers extolled the dignity of the intellect in its power to know an objective order of things, a radical intellectualization of the genesis of knowledge was ruled out. Besides, in making men keenly aware of the concrete in its existential character, the Christian religion rendered such intellectualization entirely impossible. Consequently, we find thinkers yielding a larger place to psychological, moral and religious realities, regarded as indispensable to a more adequate conception of the concrete in its fullness and depth. It is not surprising, therefore, to find a point of view emerging which embraced, in some kind of synthesis, the truths underlying intellectualism, voluntarism and actionism.

Clearly, James was impelled by a truth vehemently upheld today, that the intellect is no impersonal faculty which functions automatically, as it were, and apart from the tendential being of man and from a life in which choice and risk and experimentation play their part. True, he does not provide us with a comprehensive or even truly integral account of knowledge, for he teeters on the brink of actionism and sensism, but he throws light on aspects so often ignored, and in a way which calls for a reexamination of the problem of knowledge in its entirety. To recapitulate, we may say, then, that he has highlighted the truth that thinking cannot be dissociated from a personal drama which is our own, albeit fitting into a larger scheme of things. He has also brought out an important feature of knowledge, which can easily be assimilated into a more comprehensive philosophy, namely, the fact that our ideas have not fulfilled their function until they rejoin experience. That is, ideas are "complemental factors" of reality, finishing out their function in being carried into "the stream of experience," which "may indeed reveal far more connection and union than we now suspect." Concepts, therefore, have a teleological role, so to speak, by which they enlarge our vision of the real, provided they are redirected into experience. If James had safeguarded the objective value of the concept, while insisting on its insufficiency when viewed apart from its directive function, he could have more successfully opposed "vicious intellectualism" without drifting so dangerously close at times to a vicious anti-intellectualism.

James's primary intention is to bring intellectual activity into a closer relation to experience by enlarging the cognitive role of the latter, so that experience itself may have more and more to say regarding the validity of our concepts and their relations. Thus he is aiming at a logic of the concrete with which Christian thinkers are concerned in our own day, since they too wish to bring thinking into a more fecund relation to the inexhaustible data of experience. When James says that "all discarnate truth is static, impotent and relatively spectral," he means by discarnate truth, the truth that has been torn away from life and consequently from that wholeness of experience in which alone its characteristics and value are made manifest.

James's *Pragmatism* unleashed a fierce criticism from all quarters, inasmuch as his doctrine appeared to be a mere glorification of action and success. In an article in the *Philosophical Review* for January, 1908 (vol. xvii, p. 1), reprinted as Chapter VIII of his work, *The Meaning of Truth*, subtitled "A Sequel to 'Pragmatism,' " he complains of "the fantastic character of the current misconceptions," and sets out to show that his doctrine cannot be lightly thrust aside as "a characteristically American movement, a sort of bobtailed scheme of thought," designed for men of action generally, who "have no time or wit to study genuine philosophy." This article, which is indispensable for a better understanding of James's intentions, suggests that he himself was engaged in a continuous search for the deeper meaning of his own doctrine. At any rate, it puts his views in a more favorable light than do the popular lectures comprising his *Pragmatism*.

Somewhat nettled because his critics "boggle at every word, refusing to take the spirit rather than the letter of our discourse," James nevertheless acknowledges his own share of responsibility for the "current misconceptions." The very name "Pragmatism," with its suggestion of action, was "an unfortunate choice," he averred, and he realized that he had marred his exposition with "infelicities of expression" and carelessness of language. In fairness to James it should be said that much of his rhetorical carelessness sprang from his fondness for the popular idiom and the broad stroke, and from his desire to communicate life and meaning to every type of audience. Always insisting on the mastery of one's subject, he knew the importance of improvisation and spontaneity and trusting to one's luck. And in his more technical writing, just as on the platform, he took naturally to the free and easy and personal way of expressing himself which jarred "respectable minds" and caused many to forget that he was a master of prose style.

To James, the storm of criticism that raged around his *Pragmatism* merely betrayed an unfamiliarity with "the concrete point of view which pragmatism assumes." It is this concreteness, he explains, which marks the "whole originality" of pragmatism, not its emphasis on action, which is secondary. He is especially concerned to disabuse his critics of the idea that pragmatism is an agnostic doctrine, insisting that there could be no "worse misapprehension" than the view that our reason is incapable of attaining to the foundations of reality. "For him, as for his critics," he declares, "there can be no truth if there is nothing to be true about." While satisfactions are indispensable to the truth-building process, "I have everywhere called them insufficient unless reality be also incidentally led to," for it is an inherent relation of our belief to reality that gives us "that specific *truth*-satisfaction." Hence he concludes, "I remain an epistemological realist."

James's realism is a fact which looms large in his writings and should carry weight. Thus we find in *Pragmatism* the following, which sums up rather well his fundamental attitude: "Pent in, as the pragmatist more than anyone else sees himself to be, between the whole body of funded truths squeezed from the past and the coercions of the world of sense about him, who so well as he feels the immense pressure of objective control under which our minds perform their operations?" Again he writes in the same work, "realities mean, then, either concrete facts or abstract kinds of things and relations perceived intuitively between them." His realism is in evidence in his vivid sense of "irreducible and stubborn facts," especially in what has been called "the flux of immediate experience." His very susceptibility to the demands of the actual data of experience made him reluctant to become a full-fledged nominalist, despite his emphasis on radical individuality, for, as Ralph Barton Perry says in his magnificent biography, James retained "a modicum of Platonic realism" in somehow providing "for universals, generals and concepts, however much he might disparage them."

Let us consider James's realism for the light it may shed on the meaning of his pragmatism. Santayana has called James "a mystic in love with life." Certainly he had the mystic's sense of the plenitude of the real, and "of a certain total character in the universe" which somehow escapes the grasp of philosophical systems. This explains his sustained effort to recall men to reality and life by showing in a hundred different ways that our abstractions become an impassable barrier once we forget that reality exceeds them just as it exceeds our logic. Hungering for an authentic experience of being in its copiousness and its "primitive concreteness," he was led to view the life of mind as a process toward immediacy of knowledge, even if such immediacy is more often than not attained by means of and across our concepts. Unfortunately, James seems to go counter to much that he has written by often resorting to an ultimate sense-immediacy, as though there could be no immediacy of knowledge on a higher intuitional level.

Evidently, for James, pragmatism is an "attitude of orientation" by which man can achieve a vital contact with concrete reality and along innumerable paths, by aiming not simply at the abstract relation of the mere onlooker but at a relation that is personal, direct and immediate, and involving participation with one's whole heart and being. Thus, pragmatism seems to be the method designed for an epistemology of the person rather than of the mind taken in isolation. That is, pragmatism is a method presupposing an epistemology which embraces the whole realm of personal existence, in making a place not only for logic but for "the humblest and most personal experiences," and in being adequate to "the collectivity of experience's demands, nothing being omitted." That is why, as he insists, ideas, to be true, "must help us get into satisfactory relations with other parts of our experience," and while leaning on old truth must grasp new fact.

Before closing, it is well to point out that pragmatism is not necessarily antimetaphysical. James himself believed pragmatism to be primarily a method and, as such, capable of being adapted to any type of metaphysics. But its metaphysical affinities are clearly in evidence in the philosophy of Charles S. Peirce, one of the founders of the pragmatic movement. A logician of the first magnitude, and a profound and original thinker besides, Peirce has title to a philosophical greatness which is becoming more firmly established with each passing year. But what interests us here is that Peirce made contact with the classical tradition of thought, and particularly with medieval Christian philosophy, claiming a close affinity between his own type of realism and Scholastic realism.

In his view, pragmatism seems to be a method for engaging the mind in an actual and concrete relation to truth, and so far from being merely utilitarian or sensist, implies a metaphysics of a Platonic character. Hence his statement that the "most important consequence" of pragmatism is that "under that conception of reality we must abandon nominalism." Peirce saw fit to differentiate his own version of pragmatism from that of James by renaming it "pragmaticism," because of his aversion for what to him was the anti-intellectualistic character of James's approach, and also because he wanted to safeguard from any taint of actionism the notion of action as intimately bound up with knowledge.

Whitehead, who did so much to rehabilitate metaphysical thinking in our own day, not only acknowledged his debt to James, but also pointed out that the meaning of pragmatism must be given wider extension and not be limited by arbitrary specialist assumptions. Granting, therefore, the grave objections that can be mustered against James's form of pragmatism, we must, nevertheless, with Peirce and Whitehead, seek out the fuller meaning of pragmatism in its most general character. And we must also endeavor to show that without a proper metaphysical framework, pragmatism will keep narrowing its meaning, as it is doing among contemporary pragmatists, until it becomes totally devoid of intellectual life and is helpless before the accumulated wealth of knowledge and experience. Meanwhile, we should avoid saddling James with forms of pragmatism which lack his breadth of vision, his openness to possibilities and the whole searching character of his thought.

ROBERT C. POLLOCK

SELECTED BIBLIOGRAPHY

JAMES, William, *Pragmatism; A New Name for Some Old Ways of Thinking*. Longmans, Green.

JAMES, William, *The Meaning of Truth: A Sequel to Pragmatism*. Longmans, Green.

SANTAYANA, George, *Character and Opinion in the United States*. Scribners.

PERRY, Ralph Barton, *In the Spirit of William James*. Yale.

PERRY, Ralph Barton, *The Thought and Character of William James*. Harvard. (A two-volume edition is published by Little, Brown.)

JAMES, William, *The Philosophy of William James*. Random House (The Modern Library).

JAMES, William, *Pragmatism*. Regnery.

20

Samuel Clemens: Adventures of Huckleberry Finn

OF TWENTY-THREE LISTS of foremost American novels prepared for widely different reasons, *Huckleberry Finn* and its
near opposite, Hawthorne's *Scarlet Letter,* are always at the
top, to be followed at some distance back by other famous
works, such as Melville's *Moby Dick,* Howells's *Rise of Silas
Lapham,* or Cooper's *Last of the Mohicans.* To be sure, *Huck
Finn* is a children's classic, but it is something more as well. It
is the "something more" that concerns us here.

A children's classic demands only a limited level of reading.
This is not to say that the child does not give the whole of himself to the book he is reading, for he does so inevitably, and
often a lot more willingly than his guardians give him credit
for. No, rather the child's participation is limited only by the
inevitable limitations of his child nature. Experience of life,
reflection, larger and more complex comprehension will lend
weight, depth and wisdom, and thus make possible the more
complete appeal appropriate to the universal classic. On the first
level, *Huckleberry Finn* meets the requirements for a children's
classic, for it is a story of outward action with motives simple
enough for the child mind to grasp easily. This ease of assimilation is essential but it is not by any means the sole requirement
for a children's classic; otherwise, of course, the comic strip
would be fully comparable as an art. What distinguishes the
children's classic is that it confirms, or at least never contradicts,
the judgments of mature life. It does not matter how early one
reads *Huckleberry Finn* for the first time, or how soon or how
many times one rereads it; the important truth is that one never
has to give up an earlier interpretation. One enjoys the work

and values it for deeper reasons and for further reasons, but the original evaluation is never reversed.

The universal classic must be capable of satisfying the full and intense scrutiny of the mature mind, and as such it must engage a proportionately greater share of the reader's whole person and experience of life. The greater the classic, the more of the reader participates in the reading, as in Shakespeare, Dante, and so on. There is frequent misunderstanding on this score. It is sometimes held that a classic is measured by its appeal to all kinds of people of all age groups. *Huckleberry Finn* is not to be thought of as a classic in this sense any more than we would praise Shakespeare's classical genius because he provided slapstick scenes for his untutored audience. The presence of the groundling who applauded only the porter scene in *Macbeth* was a tribute to Shakespeare's practical wisdom as a popular artist, not to his greatness as a profound artist.

Again, we as readers may not be fully engaged by Dante because of our limitations of education, experience and reflection, but we are always aware of the deeper and fuller participation possible when our deficiencies are cleared away. In fact, the whole educative value of reading the classics is that we can grow to meet the great books at their appropriate level. *Huckleberry Finn,* as a universal classic, permits this profounder level of reading and interpretation. *Tom Sawyer,* like any other child's classic, may be read by adults, but, if so, read with only part of the mind. *Huckleberry Finn,* because of the circumstances of its composition and subject matter, is a work that not only engages the full mind but provides food for its growth as well.

When a classic is a novel, there are special considerations for evaluating it that are dependent upon its function as an art. Because it is an art, its significance will rest not on its explanation of life, as in a work of history, philosophy, science or criticism, but on its interpretation of life through its imitation of some part of life. As in every art, the work must have artistic unity. For the novel, as for the play and all other narrative arts, the unity is to be found in the action (i. e., life) as revealed in the plot. This action we most commonly speak of as the theme of the plot, and in *Huckleberry Finn* the theme is the maturing of the boy, Huck. As we shall see in a moment, the actual plot of this story is more episodic than otherwise, and this presentation of a series of incidents not integrally related to each other is an artistic blemish never fully compensated for in an otherwise almost flawless book.

In narrative art, by the fact of its role as imitating life, the incidents of life must happen to someone and in some place and time. These two elements, character and setting, are important in any novel, because of the extra unifying role they perform. In *Huckleberry Finn* the plot does not perform its unifying function, and that the work is a classic at all is due to the extraordinary presentation of the character of Huck and of the life of the midcentury Mississippi River region.

Before examining the novel for its interpretation of life, it is necessary to explain briefly why this single work is preeminent in Samuel Clemens's literary career. The writer himself gave no special accolade to it. In fact, he often expressed surprise that this single work should be spoken of as having a different order from his other writings. We now know that he was a more conscious artist than earlier critics realized and, presumably, his long delay in finishing the work was due in large part to technical difficulties—he didn't know how to end it. Perhaps his own somewhat curt relegation of *Huckleberry Finn* to his "other work" was made in deference to his artist's bad conscience about the trick chapters of Tom Sawyer's escapade with which the book closes. Indeed, if we are to find an explanation for the high place of *Huckleberry Finn,* we must look where Clemens himself could not see: first, outside the book to Clemens's life and career; second, inside, to the technical achievement of the style.

All students of the author's career point out definite stages, or changes, from the frontier gaiety of *Innocents Abroad* and *Roughing It* of his youth to the cynical despair of *Mysterious Stranger* and *What Is Man* that mark his last years. Assorted opinions have been offered in explanation of this change, ranging from the Freudian to the Marxian, none of which is without some merit, though none is totally convincing. One explanation in particular has been too long forgotten, that of George N. Shuster in an early article on "The Tragedy of Mark Twain" written many years ago for the *Catholic World.* The hypothesis offered then was soon forgotten in the light of

Van Wyck Brooks's more flamboyant accusations that Olivia Clemens had prettified and (s)mothered all Clemens's western strength and genius. Yet Shuster's perception of the materialism of frontier life and the consequent spiritual starvation of its sons is basic to any larger understanding of Clemens's career.

The middle period, in which *Tom Sawyer, Life on the Mississippi* and *Huckleberry Finn* were written, was between the excited, uproarious and belligerent swagger of the frontier humor and the brooding despair and bitter agnosticism of the last period. Parrington has called this middle period the "imaginative recollection of a youth that is past," and in one of his best sections he deals brilliantly with the books that reveal the changes in Clemens's outlook. Whatever the explanation, there was in the ten-year period from 1875 to 1885 a mood of serenity and confidence within which his best work was composed. Had *Huckleberry Finn* been attempted earlier or later than this decade it could not, in all probability, have been his greatest work. It reflects an attitude toward life that, however briefly, was his own.

Commercial success as a writer had come to Clemens in 1869 with the publication of the widely popular *Innocents Abroad.* In this and in *Roughing It,* his first two works, and in all of Clemens's writing thereafter, his intuitively grasped yet shrewdly manipulated hold on the popular fancy, especially in its lighter moments, is everywhere evident. The use of understatement, anticlimax, exaggeration, misquotation, euphemism, homely metaphor, and all such tricks of the popular humorists of the day came to him almost without effort. His facility in creating amusing scenes and situations made him one of the best-paid writers of his century. An uneven work, written in collaboration with a literary neighbor, has one of those intuitively chosen titles, *The Gilded Age,* that has been borrowed by social historians to characterize the period. The work, particularly through the memorable character of Colonel Beriah Sellers, gaily satirizes the speculative spirit of the time. Yet Twain himself was as much a victim of the speculative fever as many of the characters in his stories. The tremendous profits from the sale of his books he lost in one wildcat scheme after another. As a consequence, he was driven to writing what would please the popular fancy; the humorous sketch was ready cash. As he could talk, so could he write for the quick laugh, and good though these comic scenes are, they are some distance short of greatness.

Much of the artistic difference between *Huckleberry Finn* and *The Adventures of Tom Sawyer* is the result of a difference in style. *Tom Sawyer* is written in the simplest of all narrative devices, the third-person omniscient point of view. The author jumps from description to dialog to mind reading to comment to interior monolog to aphorism, back to dialog again, and so on. The very ease with which he shifts his position as narrator makes for ready delight on our part, but artistic unity is lost.

In *Huckleberry Finn*, Clemens adopted the first-person narrator role: Huck is telling the story, and everything that we know must come to us through Huck's mind. Carl Van Doren was the first to point out the great difference this made, but perhaps only through a direct comparison of the two otherwise similar novels can the full import of Clemens's self-imposed discipline of his overfacile imagination be perceived.

Whereas earlier a glib description of the town, the river, the island or the cave would do, now the picture had to be thought through in terms of Clemens's strikingly evocative memory. Before, when a composite language, gathered from the many parts of America that he knew, would suffice, now he had the most delicate task of the realist's craft to work out, that hardest thing to recapture, natural human speech. But most of all, Clemens had to discipline a mind always tempted to the excesses of exaggeration, grotesquerie and parody, to the range of vision of a sensitive adolescent coming to terms with life in a period of contradictory influences. Whether his choice of the method of composition was accidental or not, it is clear that the discipline of the imagination which this method imposed was essential to Twain the artist. In no other work of his were these conditions present.

Adventures of Huckleberry Finn provides a picture of a certain part of American life now gone. It vivifies life on the Mississippi of a century ago. The episodes are valuable in themselves as comments on American life, but they have that special quality of showing us human nature as unvarying throughout the changing circumstances of history. There is always in Clemens that danger of easy exaggeration which shifts portraiture into grotesquerie, yet in this book most of the pictures are authentic. Pap Finn, Huck's drunken father, is perhaps too aggressive in his pride of ignorance to seem altogether real, yet the rage of frustration, the blind unreasoning fury of his monolog "agin the guvment," in which he aggravates rather than resolves his repressions, is repeated every day in only slightly different words.

Similarly, the brilliant presentation of the picaresque rogues, the Duke and the Dauphin, seems overdone when read alone, but within the book these characters are seen in terms of what would impress Huck and so assume a true, albeit bizarre, consistency. Again, the famous so-called attack on the Southern family feud, in the Grangerford-Shepherdson episode, is not really an attack at all; rather, it is a deeply moving and sympathetic account in which no overt judgments are made. This episode takes on significance only because we are emotionally prepared for it by our understanding of Huck, through whose still somewhat limited comprehension the disastrous consequences of the feud are revealed. In fact, all of the pictures of Mississippi life take on higher significance when read in terms of the book. Even the account of the well-known type character of the old South-West, the "ring-tailed roarer," which Clemens excluded from the finished book but later printed in *Life on the Mississippi,* might have been more than a humorous but distracting episode (which must have been Clemens's reason for dropping it). Had the boaster been presented as a step in Huck's education, the sketch might well have had the same value as any of the minor episodes—Huck's girl-disguise and his fibs, which were penetrated by Mrs. Loftus; the eavesdropping on the murderers on the shipwrecked *Walter Scott,* the smallpox fib through which Huck scares off the planters who would have discovered Jim.

Huckleberry Finn, episodic though it may be in its structure, is not an episodic novel in the same sense as are the picaresque novels with which it is commonly classed. Thomas Nashe's *Unfortunate Traveler,* most of Smollet's novels, and much of Clemens's other work fit properly into this classification, but *Huckleberry Finn* is unquestionably of a superior order. In Nashe's work it would make no real difference in what order the adventures of Jack Wilton were told. Each one is as complete in itself as any other, and one could almost read the book backward without any serious artistic loss. In *Huckleberry Finn,* because the characters of the various episodes appear but once and then vanish completely from the story, there is an admitted loss of integration and dramatic intensity. Yet there is also almost complete compensation for the loss in that the incidents take on ascending importance through Huck's slow but certain growth to maturity.

This unity of the book is confirmed and corroborated by the all-pervasive symbol of the river, representing in its largest implications life itself. This all-embracing symbol is capable of a tremendous number of specific applications, but above everything it serves as the controlling symbol through which Huck's attainment of manhood is perceived.

Clemens's use of his native language is a triumph. His uniqueness is based almost solely upon this use. Only with Clemens does the native American idiom appear for the first time as the necessary instrument for significant artistic creation. The faithfulness to the rhythmic word groupings of our speech, the uncluttered sentence structure, the comparisons in figures of speech set up in terms of American experience, the word connotations which only Americans can fully understand, these and more make Clemens our first master of the American language. Increasingly, as our writers become more faithful to the native idiom and diction, it becomes difficult to translate American writing. Of all of our novels, *Huckleberry Finn* will always suffer most in translation. The influence of this language, through Stephen Crane, Sherwood Anderson, Edith Stein and predominantly Hemingway, is so pervasive that one must agree with Hemingway that "all modern American literature comes from one book by Mark Twain called *Huckleberry Finn.*"

Another level on which the greatness of this book is to be understood is its interpretation of life, a matter of special significance to the Christian reader. There are few references to orthodox Christianity in Clemens's work, and as he grew older he turned sharply away from even nominal acceptance of Christian precepts. His father was at one time a Universalist and later a self-styled "free thinker." His mother's firmly held Calvinistic traditions may have had important psychological consequences, but they had little intellectual influence on his life. With little formal education and certainly no philosophical training, he found in Voltaire and Paine the support for his agnosticism. What he knew of Catholicism, he learned from his researches into a hated feudalism, so that his attacks on predemocratic governments invariably included attacks on the religious institution he thought supported them. Even his almost scabrous attack on Christian Science is not a defense of Christianity against its threatened perversion but a blast against any optimistic view of life, even the qualified optimism of Christianity itself.

Whatever the reasons for Clemens's later cynicism may be, and his biographers are still searching for them, *Huckleberry Finn* appears before the decline. It is, indeed, not only the most optimistic of all of his works but is frequently hailed as one of the last convincing manifestations of the romantic view of life. Looked at in terms of literary history, *Huckleberry Finn* may be seen as the end-result of works he probably never read, Rousseau's *Émile* and *Nouvelle Héloise*. Although it does not seem the whole picture, there is a certain plausibility in the interpretation of this book as the last great romantic (in the sense of Rousseauistic) novel. What is Huck? He is the noble savage *par excellence*. He is not spoiled by society; his natural goodness or his native altruism cannot be perverted by church, school or custom, because he runs away from all three. Hence, when he is tempted (i.e., to turn in Jim, the runaway slave), he renounces society and all its social and religious sanctions.

But *Huckleberry Finn* is more than Midwestern Rousseauism dressed up in pseudorealistic garments. Although there is evidence for this, there is much stronger evidence for a Christian interpretation appropriate to the book's high reputation. In the Rousseauistic interpretation, Huck's resistance to temptation can only by accident have occurred where it does in the book. Presumably, Huck is freed of the evil influences of society from the very beginning of the tale, and had the occasion arisen in the first chapter instead of the thirty-first, Huck would still not have turned Jim in. But any true reading of the book makes this conjecture an impossibility. From everything we know of Huck at the beginning of the story—that he was sensitive, curious and shrewdly perceptive, yes, but that he was also

timid, without any courage but what was required for self-pres-
ervation, and vividly impressed with official learning—we realize that he would have turned Jim in with hardly a second
thought.

Indeed, not until Huck has matured can Clemens put in the
crucial temptation. On the trip he must come to love Jim, to
see him as a brother, to develop those primary virtues for
spiritual maturity, humility and charity. Before the temptation scene spoken of, there must occur a series of events as key
steps in Huck's spiritual growth. It begins with the casual acceptance of the death of others—he doesn't know the dead man
is his father, so he shrugs off the episode because it doesn't
concern him. The next step is his escape from the island with
Jim, for he becomes aware for the first time of a need for com-
panionship. Then a major step in his reaction to the leaving
of the murderers on the disintegrating ship:

Now was the first time that I had begun to worry about the men
—I reckon I hadn't had time to before. I begun to think how dreadful it was, even for murderers, to be in such a fix. I says to myself,
there ain't no telling but I might come to be a murderer myself yet,
and then how would I like it?

As another step, Huck must be brought to feel shame. He plays
a mean and frightening trick on Jim and, after Jim's simple but
profoundly moving protest, Jim

. . . got up slow and walked into the wigwam, and went in there
without saying anything but that. But that was enough. It made
me feel so mean I could almost kissed his foot to get him to take it
back. It was fifteen minutes before I could work myself up to go
and humble myself to a nigger; but I done it, and I warn't ever
sorry for it afterward, neither.

And so the self-education continues, each episode adding a
further step in the attainment of maturity. There is the bitter
disappointment when the raft misses the long-awaited junction
with the Ohio (where Jim can escape into free territory). Later,
comes the violence of the feud in which both dignified, generous and courageous families are destroyed to reveal to Huck
the horrifying effects of pride. Then the cupidity and effron-
tery of the Duke and the Dauphin, contrasted on the one side
with the gullibility of the townspeople they hoodwink and on
the other with the very moving account of Jim and his deaf

child. These and all the other so-called episodes lead directly and inevitably to what cannot but have been Clemens's intention, conscious or otherwise, that Huck becomes a man; becomes, indeed—because it is an extension only of degree, not of kind—a saint.

If it is claimed on theological grounds that saints must be baptized (as Graham Greene is theologically sound if artistically implausible in having the heroine of *The End of the Affair* baptized even though she doesn't know it), so be it. *Huckleberry Finn* makes no such overt claims to be a specifically Christian novel. Yet Huck most certainly might claim the baptism of desire, and the water of life has been a universal symbol of mankind from the river Jordan to the Mississippi.

C. CARROLL HOLLIS

SELECTED BIBLIOGRAPHY

BELLAMY, Gladys C., *Mark Twain as a Literary Artist*. University of Oklahoma.
CANBY, Henry S., *Turn West, Turn East*. Houghton, Mifflin.
DE VOTO, Bernard, *Mark Twain's America*. Little, Brown.
FERGUSON, DeLancey, *Mark Twain: Man and Legend*. Bobbs-Merrill.
CLEMENS, Samuel, *Adventures of Huckleberry Finn*. Regnery.

Postscript to the Four Volumes

IT MAY SEEM rather arbitrary for the Editor of this series to determine that it would extend no further than these four volumes. The Great Books Foundation has projected a ten-year course for discussion groups; why, then, should we not keep issuing a volume a year so as to keep up with the discussions?

A fair question, undoubtedly, which calls for a fair answer: the Editor feels that these four volumes, now completed, have achieved what they purposed to do. The Introduction to Volume I remarked that, despite all the very admirable objectives of the Great Books discussion scheme, there was a definite danger that the whole program might well bog down in aimlessness —discussants might approach the individual Great Book with no clear idea of what it treated or of what they might find in it, and depart from the two-hour discussion still quite at sea.

It was to obviate this indefiniteness that the series was projected. None of the essays has been intended to tell the discussant precisely what to think about the Great Book in advance of its discussion. Each essay has simply aimed, rather, at telling briefly what the Great Book is about—to give its topic sentence, so to speak—at placing the book in proper relationship to its own time and to the entire stream of Western culture.

The Editor hopes that those who have faithfully followed the four volumes, and who have found that their participation in the discussion groups has been thereby made more practical and fruitful, will by now have taken the hint and imbibed the method. That is to say, that they will have realized that a certain advance familiarity with the Great Book to be discussed, and with its background, far from launching the discussion on a sea of preconceptions and bias, will serve to inaugurate discussion that comes immediately to grips with the heart of the book.

If, then, those who may regret the end of this series will continue their actual participation in the discussion groups with the same intellectual keenness and the same intellectual modesty which prompted them to begin the collateral reading that here terminates, the Editor will feel properly repaid and his collaborators will share in his satisfaction.

Notes on the Contributors

FRANCIS J. BRACELAND, M.D., Sc.D. [1900-   ]

Dr. Braceland graduated from LaSalle College and Jefferson Medical College. He was Associate Professor of Psychiatry, Graduate School of Medicine, the University of Pennsylvania, and Dean of Loyola University School of Medicine. During the war he was on active duty with the Medical Corps, U. S. Naval Reserve, as Special Assistant to the Surgeon General, U. S. Navy, and later chief of the Neuropsychiatry Branch of the Bureau of Medicine and Surgery. Following this, Dr. Braceland was Consulting Psychiatrist and Head of the Section of Psychiatry at Mayo Clinic. At present he is Psychiatrist-in-Chief of the Institute of Living in Hartford, Conn. He is a member of the American College of Physicians, the American Psychiatric Association, the Society for Research in Nervous and Mental Diseases, the Society for Research in Psychosomatic Problems, the American Neurologic Association, the Armed Forces Medical Advisory Committee under the Secretary of Defense, the National Research Council as Psychiatric Consultant to the Surgeon General, U. S. Navy, and the American Board of Neurology and Psychiatry, of which he is now president.

REV. JOSEPH T. CLARK, S.J. [1911-   ]

Father Clark is Professor of the Philosophy of Nature and of Science in the Department of Philosophy at Bellarmine College, Plattsburg, N. Y., and is engaged in research on Galileo's contemporary and scientific correspondent, Gassendi, at Harvard University's Widener Library. He is a member of the History of Science Society and of The Philosophy of Science Association.

JAMES COLLINS [1917-   ]

Dr. Collins did his undergraduate and graduate work at The Catholic University of America, Washington, D. C. His doctoral dissertation was on "The Thomistic Philosophy of the Angels." He is Associate Professor of Philosophy at Saint Louis University and a contributor to many philosophical journals. He is the author of *The Existentialists: A Critical Study*.

REV. JAMES I. CONWAY, S.J. [1908-   ]

A graduate of Regis High School, Father Conway entered the Society of Jesus in 1926. After classical studies at St. Andrews-on-Hudson, and philosophical studies at Woodstock College, Maryland, he taught Latin and Greek Literature for three years at St. Peter's College, Jersey City. From 1936 to 1940 he studied theology at Louvain, Belgium. After a year of ascetical theology at the Shrine of the Martyrs at Auriesville, N. Y., he was appointed Professor of the History of Modern Philosophy at Woodstock College. From 1945 he also lectured on the History of Ancient Philosophy and in 1948 conducted the course in the texts of Aristotle at Woodstock.

He received his doctorate in philosophy from Fordham University in 1952. Father Conway was Secretary of the Jesuit Philosophical Association, editing the annual *Proceedings* from 1947 to 1951, when he was elected President of the Association. He has contributed articles to *The New Scholasticism* and *Thought*.

Rev. Joseph F. Costanzo, S.J. [1913-   ]

Father Costanzo entered the Society of Jesus at St. Andrews-on-Hudson in 1931. He did his philosophical and theological studies at Woodstock College, Maryland, where he received his Lic. Phil. and L.S.T. Fordham University granted Father Costanzo his M.A. and Ph.D. in political philosophy. He is lecturer in Fordham's philosophy and political philosophy departments. He has contributed to the *Fordham Law Review* and *New Scholasticism,* and is at present working on a volume on the History and Development of Political Philosophy.

Rev. William A. Dowd, S.J. [1884-   ]

Father Dowd, born in Cincinnati, received his primary education from the Sisters of Charity in Springer Institute and his higher training in Xavier University, with the degree of A.B. in 1905. Joining the Jesuits the same year, he followed their regular course at Florissant, Missouri, and at St. Louis University, receiving his A.M. in 1912. After a year of special study and teaching at Florissant, he taught the classics for four years at St. Marys College, Kansas. He studied theology for four years at St. Louis University, being ordained there in 1920. Three years at the Biblical Institute, Rome, were succeeded by tertianship at Tullamore, Ireland. From 1925 to the present he has been Professor of Sacred Scripture at St. Mary of the Lake Seminary, Mundelein, Ill. He has published *Memory Gems, Loyola Latin Elements* and *The Gospel Guide,* and has contributed book reviews to various Catholic publications, especially *America.* Father Dowd contributed a critical essay to Volume III of the present series.

C. Carroll Hollis [1911-   ]

Mr. Hollis graduated from Marquette University, received his M.A. at the University of Wisconsin, and is at present a candidate for his Doctorate at the University of Michigan. His teaching positions have been: Graduate Fellow at St. Louis University, instructor and Associate Professor at the University of Detroit, where he is in charge of graduate and undergraduate programs in American and contemporary literature, Chairman of the Arts and Science registration committee, a member of the executive committee of the lay faculty, and Faculty Moderator of Delta Pi Kappa, a journalistic fraternity. Mr. Hollis's published works include critical essays in the *South Atlantic Quarterly, Commonweal* and *America.* He is engaged on a study of *The Literary Criticism of Orestes Brownson.*

Helene Iswolsky [1896-   ]

Miss Iswolsky, who is Russian born, was educated at Paris University. She worked as a writer and journalist in Paris and participated in French

Catholic social and youth movements. During World War I she was a Red Cross nurse and was given the French Médaille des Epidémie. Miss Iswolsky came to the United States in 1941 and has lectured extensively. She was with the O.W.I. in World War II and then with the O.I.C., Department of State. She was visiting lecturer in Russian at Vassar College in 1947-1948 and is now instructor in the Russian Institute at Fordham. Author of *Vie de Michel Bakounine, L'Homme Soviètique, Light Before Dusk,* and *Soul of Russia,* Miss Iswolsky is a convert from Russian Orthodoxy.

REV. WILLIAM B. MAHONEY, O.P. [1916-   ]

Father Mahoney was graduated from the University of Notre Dame in 1938. He received the Lectorate in Sacred Theology from the Dominican House of Studies, River Forest, Ill., and the Doctorate of Philosophy from the Angelicum in Rome. He is a lecturer for the Thomist Association and has contributed articles and reviews to *Cross and Crown*. At present he teaches during the summer at DePaul University, Chicago, and is Associate Professor in the Pontifical Faculty of Philosophy, River Forest.

JEAN PAUL MISRAHI [1910-   ]

Columbia University granted Dr. Misrahi his A.B. in 1929 and his Doctorate in 1933. He has studied at the Universities of Paris and Nancy. He was an instructor in Romance languages at Brooklyn College from 1933 to 1938. Since 1938 he has been Assistant Professor and then Associate Professor, and was Head of the Department, of Romance Languages at Fordham University Graduate School from 1938 to 1948. He is a contributor to *Liturgical Arts, Speculum, The French Review* and other magazines. He is a member of the editorial board of *Thought* and the author of *Le Roman des Sept Sages*. Dr. Misrahi is among the contributors to Volumes I, II and III of this series on the Great Books.

REV. BERNARD I. MULLAHY, C.S.C. [1910-   ]

After attending the University of Notre Dame, Father Mullahy studied at the Gregorian University in Rome from 1932 to 1939 and received there the Licentiate in Philosophy and in Theology. With the exception of three years spent at Laval University, where he obtained his Doctorate in Philosophy in 1946, he was teacher of philosophy at the University of Notre Dame and at Moreau Seminary from 1939 to 1950. At present he is Assistant Provincial of the Western Province of the Priests of Holy Cross. His articles, dealing principally with philosophy, education and the liturgy, have appeared in *The New Scholasticism, Laval théologique et philosophique, Proceedings of the American Catholic Philosophical Association, Sign, Orate Fratres,* and *The Benedictine Review*.

ROBERT C. POLLOCK [1901-   ]

Dr. Pollock was graduated from Harvard College in 1925 and received his M.A. from Harvard University in 1927. He then taught experimental psychology and philosophy at Bowdoin College until 1930. In 1932 he received his Ph.D. degree from the University of Toronto (Institute of Mediaeval Studies). While preparing for his degree he taught at the

University of Toronto, and in 1932 joined the faculty of the University of Notre Dame. He has been on the Graduate Faculty of Fordham University since 1936. He has been a contributing editor of *Commonweal* and has contributed to *America* and *Thought*. For a number of years he was closely associated with Don Luigi Sturzo, sociologist and historian, and a founder of the Christian Democratic Party of Italy. Regarded by Sturzo as the foremost interpreter of his thought, he has written an introduction and several chapters of the work *Del Metodo Sociologico,* to which Sturzo also contributed some chapters. An English rendering of this work, called *Man in Society and History,* is being prepared for publication.

HERBERT A. RATNER, M.D. [1907-   ]

Dr. Ratner received his elementary education in the public schools of New York City. At the University of Michigan he received his B.A. (1929) and M.D. (1935) degrees and did graduate work in bacteriology, public health and nutrition. He was on the Michigan faculty of the Department of Bacteriology and the Department of Internal Medicine, and received his clinical training at their University Hospital. Following this he was appointed a Senior Member of the Committee of the Liberal Arts of the University of Chicago by Dr. Robert M. Hutchins (1937-1940). He held the post of Director of Student Health at Loyola University (Chicago) from 1942 to 1950. He was also made a member of the Department of Public Health and Preventive Medicine of the Loyola University School of Medicine in 1942, where he now holds the rank of Associate Clinical Professor. He is also the full-time Health Commissioner of the Oak Park, Illinois, Department of Public Health. He has been Medical Consultant to the Encyclopaedia Britannica Great Books Syntopicon. A Lecturer in Biology and the Great Books at the University of Notre Dame, Dr. Ratner is on the faculty of the St. Albert Magnus Lyceum of the Natural Sciences of the Dominican House of Studies, River Forest, Ill. He is also Medical Adviser to the Cana Conference of the Archdiocese of Chicago.

MATTHEW A. ROONEY, S.J. [1912-   ]

Since 1949 Father Rooney has been Professor of Philosophy at St. Peter's College, Jersey City. In that year he was granted a doctorate in philosophy at l'Institut d'Études Médiévales Albert le Grand, Université de Montréal. His previous philosophical studies were made at le Collège Philosophique, Eegenhoven, Belgium. From 1937 to 1940, before entering upon his theological studies, he taught the classics and modern languages at Gonzaga High School, Washington, D. C.

FRANCIS J. SHEED [1897-   ]

Mr. Sheed is a graduate of Sydney University, in arts and law. In 1926 he and his wife, Maisie Ward, opened the London publishing house of Sheed & Ward. The American house was opened in 1933. Mr. Sheed is the author of many books, including *A Map of Life, Communism and Man, Society and Sanity, Theology and Sanity.* He has translated some dozen works, including *The Confessions of St. Augustine,* and has edited *The Guest-Room Book* and *The Mary Book.* In addition to his writing and publishing,

Mr. Sheed has been for over thirty years a speaker of the Westminster Catholic Evidence Guild, whose purpose is to teach Catholic doctrine and explain the Catholic point of view on the street corner. Mr. Sheed assists in training the Guild speakers in London and has addressed well over three thousand street-corner and indoor meetings in England and America. He contributed a critical study on St. Augustine to Volume I of this series.

VINCENT EDWARD SMITH [1915-   ]

Dr. Smith studied at Xavier University, the University of Fribourg, Switzerland, Institutum Divi Thomae, the Catholic University of America, Harvard University and Massachusetts Institute of Technology. He taught at the Catholic University of America and at present is on the faculty at the University of Notre Dame. He is editor of *The New Scholasticism,* a journal of the American Catholic Philosophical Association, and author of *Philosophical Frontiers of Physics, Idea-Men of Today, Philosophical Physics* and *Footnotes for the Atom.*

FERNAND VIAL [1905-   ]

Dr. Vial's early studies were made at the Lycée de Digne, France; Baccalauréat-es-Lettres-Philosophie at the University of Aix-en-Provence; Licentiate in Scholastic Philosophy at the Catholic University of Lyon; M.A. and Ph.D. at the University of Michigan. He is Chairman of the Romance Language Department in the Graduate School of Fordham University, and Associate Editor of the *French Review.* His articles have appeared in the *French Review,* the *Romantic Review, PMLA, Thought* and other periodicals. His published books are: *Une Philosophie et une Morale du Sentiment* (Paris, Droz, 1938); *Contes Favoris* (New York, Harpers, 1940); *Louis Bastide* (New York, Holt, 1946); *Voltaire* (Paris, Didier, 1952).

REV. GUSTAVE WEIGEL, S.J. [1906-   ]

Father Weigel's A.B. and M.A. are from Woodstock College, Woodstock, Maryland. After ordination in 1934, he went to Rome for graduate ecclesiastical studies. He received the degree of S.T.D. from the Gregorian University in 1938. For eleven years following, he was prominent in the academic life of Chile, where he was Professor of Philosophy and Theology and Dean of the School of Divinity of the Catholic University of Chile. Since 1948 he has been professor of Ecclesiology at Woodstock College. He has written several works in Spanish and was the founder of the *Anales de la Facultad de Teología,* an annual review of theology. Father Weigel was a contributor to Volumes II and III of this series.

CHARLES G. WILBER [1916-   ]

Dr. Wilber received the degree of Doctor of Philosophy from Johns Hopkins University in 1942. He served as Chief of Altitude Training with the Air Force during World War II, Assistant Professor of Physiology in the Graduate School at Fordham University, and leader of several Arctic biological expeditions to Northern Alaska. Formerly Director of the Biological Laboratories at Saint Louis University, he is at present assistant chief of the Applied Psychology Branch of the Army Chemical Corps Medical Laboratories. His articles dealing with evolution of body fluids, cellular physiology, and Arctic biology have appeared widely.